The
Most
Glorious
Crown

The Most Glorious Crown

by Marvin Drager

WINCHESTER PRESS

All official charts of the Kentucky Derby, Preakness, and Belmont Stakes are reproduced as originally published in the *Daily Racing Form:* Copyright © 1974 by Triangle Publications, Inc. (Daily Racing Form). Reprinted with permission of copyright owner.

Photographs are from the following sources:

Keeneland-Cook: 10, 12, 18, 20, 21, 23 (all), 44 (bottom), 49, 67, 80 (top), 81 (bottom), 89, 95 (bottom), 97, 106, 116 (bottom)
Keeneland-Morgan: 116 (top), 118 (all), 119, 126, 128, 130 (all), 134, 147, 148, 150 (all)
United Press International: 2 (bottom), 25, 35, 39, 41, 47, 52, 54, 55, 56, 57 (all), 64, 66 (all), 72, 80 (center, bottom), 81 (top left, top right), 93, 110, 137, 145, 152, 156, 159, 171, 174, 181 (all), 187, 189, 192
Wide World: 26, 44 (top), 46, 58, 95 (top), 104, 112, 155, 190
Caufield & Shook: 15, 37, 42, 63, 91, 113
Bert Clark Thayer: 30, 32, 50, 84, 122, 140
Thoroughbred Racing Associations: viii, 60, 98
Churchill Downs: 2 (top), 14
Pimlico: 4 (all), 82, 177, 178
New York Racing Association: 5 (all)
Narragansett Park: 102 (all)
Knights of Ak-Sar-Ben: 59
Santa Anita: 62, 154 (top, center)
Hollywood Park: 154 (bottom)
Bert Morgan: 127, 131
King Ranch: 124, 138
Casper (Wyo.) Star-Tribune: 29 (all)

Library of Congress Catalog Card Number: 74-16864
ISBN: 0-87691-159-9

Published by Winchester Press
460 Park Avenue, New York 10022

Printed in the United States of America

To

LENORE

and

SHARON, LAURA, IRIS

"The Women in My Life"

*With love, thanks, and gratitude for the patience and equanimity
with which you endured oft-told horse tales.*

Special thanks and recognition for their generous time, cooperation, and assistance to:

John I. Day—Thoroughbred Racing Associations
Calvin S. Rainey—The Jockey Club
The late John Kennedy—The Jockey Club
Robert F. Kelley
Alfred G. Vanderbilt—New York Racing Association
William C. Steinkraus
Charles Hatton—*Daily Racing Form*
Mrs. Amelia K. Buckley—Keeneland Library
George Cassidy—New York Racing Association
Charles J. Lang—The Maryland Jockey Club (Pimlico Race Course)
Philip McAuley—Caspar, Wyoming, *Star-Tribune*
Owen A. Frank—Caspar, Wyoming, *Star-Tribune*
John A. Cypher, Jr.—King Ranch
J. K. Northway, DVM—King Ranch
Dick Nash—Los Angeles Turf Club (Santa Anita Park)
George Lobris—Narragansett Racing Association (Narragansett Park)
Stan Bowker—Knights of Ak-Sar-Ben
Robert P. Benoit—Hollywood Turf Club (Hollywood Park)
Francis Dunne—New York State Racing Commission
Bud Hyland—The Jockey Club
Pat Lynch—New York Racing Association (Aqueduct, Belmont Park, Saratoga)
Thomas S. Rivera—Chicago Thoroughbred Enterprises (Arlington Park)
William J. (Buddy) Hirsch
H. A. (Jimmy) Jones—Monmouth Park Jockey Club
William Rudy—Churchill Downs
Alex Robb—New York Breeders Service
Michael P. Sandler—*Daily Racing Form*
Fred Grossman—*Daily Racing Form*
Sam Siciliano—Pimlico Race Course
Mrs. Martha Mischo—The Jockey Club
Mrs. Marguerite Smithers—The Jockey Club
Jack Fletcher—United Press International
Marty Monroe—Wide World Photos
Humphrey Finney
Charlie Kenney—Stoner Creek Stud
Louis Weintraub—New York Racing Association
Steve Haskin—*Daily Racing Form*

and the many people in the United States, Canada, England, and France who were kind enough to take time out to respond to inquiries in the course of researching the book.

This book was prepared with a dedicated devotion to the accuracy of the information contained within its covers. Any errata which may crop up are purely unintentional, for which the author begs the reader's indulgence.

Contents

The Triple Crown trophy. The names of the three races are inscribed on it, one to each of the three sides.

Introduction

A small red box, with gold snap-lock and hinges, sits atop a tall green safe in the posh offices of the Thoroughbred Racing Associations, in New York. It contains a triangular, three-sided sterling-silver vase, approximately eight inches tall, which symbolizes the epitome of achievement for a three-year-old Thoroughbred. It is the Triple Crown of American turfdom.

Each side of the trophy represents one of the three races, which a single horse must win in a single year to earn the title. Often referred to as the three "jewels" in the Triple Crown, they are the Kentucky Derby, the Preakness Stakes, and the Belmont Stakes, three of the oldest classics of America's King of Sports.

From 1949 through 1972, every spring, the vase had been sent to its designer, Cartier, Inc., to be burnished to a painfully brilliant gloss, in anticipation of the next winner of the trophy. On the second week of June, in each of these years, the vase was returned to its red box, which was returned to its perch atop the tall green safe in the posh offices of the TRA, as yet another season passed without a recipient.

The fact is, from 1875 through 1974, the years that all three races have been in existence simultaneously, only nine horses have won the Triple Crown, making it the most elusive championship in all of sports. It was last won in 1973, and the members of this exclusive club of title-holders are: Sir Barton (1919), Gallant Fox (1930), Omaha (1935), War Admiral (1937), Whirlaway (1941), Count Fleet (1943), Assault (1946), Citation (1948), and Secretariat (1973).

In fairness to all Thoroughbreds, past and present, it should be duly noted that some extenuating circumstances ruled out at least eight possible winners. In 1890, both the Preakness and the Belmont Stakes were raced on the same day; there was a three-year hiatus in the running of the Preakness, from 1891 to 1893; Governor Charles Evans Hughes of New York banned racing in the state during 1911 and 1912, which blacked out the Belmont Stakes; and both the Kentucky Derby and the Preakness were raced on the same day in 1917 and 1922.

Although the Kentucky Derby is the most famous of the three races, it is the youngest. It was first run in 1875, on land owned by John and Henry Churchill, in Louisville, Ky. The tract eventually took on the name of Churchill Downs. Today, the race is presented on the first Saturday in May. Its official flower is the rose, which prompted sportswriter Bill Corum to coin the phrase "Run for the Roses." Perhaps its greatest importance lies in the fact that it is "the first race in which the best horses from one crop of foals meet at the accepted classic distance of a mile and a quarter," carrying 126 pounds.

The Preakness is raced two weeks later, at Pimlico Race Course, Baltimore, Md. It was established in 1873 at Pimlico, was raced at Morris

The Kentucky Derby trophy.

Churchill Downs. The photograph was taken on May 7, 1946, the day Assault won the Kentucky Derby.

Park, The Bronx, N. Y., in 1890 and at Gravesend Course in Brooklyn, from 1894 to 1908, and finally settled permanently thereafter back in Maryland. The distance is a mile and three-sixteenths, with 126 pounds, for a blanket of black-eyed Susans, the state's official flower.

Although it is the oldest of the three, the Belmont Stakes is perhaps the least popularly known. However, a combination of the heroics of Canonero II, New York City's new off-track betting system, worldwide satellite television coverage, and the largest crowd in New York racing history (81,036 people), gave the race a huge new measure of notoriety in 1971. It was founded in 1867, and is raced on the first Saturday in June, at Belmont Park, Long Island, N. Y. The distance is a mile and a half, with 126 pounds, for chrysanthemums. To aficionados of the turf, this race offers a truer picture of the quality of the Thoroughbred. By the time it is run, the three-year-old has fully matured, and the field has been weeded out, so that only the very best of the crop are entered. That is why the field is usually the smallest of all three races. Also, the distance offers the sternest test for the entry, and any defect in the horse's breeding is most apt to show up. It is because of these factors that breeders, owners, and trainers would prefer to win this one race over the other two. The stud value of a Belmont Stakes winner immediately soars, simply because more horses have proved best in stud who have won the Belmont. This is also why turfmen call it "the Test of the Champion."

The Triple Crown title was formally proclaimed in December 1950, at the annual awards dinner of the Thoroughbred Racing Associations in New York. Since there had been no candidate that year, it was decided to present the trophy retroactively to the first winner, Sir Barton. This became an annual feature at the dinner for the next seven years, until they ran out of former winners. Then the turf nabobs could only hope for a newcomer to reach the hallowed winner's circle.

Credit for initiating the movement to proclaim a Triple Crown is given unofficially to Charles Hatton, the venerable columnist of the defunct *Morning Telegraph* and present *Daily Racing Form*. It was in the early 1930s that his copy began to include the phrase "triple crown," whenever he wrote about the Kentucky Derby, Preakness, and Belmont Stakes. As with many newsmen who eschew the touch-typing system in favor of the two-finger hunt-and-peck method, Hatton tired of having to spell out the names of the races in his copy every spring, and evolved his own shortcut by referring to them collectively as the "triple crown" races. "It was rhetorically more acceptable," he claims. In time, his fellow fourth-estaters picked up the cue, and the phrase became so popular that more and more owners began to point their horses toward winning the triad of races. By 1941, newspapers were hailing the feat with banner headlines, such as: "Triple Crown to Whirlaway; Easily Takes Belmont Stakes."

The Triple Crown is not an American racing innovation. Rather, it came to us from England. There are five British classic races for three-year-olds, dating back almost two centuries. They are the St. Leger

The Preakness trophy.

Aerial view of Pimlico Race Course.

The Belmont Stakes trophy.

Aerial view of Belmont Park.

(1778), the Oaks (1779), the Derby Stakes (1780), the Two Thousand Guineas (1809), and the One Thousand Guineas (1814). Since only fillies may run in the One Thousand Guineas and the Oaks Stakes, the other three races became major tests for all Thoroughbreds in England, and, in time, the winner of all three was classified as the Triple Crown champion. West Australian, in 1853, was Britain's first Triple Crown winner.

The Two Thousand Guineas is raced at Newmarket in May, at a mile. The Derby is run at Epsom Downs on the nearest Wednesday to June 1, at a mile and a half. The St. Leger takes place on the Town Moor at Doncaster, Yorkshire, in September, over a distance of a mile, six furlongs, 132 yards. It is generally conceded that the American triple is the more difficult and demanding, because there is no long span of time between the races as there is in England.

The importance of the Triple Crown races grew apace with the evolution of the science of breeding Thoroughbred horses. Once the Thoroughbred gained a foothold in England, an unending search began to improve the bloodlines and the swiftness afoot of these magnificent animals. Consequently, their performances in the classic races became a barometer for excellence in potential breeding stock. It follows, therefore, that in addition to the traditions of Thoroughbred racing, the British handed down to us the Thoroughbred himself, as a species bred specifically for racing.

"The term 'Thoroughbred' as applied to the horse is universally accepted and recognized as applying specifically and limitedly to the equine strain which traces to the Arabian, Barb or Turk," say the editors of *Call Me Horse,* a book which devotes itself to horse racing and breeding.

The Arabian, or what is referred to as the Southern Horse (hot-blood line) in the evolution of the horse, was indigenous to Asia Minor and the Middle East, or to the neighboring lands of Persia, India, and Arabia. His lineage was traced back for five thousand years to the wild horses Honshaba and Baz, which supposedly were captured by and belonged to Baz of Yemen, the great-great-grandson of Noah. A member of the modern species of horse, the Arabian was descended from an Asiatic ancestry, and was one of two strains of this species which migrated westward from Central Asia. He had a sleek coat, beauty, speed, and stamina, and was extremely popular with sultans and kings, some of whom owned as many as 40,000, as did King Bahram in 120 A.D. By 1290 A.D., fantastic prices were paid for select horses, such as the racing filly El Karta, who went for 64,000 Turkish pounds. Stakes races of sorts were also popular between the stables of rival emirs and sultans, the races often consisting of turning loose thirsty steeds trained to run to the nearest waterhole in the desert.

The Arabian became a favorite mount of the Turks, who, with the Roman legions, brought him to the Continent during their invasions. The horse also found his way across North Africa, via Egypt, to Bar-

bary, or what is today Morocco and Algeria, where he was bred with the local stock, the new breed taking on the name of "Barb." From Africa, the Barb moved to the Continent with the Saracens, who introduced him into France, and the Moors, who took him to Spain. All of this migration resulted in the Southern Horse coming into contact with his counterpart, the Northern Horse (cold-blood line), a shaggy-haired, sturdy, vigorous beast, the second strain which migrated westward from Central Asia and settled in the desolate northern part of Europe. By crossbreeding the two strains, the Romans found that they could produce excellent chargers. Consequently, in time the Arabian horse, although not noted for being a particularly good racer, became much sought after for breeding purposes. His first appearance in England was the result of the Roman and Norman invasions.

At the outset in England, the emphasis was on producing a massive war charger, capable of carrying the tremendous weight of a man in full armor. They overdid it. The load became so great, and the horse so big and slow, that by the end of the sixteenth century both horse and warrior came to a virtual standstill. To all practical purposes they were immobilized.

The need for a lighter horse with speed and dexterity was painfully evident during the Crusades when the great knights suddenly found themselves completely outsped and outmaneuvered by the swift, streamlined Arabian flyers. One battlefield report said: "The Infidels not being weighed down with heavy armour like our knights were always able to outstrip them in pace, were a constant trouble. When charged they are wont to fly, and their horses are more nimble than any others in the world; one may liken them to swallows for swiftness." Some of these flyers were brought back to England by the knights, but King Henry VIII would have nothing of them. He was a heavy-horse enthusiast, no doubt partly because of his own massive bulk, which needed all the support he could get under him. He was so fanatical about this that he even issued an edict calling for the slaughter of all light horses and compelling concentration on weight-carrying breeds. It was after his demise in 1547 that the turnabout came.

Although the first racehorses in England to be identified by name were the Arabian stallion Arundel and the mare Truncefice, in 957 A.D., the sport of racing was introduced around 1174 during the reign of King Henry II. Horse fairs were held every Friday night outside the gates of London and were attended by earls, barons, and knights, with races run over the open fields. Except for the hiatus dictated by King Henry VIII and a brief interruption in 1654 by Oliver Cromwell, the sport was encouraged by succeeding monarchs, which eventually led to its being dubbed "the Sport of Kings." For example, James I favored Epsom Downs in the early 1600s; Charles II, called the "father of the British turf," established Newmarket as the headquarters for both racing and breeding in the middle 1600s; and Queen Anne gave Ascot its high distinction for racing between 1702 and 1714. Finally, in 1750, the establishment of the Jockey Club formalized the British Thoroughbred, as all of his breeding and racing activities were rigidly controlled by uniform rules and regulations.

During the reign of the Stuarts in the 1600s, Barbs, Arabs, and Turks were imported in great numbers. It was between 1688 and 1729 that three famous stallions arrived in England, from whom all modern Thoroughbreds trace their lineage. They were the Byerly Turk, Darley Arabian, and Godolphin Arabian or Barb. Their mating with British stock proved their supremacy to such a degree that the native breed of sires died out completely.

The Byerly Turk is thought to have been captured by Captain Robert Byerly, in 1687, when he fought the Turks in Hungary, and brought back to Byerly's home in Yorkshire. The Darley Arabian was foaled about 1702, and was shipped from Syria to Richard Darley, of Yorkshire, as a gift from his son. The Godolphin Arabian was foaled about 1724, and is said to have been a gift to King Louis XIV of France from the Emperor of Morocco. However, he was stolen from the king's stables and disappeared, until spotted by Edward Coke pulling a water cart through the streets of Paris. Coke bought the horse for three pounds, imported him into England around 1730, and presented him to his friend Roger Williams, who in turn passed him on to the Earl of Godolphin.

Organized racing in America began with the British invasion of New Amsterdam, in 1664. In addition to renaming the city "New York," Colonel Richard Nicolls, commander of the troops, established organized racing in the colonies by laying out a two-mile course on Long Island, calling it Newmarket and offering a silver cup to the best horses in the spring and fall seasons. As the sport spread in popularity, efforts were made to breed better horses. Thoroughbreds were imported from England, the first of which was the Dutton Arabian, in 1721. He was mated with the predominant native mustangs, but the results were disappointing halfbreeds.

Thereafter, aristocratic planters in New York, Maryland, Virginia, the Carolinas, and Kentucky set about in earnest to produce a truly fine Thoroughbred strain in the United States. In the next forty-five years, they imported some 113 stallions and 73 mares from England. At the same time, too, the pattern of American turfdom emerged, with New York becoming the center of racing and Virginia, Maryland, and Kentucky the centers of breeding.

From the beginning, and continuing until the Civil War, racing in America was apparently influenced by the rugged pioneer spirit of the fledgling country. The hallmark of excellence for the American Thoroughbred was stamina, rather than speed. Races were long, as much as four miles, and involved several heats. For example, on October 13, 1832, at the Union Course on Long Island, a field of America's best mares ran a total of twenty miles in one afternoon before a winner was determined. It is also pertinent that racing had become the common man's sport, as evidenced by a turnout at the same track in 1842 of between 50,000 and 75,000 fans, who paid a $10 admission charge to watch a match race between the filly Boston and the colt Fashion. It is little wonder that the original appellation was eventually changed to "the King of Sports."

After the Civil War, American racing went through a refining process. Speed became the goal and the British system the model. For one thing, distances were lowered to the classic mile and a half and then to the mile and a quarter and the mile. By the turn of the twentieth century, stamina no longer was most important, and the most common distance was three quarters of a mile. Finally, two- and three-furlong dashes came into vogue for two-year-olds, raced at the beginning of the year and leading up to a mile and a sixteenth for the best of them by October. Jockey clubs sprang up in different states to regulate breeding and racing through uniform rules. Purses were increased, too, until special races, the handicaps and stakes, took on added significance.

The one major difference between American and British racing was the track. In England, all races are run on turf, which custom dates back to the early days when the nobility gallivanted over the countryside, while in America virtually all races are held on oval dirt tracks, most of which are a mile around.

Efforts to set up clusters of races along the lines of the British Triple Crown also began after the Civil War. In 1875, Colonel Louis M. Clark, the founder of Churchill Downs, tried to promote the Endurance Handicap, Kentucky Derby, and Key Derby. New York, around 1900, offered the Withers, Belmont Stakes, and Lawrence Realization. The efforts failed, although the individual races flourished. There was just too much provincialism among turfmen, with each group refusing to recognize the other, each insisting that its own track was pre-eminent. In fact, it was a long time before the socialites of the Eastern states, who largely controlled the sport, would even allow their horses to run in the "West," at Churchill Downs. It was this stubborn attitude which impelled Samuel Riddle to keep the great Man o' War out of the Kentucky Derby, in 1920, thereby denying him a sure-bet Triple Crown.

By the same token, it was the fierce competitive spirit of a distinguished Canadian sportsman, who was most anxious for his horses to run in the 1919 Derby, that was in some respects the catalyst which brought East and West together. In fact, it was the dramatic victories of one of his Thoroughbreds in the Derby, Preakness, and Belmont that marked the beginning of a new turf tradition in America—the Triple Crown.

SIR BARTON

SIR BARTON
(Chestnut Colt)

	*Star Shoot	Isinglass
		Astrology
	Lady Sterling	Hanover
		*Aquila

Sir Barton

1

In the spring of 1971, the general opinion among turfmen was that Hoist the Flag would win the Kentucky Derby easily, and could even take the Triple Crown. A few weeks before the Derby, however, he shattered a leg during a workout at Belmont Park, which ended his racing career. As a result, there was a mad scramble to enter horses in the Derby at the last moment, Thoroughbreds who otherwise never would have made the trip to Louisville. Suddenly, everyone began to have delusions of winning the "Run for the Roses," now that the favorite was gone.

One such horse was Canonero II. Bred in Kentucky, he developed a crooked foreleg, and was sold to a Venezuelan for the modest price of $1,200. Thereafter, he became a journeyman racer, on tracks in South America and California. At the 1971 Derby, he went off in a field of twenty-two as one of the long shots, and rocked the racing world by winning handily. Most experts considered the win a fluke and the horse a freak who just happened to beat out a very bad crop of three-year-olds. Two weeks later, Canonero II became the darling of the turf, the Cinderella horse of the year, when he took the Preakness in record time. By post time at Belmont Park on June 5, he had become the "people's choice" of every two-dollar bettor, and was the sentimental favorite to become the first Triple Crown winner in twenty-three years. He finished fourth.

Spectacular as Canonero II's achievements were, they pale by comparison with those of a rather diminutive, deep-chested colt, distinctive with an irregular blaze and a richly burnished chestnut coat, who also began his career as an uninspiring two-year-old, more than a half century earlier in 1918. The following year, he too was entered in the Derby at the last moment and scored a tremendous upset victory. The big difference was that unlike Canonero II, he went on to win the other two big races and become America's first Triple Crown champion. He was Sir Barton.

John E. Madden was one of the foremost breeders at the time, and Sir Barton was foaled on his vast Hamburg Place farm, just outside of Lexington, Ky. He was by Star Shoot, out of Lady Sterling, a seventeen-year-old mare. His sire was the son of Isinglass, an English Triple Crown winner, and he was the half-brother of Sir Martin, who had been acclaimed the two-year-old champion of America in 1908. For all of his excellent lineage, he was plagued with soft shelly hooves, which he inherited from his sire. His feet were so tender that shoeing was always an intricate process. Piano felt was often inserted between the shoe and the foot, but he still walked in pain. Because of this condition, it was not unusual for him to lose his shoes in competition, and in one race later in his career, he lost all four of them.

Despite this physical problem, Madden liked the horse and kept him for his own colors. Sir Barton made his debut in the Tremont Stakes, at Aqueduct in New York City, as a two-year-old, finishing fifth. He next raced at Saratoga, in August, in the Flash, U.S. Hotel, and Sanford Memorial classics for freshmen horses and lost in each race. Although his showing was rather dismal, he still displayed an ability for good speed.

Attending the Saratoga meeting that August was John Kenneth Levison Ross, a former commander of a World War I destroyer in the Royal Canadian Navy and the scion of a distinguished Dominion family which helped to found the Canadian Pacific Railway. He had started a stable in 1915. With him was his trainer, H. G. Bedwell, a former Oregon cowboy who had a reputation for restoring broken-down horses to winning form. Both men were looking over the year's crop. Madden knew of Ross's desire to add to his string, and encouraged him to consider Sir Barton. He had become disenchanted by his performances, but still felt that with the proper handling the colt had the ability to become a winner. By the end of August, Ross and Bedwell had arrived at the same conclusion. They paid $10,000 and went home with the horse.

Commander J.K.L. Ross (right), owner of Sir Barton, with his trainer, H. G. Bedwell.

Their immediate objective was to prepare him to run in the Futurity Stakes, at Belmont Park, on September 14. In the meantime, he was used to help train the top horse of the Ross stable, Billy Kelly, another two-year-old who soon found it tough trying to keep pace with his new stablemate. The immortal Earl Sande, then just a youngster, rode Sir Barton in the Futurity. Although there was little hope that he would finish in the money as he went off at 15 to 1, the colt flashed across the finish line second to Dunboyne with a surging burst of speed, even though he had been boxed in until the last furlong. Nevertheless, the 1918 season ended with victory still eluding the chestnut colt.

All through the winter, Ross thought only of the Kentucky Derby, and of how his Billy Kelly could beat his arch rival, Eternal, who had been the winner in a match race by the two at the Laurel Race Course in Maryland. When the time came to ship to Kentucky, it was decided at the last moment to send Sir Barton along as a running mate. Shortly thereafter, Ross and Bedwell evolved a strategy for the race, and Sir Barton was also entered in it. The plan was for Sir Barton to take the lead at the start and set a fast pace, to kill off the top competition, Eternal and Under Fire. When they had been run into the ground, Billy Kelly would then breeze by for the win. Earl Sande was given the choice of horses, naturally picking Billy Kelly. Johnny Loftus, who had won the Derby in 1916 on George Smith and was considered a master of pacing, was assigned to Sir Barton, with the instructions to give him his head and let him run for as long as he could. But for the fact that he was paired with his stablemate, Sir Barton would have left the post at 50 to 1 instead of as a favorite. He was still a maiden in search of his first taste of victory.

Among his other sportsman qualities, Ross was noted for his eagerness to accept a challenge, dare, or side bet. A few months before the Derby, he was seated with friends in a restaurant when he was approached by a "yeasty-faced little man" who started up a conversation on the forthcoming race, on his belief that Eternal would win it, and on his desire to bet on the results. As Ross's son recalled the incident in his book *Boots and Saddles:*

"My father, in his usual courteous manner and, I might say, with typically fast response to a dare, asked what amount the stranger wanted to bet. He told me later he expected an answer around or below $100.

" 'Would fifty thousand suit you, Commander?'

"At first my father thought it was a joke, but he didn't hesitate to reply.

" 'That would suit me well, sir. Provided you produce some guarantee of payment should you lose.' "

The stranger seemed insulted, which was understandable to Ross's friends, for they knew the stranger. He was Arnold Rothstein, the noted gambler, who had yet to make his reputation as one of the supposed principals behind baseball's infamous "Black Sox" World Series scandal in 1919. However, he did enjoy a good reputation in the underworld for paying off his debts. As a result, the wager was made, but with the understanding that it would be off if neither horse finished in the money.

Derby day found the track heavy from a night of rain. The race went according to plan for a mile and an eighth. Sir Barton ran well out in front as the field thundered past the stands to the first turn. He was moving effortlessly, and increased his lead to three lengths by the top of the stretch. At the one-eighth pole he was supposed to fade. Instead, he went to a five-length lead. "There was no Billy Kelly. But neither was there anybody else," wrote young Ross. "Sir Barton crossed the finish line with his ears pricked and with Loftus standing in the stirrups glancing over his shoulder wondering what happened to the rest."

Billy Kelly came in second, Under Fire third. It was the first time in the history of the Kentucky Derby that the one-two horses wore the same colors. It was also the first time that a maiden had won the Derby, and the racing world rubbed its eyes in disbelief. The mud and other excuses were cited for the poor showings of the favorites. Regardless of these, the knowledgeable railbirds conceded that the spectacular victory was of major consequence. The Derby, according to them, was "just another horse race" until Sir Barton put it on the map. The race also proved that Mr. Rothstein was a man of his word. A few days later, Commander Ross received payment.

Sir Barton leads Billy Kelly as he becomes the first maiden ever to win the Kentucky Derby.

Sir Barton, with jockey Johnny Loftus up, is held by trainer Guy Bedwell in the winner's circle after his upset victory in the Kentucky Derby.

Official chart of Kentucky Derby.

42305 FIFTH RACE—1 1-4 Miles. (May 9, 1914—2:03⅖—3—114.) Forty-fifth Running KEN-TUCKY DERBY. $20,000 Added. 3-year-olds. Allowances. Net value to winner $20,825, second, $2,500, third, $1,000; fourth, $275.

Index	Horses	A Wt PP St	¼	½	¾	Str	Fin	Jockeys	Owners	Equiv. Odds Str't
39683²	SIR BARTON	wв 112½ 1 1	1²	1½	1²	1½	1⁵	J Loftus	J K L Ross	†260-100
(42081)	BILLY KELLY	w 119 11 8	3½	3⁴	2⁸	2⁴	2¹	E Sande	J K L Ross	†
42227²	UNDER FIRE	w 122 7 11	9½	9½	6½	3¹	3¹	M Garner	P Dunne	1915-100
42227	VULCANITE	w 110 6 10	10½	5ʰ	4½	4¹	4⁶	C Howard	W F Polson	7000-100
42227³	SENNINGS PARK	wв 122 8 9	6²	4½	5½	5¹	5¹	H Lunsf'rd	O A Bianchi	§1410-100
42222³	BE FRANK	w 119 2 6	7ʰ	7½	7½	6½	6½	J Butwell	C M Garrison	2745-100
(41177)	SAILOR	wв 119 10 12	12	10²	10½	8½	7⁸	J McIntyre	J W McClelland	‡210-100
42227	ST. BERNARD	w 119 4 2	5ʰ	6¹	9¹	7²	8²	E Pool	B J Brannon	§
(42227)	REGALO	w 117 9 7	8²	8¹½	8¹	9²	9⁴	F Murphy	Gallaher Bros	605-100
(41798)	ETERNAL	w 122 5 3	2½	2½	3½	10⁵	10¹⁰	A Schu'g'r	J W McClelland	‡
38508	FROGTOWN	w 119 12 4	11²	11½	11²	11¹⁰11²⁰	J Morys	W S Kilmer	2245-100
(42137)	VINDEX	w 122 3 5	4ⁿᵏ12	12	12	12	W Knapp	H P Whitney	815-100

†Coupled in betting as J. K. L. Ross entry; ‡J. W. McClelland entry. §Mutuel field.

Time, 24⅕, 48⅖, 1:14, 1:41⅘, 2:09⅖. Track heavy.

$2 mutuels paid, J. K. L. Ross entry, $7.20 straight, $6.70 place, $6.00 show; Under Fire, $10.80 show.

Equivalent booking odds—J. K. L. Ross entry, 260 to 100 straight, 235 to 100 place, 200 to 100 show; Under Fire, 440 to 100 show.

Winner—Ch. c, by Star Shoot—Lady Sterling (trained by H. G. Bedwell; bred by Messrs. Madden & Gooch).

Went to post at 5:10. At post 4 minutes. Start good and slow. Won easily; second and third driving. SIR BARTON raced into the lead at once and, well ridden, led under restraint until reaching the stretch, where he was shaken up and easily held BILLY KELLY safe in the last eighth. BILLY KELLY held to his task well, was under restraint in the early running and finished gamely. UNDER FIRE gained steadily from a slow beginning and finished fast and gamely. VULCANITE ran well and finished close up. ETERNAL was done after going three-quarters. REGALO ran disappointingly. SENNINGS PARK tired in the stretch.

Scratched—(42257)Corson, 122; 42142³Clermont, 122.

Overweights—Sir Barton, 2½ pounds.

The common judgment of Sir Barton's victory, just as of Canonero II's in 1971, was that it was a freak happening, but wait until the Preakness. In 1919, winning both was no mean trick, because Pimlico staged its event just four days later, on May 14, leaving little time for training. There was also the risk of a horse developing shipping fever or being injured while moving from Louisville to Maryland on such short notice, at a time when transportation was a lot slower and full of risks for such a fragile commodity as a Thoroughbred horse.

Nevertheless, Sir Barton went off as a $1.40 to $1.00 favorite. His nearest and strongest competitors were Eternal, 9 to 1, Sweep On, 15 to 1, and Dunboyne, 4 to 1, in a field of twelve.

Official chart of Preakness.

42339   FOURTH RACE—1 1-8 Miles. (May 17, 1911—1:51—3—112.) Twelfth Running PREAK-
NESS STAKES. $25,000 Added. 3-year-olds. Allowances. Net value to winner
$24,500; second, $3,000; third, $2,000; fourth, $1,000.

Index	Horses	A Wt PP St	¼	½	¾	Str	Fin	Jockeys	Owners	Equiv. Odds Str't
(42305)	SIR BARTON	wB 126 8 3	1¹	1¹	1²	1⁶	1⁴	J Loftus	J K L Ross	†140-100
42305	ETERNAL	w 126 2 1	4½	3¹	2¹	2¹	2³	A Schu'g'r	J W McClelland	920-100
(42250)	SWEEP ON	wSB 126 3 2	3²	4½	4²	3⁸	3²	L· McAtee	W R Coe	‡1555-100
42274²	KING PLAUDIT	wB 114 9 4	2¹	2½	3²	4³	4¹½	L Lyke	Brookside Stable	5325-100
(42297)	OVER THERE	w 122 4 10	8½	8³	7³	7⁶	5ⁿᵏ	H Myers	W R Coe	‡
42291²	ROUTLEDGE	w 122 12 5	5¹	5½	5ⁿᵏ	6½	6ʰ	E Ambr'se	W M Jeffords	7080-100
42305	VULCANITE	w 114 1 7	7¹	7ʰ	8¹	8⁸	7¹½	R Troxler	W F Polson	3945-100
42121³	MILKMAID	w 109 6 6	6ⁿᵏ	6²	6²	5½	8³	E Sande	J K L Ross	†
42291	DRUMMOND	wB 114 7 9	9½	9½	9²	9¹	9½	A Johnson	M Shea	14500-100
42222	YURUCARI	w 114 11 8	11	10½	10⁵	10⁸	10¹⁸	T Rice	Quincy Stable	12540-100
42250	DUNBOYNE	w 126 5 11	10²	11	11	11	11	L Ensor	P A Clark	420-100
42305	VINDEX	wB 115 10	Left at the post.					W Knapp	H P Whitney	365-100

†Coupled in betting as J. K. L. Ross entry; ‡W. R. Coe entry.

Time, 23⅖, 47½, 1:13, 1:39½, 1:53. Track fast.

$2 mutuels paid, J. K. L. Ross entry, $4.80 straight, $3.20 place, $2.70 show; Eternal, $7.50 place, $6.00 show; W. R. Coe entry, $5.00 show.

Equivalent booking odds—J. K. L. Ross entry, 140 to 100 straight, 60 to 100 place, 35 to 100 show; Eternal, 275 to 100 place, 200 to 100 show; W. R. Coe entry, 150 to 100 show.

Winner—Ch. c, by Star Shoot—Lady Sterling (trained by H. G. Bedwell; bred by Messrs. Madden & Gooch).

Went to post at 4:21. At post 5 minutes. Start good and slow. Won easily; second and third driving. SIR BARTON went to the front while rounding the turn into the backstretch, setting a terrific pace, drew away into a long lead in the last quarter and was eased up at the finish. ETERNAL was a forward contender from the start, met with no mishaps and ran a game race. SWEEP ON was always prominent in the running, but was tiring at the end. DUNBOYNE began sideways in behind the other horses and had no chance. KING PLAUDIT ran a good race. OVER THERE made a fast finish. ROUTLEDGE and VULCANITE ran well.

Scratched—42221³Terentia, 117; 42291³Natural Bridge, 114; 42273³Pride of India, 114.

Overweights—Vindex, 1 pound.

This time, Ross and Bedwell had Earl Sande ride another stablemate, Milkmaid. The plan called for him to wheel in and break up the general alignment in as legitimate a fashion as would pass the inspection of the starter, in order to allow Sir Barton to find a favorable position. Loftus, on the other hand, was merely told to "get out to the front as soon as possible and stay there." Unlike the Derby, the track was fast.

Once more, Sir Barton needed little urging. He swept out front at the start and was never headed, winning over Eternal by four lengths. As for Milkmaid, the filly, she found too many colts around of more than passing interest for her to take the race seriously. The Preakness made many believers out of doubters. Sir Barton had arrived.

With the Kentucky Derby and the Preakness under their belts, Ross and Bedwell refused to ease up the pressure to keep their colt razor-sharp. They entered him in the Withers, at Belmont, on May 24. Here it was decided to let Eternal take the lead into the stretch. The race, at that time, was run clockwise, and Bedwell in training had observed Eternal's tendency to bear out and away from the rail at the final turn. Loftus, therefore, trailed the horse until the homestretch and then moved Sir Barton inside Eternal, to win by three lengths as he made up his lost distance with the maneuver.

This victory sent the fans stark raving mad for Sir Barton, and they looked forward to the Belmont Stakes, on June 11, with excruciating impatience. The Belmont would be the true test for the colt, with nobody doubting that he would win, even though the distance would be longer than he had ever run. In 1919, the race was at a mile and three-eighths, instead of the mile and a half that it is today. So confident was the public that they established him a whopping 7 to 20 favorite.

By now, Sir Barton began to display a personality distinctly his own. Perhaps it was the assurance born of winning. The fact is, he made everyone aware of him in the stable. He had a nasty disposition, no doubt partly because of his sore feet. He ignored horses, despised humans, and hated pets. He preferred to remain aloof and was a thorough snob. On top of this, he gave his trainer fits. In track parlance, he was not a "generous horse," and would extend himself only when he was made to believe that he was in a real race. As a result, Bedwell had to resort to the subterfuge of using fresh horses in relays to pace him, and was often heard to say ruefully: "To get him fit you have to half-kill him with work—and a lot of other horses as well." Ross's son tried to explain it another way. "Horsemen speak of Thoroughbreds with this faraway gaze as 'having the look of the eagle' and they believe that it is invariably the sign of greatness. Sir Barton was an irascible, exasperating creature. But he had the look of the eagle."

He proved his mettle in the Belmont Stakes, when he "pulverized" the opposition, winning in a canter by five lengths while setting a new American record of 2:17^2/$_5$. In the process of becoming the first Triple Crown winner, he also was the first colt to include the Withers in this victory skein, a feat that was not to be duplicated until twenty-four years later, in 1943, by Count Fleet. Therefore, when 1919 came to a

Official chart of Belmont Stakes.

42784 FOURTH RACE—1 3-8 Miles. (June 16, 1917—2:17⅗—3—126.) Fifty-first Running BELMONT STAKES. Guaranteed Value $10,000. 3-year-olds. Weight-for-Age. Net value to winner $11,950; second, $1,500; third, $750.

Index	Horses	A	Wt	PP	St	¼	½	¾	Str	Fin	Jockeys	Owners	O	H	C	P	S
(42499)	SIR BARTON	w₿	126	1	1	2²	2⁸	2⁵	1³	1⁵	J Loftus	J K L Ross	2-5	2-5	7-20out	—	
42725²	SWEEP ON	w₿	126	3	2	3	3	3	2½	2⁸	C F'b'ther	W R Coe	†2	12-5	12-5	out	—
42751²	NATUR'L BRIDGE	w	126	2	3	1²	1⁸	1¹	3	3	L McAtee	W R Coe	†2	12-5	12-5	out	—

†Coupled in betting; no separate place or show betting.
Time, 2:17⅗ (new American record). Track fast.
Winner—Ch. c, by Star Shoot—Lady Sterling (trained by H. G. Bedwell; bred by Messrs. Madden & Gooch).
Went to post at 4:09. At post 1 minute. Start poor and slow. Won easily; second and third driving. SIR BARTON, after beating the gate, indulged NATURAL BRIDGE with the lead over the Belmont course, then easily took the lead after entering the main course and, drawing away, was easing up at the end. SWEEP ON was saved under early restraint and made a vain challenge at the homestretch entrance, but tired near the end. NATURAL BRIDGE tired badly after pacemaking to the homestretch.
Scratched—42641²Pastoral Swain, 126; 42725 Over There, 126.

close, there was no question but that he was the top horse of the year, having humbled most of the finest Thoroughbreds in the country. He had raced thirteen times and had won eight of these. He had campaigned so much that Commander Ross seriously considered retiring him, rather than entering him into the grueling handicap schedule of 1920. His sore feet were the big question marks for the coming year.

The owner's reservations about his colt's performance in 1920 proved to be about 50 percent justified. Sir Barton had an on-and-off spring and, overall for the year, won only five of the thirteen races he started. He was alternately brilliant and mediocre. More significantly, his championship crown was challenged by a newcomer to the ranks of the American Thoroughbred, a colt whom many have called a superhorse, "the horse of the century," one whose influence is still felt to this day. He was Man o' War, and Sir Barton would have to reckon with him before the year was up.

Man o' War.

It was March 29, 1917, at the Nursery Stud of Major August Belmont near Lexington, Ky., the year America entered World War I. A broodmare groom opened the foal book, made a routine entry, "chestnut colt, by Fair Play, out of Mahubah," and thereby commenced the dramatic story of "the greatest Thoroughbred of all time." The colt was a red chestnut, marked with a star and an indistinct, short, gray stripe in his forehead. It was Louis Feustel, his eventual trainer, who nicknamed him "Big Red." In setting down his early appraisal of the horse, he wrote: "Very tall and gangling . . . thin and so on the leg as to give the impression of ungainliness one gets in seeing a week-old foal." But he was high on the horse, because he so admired his sire, Fair Play, the best stallion on the farm, even though Mahubah was an untried mare of English extraction.

In the spring of 1918, Major Belmont announced that because of his involvement in the war effort he would sell his crop of 1918 yearlings. He offered the lot to Samuel Doyle Riddle for $42,000. Riddle was a fifty-seven-year-old textile magnate from Glen Riddle, Pa., who had been a horse enthusiast since childhood. By the time he was twenty-one, his reputation as a fearless rider on the Pennsylvania-Maryland hunt circuit had been firmly established. He also began his racing stable at that time, subsequently building Glen Riddle Farm into one of the major breeding centers of American Thoroughbred racing.

When the offer was made, Feustel was training Riddle's small stable. He had been a youngster with the Belmont stable in the days of Fair Play, and had never lost his admiration for the horse. Therefore, he urged his employer to purchase a colt by Fair Play. As a result, Riddle sent the trainer and an assistant, Mike Daly, to Kentucky to look over the Belmont yearlings. On their return, they reported that the horses were rather undersized and the offer was turned down. Belmont finally shipped the yearlings to the Saratoga Sales in August, at which time Riddle and Feustel noticed the big-framed, long-legged colt, now tagged with the impressive name Man o' War, courtesy of Mrs. Belmont.

"You said the yearlings were undersized," a puzzled Riddle said to his trainer. "Surely this colt is big enough."

"But we don't remember seeing the colt when the yearlings were shown to us in Kentucky," replied the equally puzzled trainer.

Riddle had been thoroughly honed in the whys and wherefores of horse trading and, armed with the knowledge of Feustel's enthusiasm for the colt's sire, suspected that the major was apparently so taken with him that he wanted to hold him out of the sale. All of this made Riddle more determined to buy him at any price. Belmont, on the other hand, did in fact want to keep the horse, but feared that the sale of the other yearlings would suffer if he held onto him.

The auction was held on August 17, and the bidding for the horse reached $4,900, with some fifteen persons reportedly willing to pay this sum. Riddle raised it $100, and the sale was completed. Interestingly enough, he at first never considered the colt for racing, rather figuring

Samuel Riddle (right), owner of Man o' War, and his trainer, Louis Feustel.

he would make a good hunter because of his size. It was Riddle's wife who persuaded him to leave this decision to Feustel.

At the very beginning, they ran into trouble with the colt. It was almost impossible to break him. "He fought like a tiger. He screamed with rage, and fought us so hard that it took several days before he could be handled with safety," recalled Riddle. Once he was broken, though, he displayed a tremendous speed, the likes of which none of his handlers had ever seen. As a two-year-old, in 1919, he literally scorched every race track he ran on, winning nine of the ten races he started. His only defeat was by Upset, in the Sanford Memorial at Saratoga, a loss that has been charged by some to a bad ride by jockey Johnny Loftus, and by others to the starter, C. H. Pettingill, who allowed the race to get off while Man o' War was standing broadside to the barrier when the flag was dropped. The end of the year found him unquestionably the number one horse of his class, with earnings of $83,325.

Between his two- and three-year-old forms, he emerged as a giant. He had the size and power of a sprinter, with the conformation of a stayer, and he struck fear into the hearts of all who opposed him. He was "muscled enormously, and full of the flowing spirit of the Fair Plays. His action was high and his courage matched it and when he had a horse to go with him, he did not run as much as hurtle," is the way turf historian Joe Palmer described him. He did everything with a flair, even when he ate, consuming twelve to thirteen quarts of oats and all the hay they could give him in a day. He was so ravenous that they had to put a bit in his mouth while he was feeding to keep him from eating too fast.

In 1920, he won all eleven races in which he started, including the Preakness, Withers, Belmont, Stuyvesant Handicap, Dwyer, Miller, Travers, Lawrence Realization, Jockey Club Gold Cup, Potomac Handicap, and Kenilworth Gold Cup. He set five records on the way, and wound up the year with winnings of $166,140, the first Thoroughbred to earn over $200,000. He had everything, in the view of C. W. Anderson, "blinding speed, stamina to go any distance and a love for running that is the heart and core of a fine horse. He smothered his opposition and overran his finishes by furlongs."

In all of the annals of Thoroughbred history, no other horse was ever compared to some of the greatest champions of sports the way "Big Red" was by the distinguished sportswriter Grantland Rice. "Man o' War was something different—something extra—as great a competitor as Ty Cobb, Jack Dempsey, Tommy Hitchcock, Ben Hogan, or anyone else . . . he had a furious desire to win." A classic example of this was the Lawrence Realization, in which all of the other competing horses were scratched. To avoid disappointing the crowd, the track sent in an

Man o' War, with Johnny Loftus in the irons, finishes second to Upset in the Sanford Stakes at Saratoga. This loss ranks as one of most spectacular upsets in turf history. Coming in third is Golden Broom.

entry, Hoodwink, with a ten-pound advantage. The result of the race was a foregone conclusion, but Man o' War's jockey, Clarence Kummer, was given instructions to hold him back and win by not too big a margin. It was a tall order. At the end of a quarter-mile, Man o' War was twenty lengths ahead. Try as he might, Kummer just could not hold his horse in, and he won by a modestly estimated one hundred lengths. It was an arbitrary measurement, as Hoodwink had been eased when hopelessly beaten. Still, the margin of victory was by nearly a quarter of a mile, and in record time.

The spectacular success of Man o' War soon brought about the obvious offers to purchase him. Riddle turned down all of these out of hand, with the exception of one from W. T. Waggoner. The wealthy Texan first suggested $500,000, then raised the figure to $1,000,000. When he was still turned down, he continued to persist, claiming that everything had a price. With that, he signed a blank check and told Riddle to fill in the numbers. The reply to this became a classic in racing lore. "You go to France and bring the sepulchre of Napoleon from Les Invalides. Then you go to England and buy the jewels from the crown. Then to India and buy the Taj Mahal. Then I'll put a price on Man o' War." Years later, the horse's devoted groom, Will Harbut, reported it another way. "A man came here and offered a million dollars for him, and Mr. Riddle said no, lots of men might have a million dollars, but only one man could have Man o' War."

As the 1920 racing season progressed into the Saratoga meet, it became evident that the one horse who bid well to steal some of the thunder from "Big Red" was the Triple Crown champion. Although his victories were far fewer in number they were almost as impressive. In fact, Sir Barton was among the leaders of the year's handicap division. It was at Saratoga that the abilities of the two colts came into sharp focus. Their performances in several races were almost identical.

Man o' War had two distinguished victories, the Miller and the Travers. In the latter, he equaled the record for the mile and a quarter distance, which Sir Barton had set in the Saratoga Handicap. On the other hand, Sir Barton in the Merchants' and Citizens' covered the distance Man o' War had run in the Miller by a full second faster while carrying two extra pounds. The feats fed fuel to a public clamor for the two horses to meet in a match race, head to head, to determine the better of the two.

Pressure for the race became so intense that both Riddle and Ross relented and agreed to the meeting. They decided to accept the first $50,000 offer to come along. It was made by A. M. Orpen, a Toronto promoter who controlled Kenilworth Park, at Windsor, Ontario, who then increased it to $75,000, plus a $5,000 gold cup. He knew that Colonel Matt Winn, of Churchill Downs, was also eager for the race, and tried to head him off with an irresistible offer. Both owners accepted the proposal, just a few hours before a telegram arrived from Winn with a $100,000 offer.

Sir Barton, ridden by Earl Sande, beats Exterminator in the Saratoga Handicap in record time for the mile and a quarter.

Earl Sande rides Sir Barton (on rail) to a win over Gnome in the Merchants' and Citizens' Handicap at Saratoga. He ran the mile and three-sixteenths a full second faster than Man o' War's time for the same distance.

Thus, the first "race of the century" was set. It would be the best of America versus the best of Canada, a great international event to determine the top horse on the North American continent. It was a natural, one to excite any turf fan. The terms of the race were quite simple. Only the two colts would run, under weight-for-age conditions, the four-year-old Sir Barton to carry 126 pounds and the three-year-old Man o' War 120 pounds. The distance of the race would be a mile and a quarter, and it would be run on October 12. It was also stipulated that if either horse failed to start, the other was to "walk over" for the gold trophy only. In other words, the horse need only to walk around the track and over the finish line to be declared the winner.

In actuality, neither owner was particularly in need of the purse. To Riddle, it was the means to the end of making "Big Red" the leading money-winning Thoroughbred, the first to top the $200,000 mark. For Ross, who had become one of the most popular figures in the American turf world, even described by some at the time as "the best sportsman Canada ever sent to this country," winning the race and the large purse would enhance his country's position as a leader in Thoroughbred racing.

Sir Barton arrived in Windsor from Laurel, Md., five days before the race, and almost immediately was the target of a barrage of adverse newspaper stories. It was reported that he was training poorly, that trainer Bedwell was drinking, that the Kenilworth track was too hard for his sore feet. Bert E. Collyer of the Chicago *Evening Post,* for one, wrote in appraising the horse's last workout at Laurel: "Let it be said that he is a horse of moods and hard to train. Bedwell may be a wizard, but it is my firm conviction that his charge has been in better shape than he will be on Tuesday." Bedwell was quick to dispute this. "Sir Barton is doing all I have asked him in his work for the race," he told the press. "He is ready to run as fast as he has in the past and I look for him to render a brilliant account of himself. I am making no predictions, but I believe Sir Barton will not disgrace himself in the most pretentious effort of his successful turf career."

Actually, Ross and Bedwell were concerned with the question of who their jockey would be. Clarence Kummer, who had ridden Sir Barton, was already set to mount Man o' War, while Johnny Loftus, who had also ridden him, had had his license revoked and was out of racing. That left Earl Sande, then just twenty-one and contract jockey for Ross. There was talk that he had a nervous stomach from dieting to keep his weight down, that he had displayed timidity in his riding of late, and that Bedwell feared he might get the jitters, the way he had when he rode Ross's Billy Kelly in a match race with Eternal two years before and lost.

Both owner and trainer finally decided to wait until the day of the race before making up their minds. In the meantime, they sneaked in a standby jockey, just in case. He was Frank Keogh, a veteran of the track, who rode for Admiral C. T. Grayson and Samuel Ross, of Washington, D.C. The admiral was the personal physician of President

Woodrow Wilson. Keogh was merely told to report to promoter Orpen at Kenilworth on October 11, without being advised why. The next morning, on the day of the race, Ross and Bedwell watched Sir Barton in a workout. The horse did not seem to be razor-sharp, and Sande appeared to be in an extreme state of anxiety. It was at that moment that Ross made his decision to have Sande stand down. He broke the news to the young man in the jockey's room just about an hour before the race, and Sande sat down and cried. The owner then released a statement to the press. "I have determined to substitute Jockey Frank Keogh for Earl Sande on Sir Barton in today's race for the reason that my boy is not in good form, as his recent performances will show." He insisted that there was no prejudice toward Sande involved, that it was only for the good of the horse.

Man o' War also had a few anxious moments. He had struck himself in the Potomac Handicap, at Havre de Grace, Md., and, according to trainer Feustel, started to bow a tendon. His leg also filled once while preparing for the special, but he surmounted this and was fit on the morning of the big race.

The net result of these pre-race speculations and happenings was that Man o' War was made the overwhelming favorite, at 5 to 100, and Sir Barton the underdog, at 550 to 100. The match was the fourth race on the program of the day, and the bulging stands included many celebrities of the turf world, such as Joseph Widener, William Woodward, August Belmont, John Madden (who had bred both horses), and Enrico Caruso, the Metropolitan Opera star. *Untrue he bred Sir Barton, Belmont bred Man o' war*

Man o' War follows lead pony toward the starting line for his match race with Sir Barton in Canada Clarence Kummer is up.

The jockeys had been given identical instructions—get to the front and stay there. Man o' War was fractious at the barrier, which was located at the near turn of the track. Sir Barton, on the rail, was more docile and broke first with the flag. His inside position gave him a temporary advantage, as they moved into the stretch for the first sweep past the stands. The lead was short-lived, for Man o' War caught up quickly and went ahead to stay after they had traveled only sixty yards. "He actually galloped the Ross colt dizzy in the first mile and drew away so easily in the final quarter of a mile that he was never fully extended," reported the New York *Times*. Despite this, he won by seven lengths in 2:03, a new track record which clipped $6^2/_5$ seconds from the old mark. It was a ridiculously easy victory, a race which the press labeled as a "farce," a "great spectacle, hardly a great race." Some critics blasted the race, saying it should never have been run, that Sir Barton should never have been allowed to race because of his sore feet. There was no doubt but that he had been completely outclassed and humbled. Commander Ross was among the first to admit to the superiority of Man o' War, not only over his own horse but over any other one around, when he rushed over to Samuel Riddle's box to offer congratulations.

Man o' War races to a seven-length victory over Sir Barton. Frank Keogh is in the saddle of the Triple Crown champion.

The reporter for the *Times,* in assessing the talents of the horse after the race, wrote: "As it is, even with the scalp of Sir Barton dangling from his belt, Man o' War has yet to show just how fast he can run." Riddle himself could not provide the answer to this. "We don't know to this day how fast he was," he said, "as we were afraid to let him down; knowing his intense speed, we feared he might injure himself." He was even more expansive in his praise on his return to Glen Riddle two days later, when he told a cheering welcoming crowd: "The colt lived up to expectations at Windsor. He just caught Sir Barton and romped ahead of him at every step. The crowds went wild. Many believed that the advance reports about Man o' War were exaggerated, but when Kummer, his jockey, let him out, hats went up in the air, women shrieked, race track men who had never seen the colt before gasped in astonishment; and few of the 30,000 persons who crowded every inch of the track went home without getting hoarse."

The race was not without a number of interesting sidelights. Its purse was the richest prize ever offered in a turf event on the North American continent. It drew the largest crowd ever at a Canadian track. The fans at the track bet $132,000 on Man o' War, and only $14,000 on Sir Barton. It was also the first horse race to be filmed in its entirety over a circular track. The photographer was Edward Muybridge, who forty years earlier had produced the first record on film of a running animal. At that time, he had used twenty cameras, lined up at close intervals on a straight track, with silk threads stretched across the track tripping the camera shutters as they were broken by the horse. This time, he used fourteen cameras, and the film was later shown in a Broadway theater at reserved-seat prices.

Top news events manage to attract myths which, in later years, are accepted as fact. They add extra color and excitement to future descriptions of the action, even though there is not much truth in them. The match race of Sir Barton and Man o' War was no exception, and a recounting of it some eighteen years later by Charles Parmer, in his book *For Gold and Glory,* is a case in point. It told of what happened when Man o' War caught up to Sir Barton just after the race started. "They swept down the stretch, Man o' War fighting for his head. After a quarter-mile, Kummer's left stirrup broke from weight and pressure. The boy, in catching to hold on until he could get balanced again, had to give Man o' War his head. The latter ran the next 150 yards like a wild creature, opening a big gap between him and Sir Barton before Kummer could steady him. Sir Barton was never able to gain a foot, and the farther they ran the more he fell behind."

Another story, carried by *The Blood-Horse,* revealed that "Feustel said he found after the race that Man o' War's stirrup leathers had been cut, but the job had been done badly, and the straps had held." The fact is, neither account is accurate. Man o' War merely bounded forth with his tremendous sweep and power and he was not to be denied. There was no tampering with his tack before the race.

It has been said that Man o', War broke some of his opponents' hearts. Is this another myth? Obviously, there is no sure reply to the question. Nevertheless, it is true that America's first Triple Crown champion was never the same again after the match race. Commander Ross did race him three more times in the fall of 1920, but he won none, though finishing second once and third twice. The fire seemed to be gone, and he was retired to stud.

It was all downhill thereafter, and the end of this great and colorful Thoroughbred's saga was sorrowful. Sir Barton began his first stud season in 1921, when a few mares were bred to him. The next year, Commander Ross decided to sell him for $75,000 to B. B. and Montfort Jones, the owners of Audley Farm, near Berryville, Va. The brothers had sold off their oil holdings in Oklahoma, and had gone into the even more speculative business of breeding and racing Thoroughbreds, eventually building their operation into one of the most productive centers in the country. The story is that Sir Barton was their first stallion, or one of their first, and that it was at the recommendation of John Madden, the man who had brought the horse into the world and had sold him to Commander Ross, that they purchased him.

The record book indicates that he was unimpressive in stud. But, according to Hobson McGhee, former manager of Audley Farm, "he had a lot of winners. He was bred to good mares. His book was full most every year. Mr. Jones had so many good mares of his own, ninety to a hundred, at Audley that we didn't care particularly about attracting outside mares to breed to him. He was advertised at $1,000 stud fee, which was pretty good at the time." Sir Barton's best offspring was Easter Stockings, the filly who won the 1928 Kentucky Oaks and purses totaling $85,310. The fact is, the most prominent racers of his get were fillies, according to the former manager of the farm. "I think you can say that it figured to be that way. Sir Barton, on his breeding, came from horses that stood out on the bottom side . . . Sir Barton's was a strong distaff line, more than his sire's side."

The stallion remained on the farm for eleven years, when he was turned over to a U.S. Remount Station, near Front Royal, Va., in 1933, at the age of seventeen. A Colonel Wall was the commanding officer, and apparently was a friend of the Jones brothers. Nobody seems to know why the horse was sent away, particularly since the Joneses held on to pensioners at Audley. The story is equally obscure in that Sir Barton is said to have also wound up at a U.S. Remount Station at Fort Robinson, Nebr., that same year, with his stud fees reported to be between $5 and $10. Then, later in the year, he was purchased by a Dr. J. R. Hylton, of Douglas, Wyo., who owned a string of race horses. The good doctor brought the Thoroughbred to his La Prele Creek ranch in the foothills of the Laramie Mountains, some eighteen miles from Douglas, where he lived out the rest of his years. Sir Barton, America's first Triple Crown champion, died on October 30, 1937, when he was twenty-one years old. He was buried near the paddock on the ranch, in a plot enclosed by a picturesque post-and-rail fence, with a sandstone marker inscribed by the foreman's wife.

Sir Barton grazes in his corral on the Wyoming ranch of Dr. J. R. Hylton in 1934. He died three years later at the age of twenty-one.

Gravesite of Sir Barton in Douglas, Wyo. The famous racer had originally been buried on the Hylton ranch.

Man o' War with his devoted groom Will Harbut. Over 1,323,000 people visited him during his days of retirement.

For over thirty years, the famous racer reposed in quiet obscurity on the Hylton ranch until in 1968, through a Jaycee-sponsored project, Sir Barton once again came into prominence. His remains, carefully exhumed from their original resting place, were put beneath a handsome equestrian statue in Washington Park at Douglas—a site which is one of the area's foremost tourist attractions today. It is only fitting that the horse was so honored, albeit the tribute was not without a bit of irony despite the good intentions of the Douglas citizenry. He did suffer one more indignity. It appears that the heroic statue is not a likeness of Sir Barton. Rather, it is a fiberglass replica of "a" horse, produced as a stock item by a Montana company, whose specialty is life-sized models of large animals.

Man o' War also came to the end of his competitive days with the Kenilworth race. Samuel Riddle feared the weights that would be assigned to him if he participated in the handicaps in his fourth year. He had had a sample of this earlier in 1920, when the horse was asked to carry as much as 138 pounds. Thus, he was retired to stud, and wrote a new and glorious chapter to an already phenomenal career. His first foals reached the races in 1924. Out of his second crop came Crusader, the first of his offspring to exceed $200,000 in earnings. Man o' War, in 1926, headed the sire list, as his sons and daughters won a record-breaking $408,137. He became a headliner once again in 1937, when his son, War Admiral, captured the Triple Crown, and his grandson, Seabiscuit, became one of the turf's greatest campaigners and money-winners, and the two locked heads in one of the most exciting battles ever witnessed on an American race track.

Man o' War lived out his days on his owner's Faraway Farm in Kentucky, where over 1,323,000 people visited him. He died in 1947. By a conservative estimate, the initial investment of $5,000 that Samuel Riddle made in purchasing him paid off over $4,000,000, in purses won by him and his progeny and from stud fees. His epitaph was a remark made by Will Harbut, his groom: "He wuz the mostest horse."

GALLANT FOX

GALLANT FOX { *Sir Gallahad III { *Teddy
(Bay Colt)   Plucky Liege

             Marguerite { Celt
                          *Fairy Ray

Gallant Fox

Early in 1925, Arthur B. Hancock was faced with a pressing problem. The master of Claiborne Farm, one of the country's prime Thoroughbred breeding centers near Paris, Ky., had lost two sires, and was sorely in need of a first-class stockhorse. The knotty matter was resolved before the year was out, but the breeder could hardly have envisaged the chain reaction of events that followed, which added brilliant pages to the history of Thoroughbred racing in America.

It was in March that his attention was first drawn to photographs of a French-bred colt, Sir Gallahad III, as he won the Lincolnshire Handicap in England in a gallop. Sometime later, he again saw pictures of the horse beating Epinard in a match race in Le Sport Universal in France. There was something about his bearing that grabbed him. It was a hunch at first, but it nurtured into a strong desire when he learned the colt's impressive pedigree.

His sire, Teddy, of the Bend Or line through a chain of Ajax-Flying Fox-Orme-Ormonde, had been the outstanding stallion of 1923 in France, and one of that country's best in fifteen years. Plucky Liege, his dam, had dropped a whole cluster of distinguished sons and daughters, while he himself had chalked up an impressive skein of wins and purses in three years of campaigning, before retiring to stud in 1925. The statistics had sufficient weight to warrant further investigation. Hancock therefore cabled the British Bloodstock Agency, requesting an inquiry to determine if Sir Gallahad III's owner-breeder, Captain Jefferson Davis Cohn, would consider selling him.

A favorable response was received. Accompanying it was an option on the horse until the last day in November, and an invitation to visit the Normandy stud farm. Hancock would be allowed to inspect the stallion and the mares bred to him in the spring, to confirm his fertility and good health. Encouraged by this, the Kentucky breeder next contacted three aristocrats of the American turf—banker and chairman of the Jockey Club William Woodward, department store tycoon Marshall Field, and Wall Street broker Robert A. Fairbairn. He explained his plan and proposed that they form a syndicate with him to help finance the venture. The three agreed, but only if he recommended it after inspecting the horse.

Hancock sailed at once for France, landing in Cherbourg on November 24. He visited the farm the following day, met with Cohn at the Ritz in Paris the day after, and concluded the deal the next morning. The price was in the vicinity of $150,000, but included all freight and insurance costs.

Little time was wasted thereafter in bringing the prize stallion to America, and in style too. He was shipped to Boulogne, then to London, and, finally, to the United States aboard the liner *Minnetonka,* in special quarters prepared for him on one of the passenger decks. Upon his arrival in New York on December 15, he was met by a special float that transferred him to a private railway express car, made available by Woodward, for the trip to Kentucky. He finally reached Claiborne, safe and sound, to begin his first stud season on American soil in the spring of 1926; something like forty mares were awaiting the pleasure of his company.

"It may be fitly said that he was destined to exercise a more potent influence upon the American breeding fabric than any other stallion imported for many years, and that this animal marked the beginning of a new development in our stud history," is the appraisal voiced by the noted turf historian John Hervey, who wrote under the pen name of "Salvator." His first issue came of racing age in 1929. They numbered twenty-three, fifteen of which went to the post, with seven winning fifteen races. All told, they earned a total of $47,947. However, the following year, with only two- and three-year-olds representing him at the track, Sir Gallahad III established a new world's record, when sixteen of his get won forty-nine races and purses adding up to $422,200. It topped Man o' War's record of 1926, when twenty-six of his offspring won forty-nine races and earned $408,137.

One of the mares scheduled for a date with the French stallion in the breeding shed was William Woodward's Marguerite. He had purchased her in 1921 at Saratoga from a lot of yearlings put up for sale by Arthur Hancock. She was English-bred, and the banker paid $4,700 for her, simply because he fancied the chestnut filly. She was broken at his Belair Farm, in Prince George's County, Md., after which she made her racing debut at Belmont on May 27, 1923. She went off at 15-1 and finished last. It was also her last race, because she seemed to wrench her back, failed to respond in training, and was finally retired the following year. Her owner was not concerned, since he had felt all along that she would do better as a broodmare.

Her first foal was a colt in 1925, followed by a filly the next year. Then, on March 23, 1927, to the cover of Sir Gallahad III, she dropped a hard bay colt, with black points, a blaze face, and coronets marked with white. They named him Gallant Fox, and it was largely because of his illustrious accomplishments in racing three years later that his sire became the world's leading stallion.

William Woodward was a rather unique owner. He cared little for the two-year-old stakes races, such as the Futurity and the Hopeful. Rather, he looked forward to the classics—the Kentucky Derby, Preakness, and Belmont Stakes. Consequently, after the yearling Gallant Fox was weaned at the Belair Stud, he was shipped to the Belair stable at Aqueduct Race Track in New York, to come under the care of the great trainer "Mr. Fitz," James "Sunny Jim" Fitzsimmons. He was to be brought along slowly for the rigors of the three-year-old campaign.

It was no surprise, therefore, that his two-year-old season was somewhat unimpressive, at least at the outset. He made his debut at Aqueduct on June 24, 1929, raced greenly, but finished a strong third behind the winner, Desert Light, in a field of ten. Five days later, he was out again in the six-furlong Tremont Stakes with twelve other horses. He finished eighth, the only time in his career he ever wound up out of

Trainer James "Sunny Jim" Fitzsimmons. The photograph was taken in 1938, after he had saddled two Triple Crown champions.

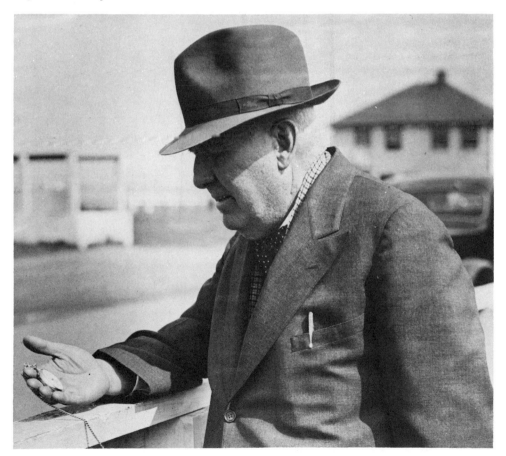

the money. The result was no surprise to his trainer, since he had become accustomed to an infuriatingly bad habit of the colt—curiosity. "The Fox" was simply nosy about all that was going on about him, which kept him from settling down to business. The Tremont was an example. Fitzsimmons claimed, "He was so interested in the others that he forgot to leave the barrier until he saw them running down the track away from him, when he started after them and did pass five of them."

Finally, on July 29, Gallant Fox broke his maiden, "closing like a lion" from third in the stretch, to take the Flash Stakes at Saratoga by a length and a half. The win convinced Woodward and Fitzsimmons that they had a rather good horse in training. Nobody was particularly upset, therefore, when he lost the next three races, the U.S. Hotel Stakes, Futurity Trial, and Futurity. Each race found him running stronger. His final outing of the year was in the Junior Champion Stakes at Aqueduct, on September 28. He caught the leader, Desert Light, with an eighth of a mile to go, wrote Neil Newman, the respected turf writer with the distinctive *nom de plume* "Roamer," "swept past him as if he were anchored and won with his head on his chest by two lengths." This race stamped Gallant Fox as a high-class colt, and his name from that time on was mentioned in all discussions about the three-year-old classics of 1930.

So, as the colt prepared to spend the winter at Aqueduct, he did, indeed, become the talk of the turf. Before the year was up, both Whichone and Boojum, the Harry Payne Whitney precocious speedsters, were withdrawn from the Kentucky Derby of 1930 because of leg problems. The only other horse that rated with the track fans was the Kentucky-bred Desert Light, and Gallant Fox had already beaten him. Reflecting in retrospect on the colt's sudden elevated status, "Roamer" commented: "As a two-year-old Gallant Fox was a first-class race-horse, but I doubt if any outside of his immediate circle, prior to the running of the Junior Champion Stakes the latter part of September, suspected that he was a potential champion and record maker." Whatever doubt existed evaporated progressively as the winter of 1929 eased into the spring of 1930.

A fusing of factors within a relatively short span early in the year virtually guaranteed a phenomenal racing season for Gallant Fox. First off, he weathered the rigors of a New York winter with ease, growing and developing into a handsome, powerful frame, an inch over sixteen hands tall and weighing some 1,200 pounds. Then, once the snow had disappeared from the track, James Fitzsimmons laid out a grueling training campaign for him. Although he was not entered in any races until the Wood Memorial in April, he nevertheless trained as though he were preparing for an outing any day. The fact is, they had him sizzling through eight furlongs in 1:41 as early as March. Also, Gallant Fox seemed to have put to rest his insatiable curiosity about things around him and was all business. Finally, Earl Sande decided to come out of retirement and become the colt's regular jockey. They became the dream team of the year, one of the best of all time.

Actually, it was as late as April before Sande made his move back to the track. He had begun riding as an amateur in his home town of American Falls, Neb., at the age of ten. In 1918, he turned professional as an apprentice in New Orleans, from which point he rose to the top of his profession, and was lionized with the same awe and admiration as was Babe Ruth in baseball. By 1923, he was the highest-paid rider, a far cry from the youngster with the nervous stomach who had been taken off Sir Barton for the match race with Man o' War. Sande finally retired in 1928, when making weight became something of a chore. He turned to training and owning his own string. The venture was anything but a success, and he eventually wound up $75,000 in debt. With the death of his wife, and still only thirty-four years old, he began to yearn for the track. He started working out to see if he could regain some of his old finesse. Then, as the important Wood Memorial on April 26 approached, he was prevailed upon to ride Gallant Fox in the colt's first race at three. For the jockey, it was his first competitive ride since September 1928.

Earl Sande and Gallant Fox, the turf dream team of 1930. The colt's right eye had too much white around the pupil, giving it the appearance of a "wall eye," which some said threw fright into his rivals.

"Sande has a spell to which horses seem unable to refuse response," reported Vernon Van Ness in the New York *Times*. "And most horsemen will tell you that Sande is the only real genius among jockeys they have ever seen." Going off at 8-5 in the mile and seventy yards race, the Gallant Fox–Earl Sande duo romped to a four-length victory. At the outset, Crack Brigade jumped out into an early lead, as the rest of the field closed in and pinched off the Belair colt. Into the far turn, he was still boxed in on the rail, whereupon Sande eased him back and made a move around the field on the outside. As he came on, Desert Light challenged him, at the same time forcing him still farther away from the rail. The strategy failed, for Gallant Fox just kept going, reaching the leader at the quarter pole and galloping home as he pleased, in 1:43$^3/_5$, while carrying 120 pounds as if the weight were a mere nothing.

Followers of the turf said the win created more excitement and enthusiasm with the 20,000 fans at the track and throughout the racing world as to the horse's prospects in the upcoming Preakness and Kentucky Derby than had been shown in a horse in years, particularly since all of the horses who ran in the Wood were Derby candidates. Unfortunately for Desert Light, the second favorite of the race, he bowed a tendon and was lost for the season.

Thirteen days later, on May 9, it was Preakness time at Pimlico. This was one of the years when the race was run before the Kentucky Derby. A field of eleven Thoroughbreds went to the post, and once again Gallant Fox was in trouble at the outset. Running on the rail, he "lacked early footing," was passed, pocketed, and lost even more ground on the clubhouse turn. Moving into the backstretch next to last, Sande's golden touch with a horse became evident, when he started what was described in the *Times'* account of the race as "the most electrifying dash that has been seen in Maryland in many a day. Finding a hole here and a gap there, Sande snaked his way through the field and was third at the far turn," having made every other horse look like they were on a treadmill. He was second at the top of the stretch, at which point Sande gave his charging mount a breather, before moving to within a head of the leader at the mile. A neck-and-neck battle for the lead was joined with Crack Brigade, who "couldn't stand the strain and gave just a little" 150 yards from the finish line, enough to wind up second by three-quarters of a length. The time was 2:00$^3/_5$, and the crowd of 51,925, including Vice President Charles Curtis, tried to figure out how the horse had pulled off the victory, when he appeared to be so hopelessly lost on the first pass of the grandstands.

The accolades tumbled forth in a gush. Bill Corum, in the New York *American*, crowed: "The squarest shooting kid that ever clucked in the ear of a race horse came back to the big time to give us as masterly an exhibition of horsemanship as ever he flashed when his name was a byword of the turf." "Roamer" wrote: "This race demonstrated that Gallant Fox did not have to have everything his own way during the race,

Gallant Fox, with Earl Sande up, drives down the home stretch to win the Preakness by three-quarters of a length over Crack Brigade.

Official chart of Preakness.

47354
May-9-30-Plm

FIFTH RACE—1 3-16 Miles. (Big Blaze, Nov. 13, 1924—1:58⅗—3—118.) Thirty-ninth Running PREAKNESS STAKES. $50,000 Added. 3-year-olds. Entire Colts and Fillies. Weight-for-Age. Net value to winner $51,925; second, $5,000; third, $3,000; fourth, $2,000.

Index	Horses	A	Wt	PP	St	½	¾	1	Str	Fin	Jockeys	Owners	Equiv. Odds Str't
(46944)	GALLANT FOX	wB	126	1	2	8nk	3²	2⁴	1h	1¾	E Sande	Belair Stud Stable	100—100
47197²	CRACK BRIGADE	ws	126	8	3	2½	2h	1h	2⁸	2⁶	G Ellis	T M Cassidy	1145—100
47154³	SNOWFLAKE	wB	121	2	1	6nk	8½	4½	3h	3¹½	A Rob'ts'n	W J Salmon	†900—100
47197³	MICHIGAN BOY	w	126	6	9	10¹	7h	5³	4³	4¹½	J Shelton	J L Pontius	1475—100
(47006)	GOLD BROOK	w	126	9	6	4¹½	4nk	3¹½	5³	5h	J Maiben	Howe Stable	‡1675—100
47198	SWE'T SENTIMENT	w	126	7	4	3h	5²	6h	6³	6³	F Col'letti	Seagram Stable	1175—100
(47197)	WOODCRAFT	w	126	5	11	11	10½	10¹	7h	7nk	E Ambr'se	Audley Farm Stable	1695—100
(47234)	ARMAGEDDON	w	126	11	8	7½	9¹	9³	9²	8h	J Eaby	W M Jeffords	1205—100
(47071)	SWINFIELD	w	126	10	7	5h	6h	8¹	8³	9¹½	L Schaefer	W J Salmon	†
46951³	FULL DRESS	w	126	4	10	9h	11	11	11	10¹½	J McCoy	Glen Riddle St'k F'm Sta	2030—100
(47062)	TETRARCHAL	w	126	3	5	1²	1nk	7¹	10½	11	W Kelsay	Howe Stable	‡

†Coupled as W. J. Salmon entry; ‡Howe Stable entry.

Time, :23⅗, :48, 1:13⅗, 1:39, 2:00⅖. Track fast.

	┌$2 DONATIONS PAID┐			┌EQUIVALENT BOOKING┐		
GALLANT FOX	$ 4.00	$ 4.30	$ 2.90	100—100	115—100	45—100
CRACK BRIGADE		7.20	4.60		260—100	130—100
W. J. SALMON ENTRY			3.70			85—100

Winner—B. c, by Sir Gallahad III.—Marguerite, by Celt (trained by J. Fitzsimmons; bred by Belair Stud).

WENT TO POST—5:02. AT POST—6¼ minutes.

Start good out of machine. Won driving; second and third easily. GALLANT FOX, in trouble on the first turn, went to the outside in the back stretch, caught the others with fine speed and, given a breathing spell when in contention, responded gamely to wear down CRACK BRIGADE and, ridden out, was drawing away at the end. CRACK BRIGADE forced a good pace and raced TETRARCHAL into submission and held on gamely after taking the lead. SNOWFLAKE, shuffled back at the half-mile post, recovered and finished gamely. MICHIGAN BOY improved his position slowly, but could not menace the leaders. GOLD BROOK offered a strong challenge on the turn, but tired at the end. SWEET SENTIMENT could not keep up. WOODCRAFT began slowly and was never a factor. TETRARCHAL showed fine speed for seven-eighths and quit badly.

and also proved that the experience of Sande was an invaluable asset to Gallant Fox's natural ability." Sande was somewhat more laconic. "I didn't call on him until we hit the furlong pole. Then he came on with a rush and hung it on Crack Brigade." "Mr. Fitz" was equally matter-of-fact. He professed not to have been worried, that "when he got close to the leader, I knew it was all over." The day was a heady one, indeed, for the principals. Sande and Woodward enjoyed the savor of their first Preakness victories, while the colt achieved status. According to "Roamer," "Gallant Fox had now attained national prominence, and was affectionately referred to by his admirers as 'The Fox of Belair.' "

In a driving rain, 60,000 fans turned out for the fifty-sixth running of the Kentucky Derby on May 17. There was a festive air despite the weather, what with the presence of the Seventeenth Earl of Derby, who had been invited to visit the United States by Joseph E. Widener, president of the Westchester Racing Association in New York. There were fifteen starters, with "The Fox" favored at 11-10. Next in line was the Kentucky-bred Tannery. "Roamer" was hardly impressed with the field. "When the list of his prospective rivals was canvassed," he lamented, "not one had credentials of a first-class horse. Yet local pride in Kentucky was so great, coupled with an animosity toward anything hailing from the east, that a locally owned horse called Tannery was heralded as a real menace to Gallant Fox and many loyal Kentuckians were firmly of the opinion that 'Pritchard's horse' [Tannery] would win the honors. This belief was held by some horsemen who had spent their lives around race tracks, and can only be ascribed to the intense chauvinism that sways many 'Hard Boots' in intersectional contests."

The race was almost a duplicate of the Preakness. Gallant Fox started slowly, in fifth position going past the grandstands after leaving the gate. However, as the field entered the backstretch, it was the beginning of the end, and the only question that remained was by how much he would win. Sande moved "The Fox" to the outside and "closed on the leaders with a show of power that made those who had seen his Preakness rush chuckle," marveled the *Times'* Bryan Field. For a moment, three horses raced together as a team—Gallant Knight, Tannery, and Gallant Fox. Then "The Fox" made his move, and when Crack Brigade tried to keep up with him, "Sande looked over his shoulder, slapped Gallant Fox once or twice and Gallant Fox moved away and daylight grew between his heels and Crack Brigade's nose." In the stretch it was all too "clear that a horse running in hand with power in reserve was not going to be beaten by horses failing to gain when under the bat." At the wire, he was just coasting, coming in two lengths in front of Gallant Knight, in 2:07$^3/_5$.

The victory inspired Damon Runyon to lead off his story on the race with a verse that said in part:

> "Why it's that handy
> Guy named Sande,
> Bootin' a winner in!"

Gallant Fox roars through driving rain to beat Gallant Knight in the 1930 Kentucky Derby. This victory was Sande's third Derby.

Official chart of Kentucky Derby.

47619
May-17-30-C.D.

FIFTH RACE—1 1-4 Miles. (Track record: Woodtrap, May 21, 1921—2:03⅕—7—106. Derby record: Old Rosebud, May 9, 1914—2:03⅖—3—114.) **Fifty-sixth Running KENTUCKY DERBY.** $50,000 Added. 3-year-olds. Net value to winner $50,725 and gold cup valued at $5,000; second, $6,000; third, $3,000; fourth, $1,000.

Index	Horses	A	Wt	PP	St	½	¾	1	Str	Fin	Jockeys	Owners	Equiv. Odds Str't
(47354)	GALLANT FOX	wB	126	7	8	4¹	1¹	1²	1²	1²	E Sande	Belair Stud Stable	119-100
47396³	GALLANT KNI'HT	wB	126	8	7	7¹	6½	3³	2½	2²	H Schutte	Audley Farm Stable	2273-100
47475²	NED O.	w	126	3	3	12¹½	13ʰ	9½	4ʰ	3¹	J D M'ney	G W Foreman	2579-100
47260	GONE AWAY	wB	126	10	14	14¹½	11¹½	7½	5²	4⁴	M Garner	Wm Ziegler Jr	5292-100
47354²	CRACK BRIGADE	ws	126	6	13	6¹	4ⁿᵏ	2ʰ	3ʰ	5½	G Ellis	T M Cassidy	1662-100
47401	LONGUS	wB	126	1	15	15	14⁴	10ʰ	7¹	6²	R O'Brien	R C Stable	†1812-100
(47475)	UNCLE LUTHER	w	126	2	12	8¹½	8ʰ	6¹½	6¹	7²	R Creese	L Stivers	†
(47169)	TANNERY	w	126	12	2	3¹	3¹	5ʰ	8¹½	8ʰ	W Garner	E F Prichard	312-100
47475	BR'DWAY LIM'T'D	wB	126	14	11	10½	12¹½	12³	10²	9½	P Walls	Three D's Stk Fm Sta	‡5043-100
(47520)	ALCIBIADES	w	121	4	4	1²	2½	4ʰ	9ʰ	10ʰ	L Jones	H P Headley	†
40366²	KILKERRY	w	126	9	9	11¹½	10ʰ	11½	11⁴	11⁴	T May	Three D's Stk Fm Sta	‡
47169²	BREEZING THRU	wB	126	13	6	13¹	9²	14ʰ	13¹	12⁸	J Smith	E R Bradley	§875-100
47169³	BUCKEYE POET	wB	126	15	5	2ʰ	5¹½	8¹½	12²	13¹	E Legere	E R Bradley	§
47396	HIGH FOOT	w	126	5	1	5ʰ	7¹	13½	14⁸	14⁸	C Meyer	Valley Lake Stable	2288-100
47475	DICK O'HARA	w	126	11	10	9²	15	15	15	15	N Barrett	P H Joyce	†

†Mutuel field.   ‡Coupled as Three D's Stock Farm Stable entry; §E. R. Bradley entry.

Time, :23⅗, :47⅘, 1:14, 1:40⅘, 2:07⅘.   Track good.

	—$2 MUTUELS PAID—			—EQUIVAL'NT BOOKING ODDS—		
GALLANT FOX	$ 4.38	$ 3.76	$ 3.42	119—100	88—100	71—100
GALLANT KNIGHT		14.60	8.78		630—100	339—100
NED O.			10.14			407—100

Winner—B. c, by Sir Gallahad III.—Marguerite, by Celt (trained by J. Fitzsimmons; bred by Belair Stud).

WENT TO POST—5:00. AT POST—2½ minutes.

Start good out of machine. Won easily; second and third driving.

GALLANT FOX, in extremely close quarters for the first three-eighths, raced into the lead on the outside after straightening out in the back stretch, held command under restraint thereafter and won with something in reserve. GALLANT KNIGHT began slowly, worked his way up with a big loss of ground, offered a mild challenge entering the final eighth, but tired badly near the end. NED O. began improving his position after five-eighths, lost ground on the last turn, but finished resolutely. GONE AWAY, on the extreme outside throughout, moved up fast on the stretch turn, but quit in the final eighth. CRACK BRIGADE, sent up with a rush after five-eighths, loomed up menacingly on the stretch turn, then quit. LONGUS came from far back in the stretch. TANNERY tired badly after racing prominently for seven-eighths. HIGH FOOT and ALCIBIADES tired. KILKERRY pulled up sore. BUCKEYE POET had early speed.

Scratched—47396 Busy, 126.

Overall view of the winner's circle as Gallant Fox, Earl Sande, William Woodward and Lord Derby partic-
ipate in the Derby victory ceremonies.

"Why it wasn't even close," he went on. "Gallant Fox, pride of the East, with the old master mind of the horseman sitting his saddle as easily as if he were in a rocking chair on a shady veranda, galloped off with the $50,000 Kentucky Derby." Even Lord Derby was convinced early. Watching the colt move into the stretch out in front, he turned to William Woodward, said a tersely, "Fine stuff," and looked for the route to the winner's circle for the presentation ceremonies. The crowd erupted with a tremendous roar, when Gallant Fox returned from the track, cheering as much, or more, for Sande.

Some interesting facts showed up in news accounts later on. The victory, for example, was Sande's third in the Derby, his others being with Zev (1923) and Flying Ebony (1925). He thus became the first modern jockey and first white man to accomplish this, since the black Isaac Murphy set the standard in the nineteenth century. William Woodward's investment in Sir Gallahad III paid off for him with his first Derby win. On the other hand, Gallant Fox rewarded his backers with a modest $4.38 for $2.00, or about 4-5, the shortest price in the classic since Old Rosebud won it in 1914. CBS radio, over a network of seventy stations, with Ted Husing the announcer, and NBC radio, with fifty stations and Graham McNamee and Clem McCarthy at the microphones, broadcast the race from trackside. One filly, Alcibiades, ran and came in tenth. Celebrities were in ample supply among the crowd, causing one reporter to note that "Clem McCarthy . . . who dotes on notables when chatting with his audience, ran himself bowlegged collecting names." This was the first time that stall gates were used at the start in a Derby. The pari-mutuel figures showed that $582,384 was bet on the race, of which $207,706 was placed on "The Fox." He picked up a tidy purse of $50,725, plus a $5,000 gold cup, which brought his total earnings, including the $19,890 in 1929 and the purses from the Wood and Preakness, to a very respectful $132,690.

Excitement among racing fans now began to inch up, reaching a fever pitch by June 7, the day of the Belmont Stakes. The race would see the first meeting of Gallant Fox and Whichone, regarded by many as perhaps the greatest juvenile in many a year in 1929. He had beaten Gallant Fox in the Futurity, and had earned over $100,000, to become the top two-year-old money-winner. However, he had been withdrawn from racing toward the end of the year when he developed bad knees, but had been pointed ever since toward a second meeting with Gallant Fox in the Belmont. He came up to the race in excellent condition, following a fine victory in the Withers. His jockey, too, was the extremely capable Raymond "Sonny" Workman.

Respect for the two outstanding colts was obvious when only two other horses, Questionnaire and Swinfield, dared to face them. Furthermore, the capacity crowd of 40,000 sent "The Fox" off at 8-5 and Whichone at 4-5. "The classes preferred Whichone, the masses Gallant Fox," said "Roamer." "It is the fashion of the so-called experts to favor a champion until he is beaten and tradition was adhered to in this instance to the letter." There still was doubt that the Belair colt had beaten much, despite his wins in three major races.

A drizzle was in the air when the four horses marched to the starting gate. Now, Earl Sande shot "The Fox of Belair" to the front right off. Sonny Workman preferred to hold back. The Harry Payne Whitney colt "was sawing wood in last place," seemingly trying to conserve energy. Sande also moved Gallant Fox out from the rail for better footing, giving up ground in the process and enabling Whichone to gain somewhat. The crowd was tense with excitement. "They were seeing a seemingly invincible horse held even by a colt which was supposed to have beaten only mediocre opposition in the Preakness and Kentucky Derby," the *Times* reported. They also saw Sande hand-ride his mount and still draw away, while Workman went to the whip in vain, losing by three lengths. The time was 2:31$\frac{3}{5}$, topping Crusader's 1926 record by $\frac{3}{5}$ second, but behind Man o' War's track record for the mile and a half of 2:28$\frac{4}{5}$. Damon Runyon had kept his eyes glued on the red-hooded Woodward colt, almost mesmerized. "Through the leaden-grey mist of a rainy Long Island afternoon, 'that red-headed horse,' Gallant Fox . . . galloped to his greatest triumph in winning the Belmont Stakes . . . the horse hadn't gone a hundred yards when Sande's heels drummed vigorously at Gallant Fox's satin sides and the bright hood shot out to the front. And there it stayed." It was a rather easy victory for the new Triple Crown champion, the first since Sir Barton. The race was also the richest Belmont, worth $66,040 to Gallant Fox. This brought his total earnings to $198,730 and established him as the eighth leading money-winner. Subsequently, it was learned that Sande rode despite being patched up, following a car accident. There was just no way he would allow himself to be replaced. As the day came to a close, hardly anyone was prepared to bet that Gallant Fox would ever be beaten again.

The next two races appeared to confirm this. Three weeks later, on June 28, he waltzed in by three lengths in the Dwyer Stakes at Aque-

Gallant Fox becomes America's second Triple Crown champion as he crosses the finish line four lengths in front of Whichone in the Belmont Stakes.

Proud owner William Woodward leads Gallant Fox to the winner's circle.

48551
June-7-30-Bel

FIFTH RACE—1 1-2 Miles. (Man o' War, Sept. 11, 1920—2:28⅘—3—118.) Sixty-second Running BELMONT STAKES. $25,000 Added. 3-year-olds. Net value to winner $66,040; second, $7,500; third, $3,000; fourth, $1,000.

Index	Horses	A	Wt	PP	St	½	¾	1	Str	Fin	Jockeys	Owners	O	H	C	P	S
(47619)	GALLANT FOX	wb	126	1	2	1²	1¹	1²	1¹	1³	E Sande	Belair St'd St	8-5	8-5	8-5	1-4	out
(48190)	WHICHONE	wb	126	3	4	4	3³	3¹⁰	2³	R W'kman	H P Whitney	4-5	5	4	7-10	1-6	out
(48325)	QUESTIONNAIRE	wb	126	4	4	2²	2ʰ	2½	2ʰ	3²⁰	A Rob'ts'n	J Butler	8	10	10	2	1-4
48190²	SWINFIELD	w	126	2	1	3¹	3³	4	4	4	L Schaefer	W J Salmon	30	30	30	4	1

Time, :23⅘, :37⅘, :50½, 1:03⅘, 1:16, 1:28⅘, 1:41, 1:54, 2:07, 2:31⅘. Track good.

Winner—B. c, by Sir Gallahad III.—Marguerite, by Celt (trained by J. Fitzsimmons; bred by Belair Stud).

WENT TO POST—4:24. AT POST—1 minute.

Start good and slow. Won easily; second and third the same.

GALLANT FOX was rushed into the lead at the start, was rated along under restraint and, given a breathing spell passing the half-mile post and again on the far turn, drew away when called upon and then came wide entering the stretch, finishing with speed in reserve. WHICHONE was taken under restraint in the early stages, but did not stride freely in the greasy going, responded when called upon on the far turn and finished gamely on the inside of the winner. QUESTIONNAIRE, close up throughout, saved much ground turning for home, but could not menace the leaders. SWINFIELD made a determined effort when called upon, but quit badly and was eased up at the end.

Scratched—48399 Flying Gal, 121.

Official chart of Belmont Stakes.

duct. In the opinion of "Roamer," "The horse knew he was master of the situation and refused to exert himself unnecessarily." As a result, his stature leaped. He became the first horse to win five great three-year-old stakes—the Wood Memorial, Preakness, Derby, Belmont, and Dwyer. He also picked up an additional $11,500, which carried his earnings past the $200,000 mark, thereby moving him to the top spot as the leading money-winner of the year. Once again, Sande was a doubtful starter, having injured a leg a fortnight before when he was unseated by a horse. Then, in Chicago on July 12, he took the Arlington Classic, winning by just a neck after a head-and-head duel with Gallant Knight down the stretch. It was his sixth consecutive win, and no horse in the history of the American turf had ever won the big races in the order that he had, all within just sixty days.

Now, to some, he was unquestionably America's "greatest horse since Man o' War." John Hervey saw him as a heroic figure. "His head is clean and hawklike with quick, nervous eyes. . . . To the eye he looked a bit high off the ground when in training, he stood on his feet with the poise of an athlete and there was about him an air of intense, almost flowing, vitality and dynamic force." Bryan Field ranked him with a "kingly host." "Gallant Fox is a horse of individuality and magnetism, and thus far has behaved in the opposite manner to the tempestuous Man o' War, who was a devil to break and a big, raw colt to handle and train as a two-year-old. He gives the impression of unusual grace and distinction and his symmetry and harmony have attracted thousands of admirers, as did Man o' War's effervescent temperament." It was as if he knew he was king, Field continued, for he was contemptuous of training workouts, refusing to extend himself. "Mr. Fitz" had to use relays of horses to counter this to keep his speed keyed—shades of Sir Barton. There were no other horses in the barn who could keep up with him.

There was even talk of an "evil eye," which threw fright into his rivals when he looked at them. Both of his eyes were bright and flashing,

Gallant Fox beats Xenofol in the Dwyer to continue his spectacular skein of stakes victories.

but one had too much white around the pupil, giving it the appearance of a "walleye," and the horse the impression of having a wild, staring expression. They even said he was something of a rogue, since he raced with blinkers. Jim Fitzsimmons, however, cleared up this canard. The trainer refused to remove the blinkers because he was a superstitious sort. The colt had won his first race wearing them, and "Mr. Fitz" did not want to change his luck. Instead, he merely cut away most of the blinkers, because he was afraid that Gallant Fox would risk defeat by easing up if he moved too far in front of the field and failed to see any of his opponents. "He seems to know he's a race horse and he knows what's going on," continued Fitzsimmons. "I let him run his own races pretty much and that's one reason Sande makes an ideal jockey for him," Bryan Field concurred. Sande had good hands and a good seat and understood horses, he wrote, "but when he lays in behind a horse's ears and croons to him something happens with that horse which does not happen with other horses."

So it was, coming up to the prestigious Travers on August 16, the oldest race in America, dating back to 1864. It shaped up to be a *pièce de résistance* of the Saratoga season, since it marked the third impending meeting between Gallant Fox and Whichone, who by now claimed victories in the Ballot Handicap, Saranac, Withers, and Whitney stakes races. Only two other horses, Sun Falcon and Jim Dandy, were entered. "The Fox" was favored at 1-2, and Whichone was 8-5. An indication of the value of the others was the 100-1 price on Jim Dandy. The New York *Times'* John Kiernan reasoned that the fans were willing "to back the Flying Earl any time he goes to the barrier on anything faster than a clotheshorse."

The weather was extremely uncooperative, a heavy downpour the night before leaving the track in horrible shape. It was in such bad condition on the morning of the race that track officials, in a desperate effort to dry it out, placed "dogs," forty-foot wooden beams at right angles to the inside rail around the track, to prevent horses from exercising in that area. Consequently, the middle area was pretty well cut up by post time. At the outset, it was virtually a match race between "The Fox of Belair" and Whitney Stable's Whichone. Going into the clubhouse turn, they were battling tooth and nail, head and head, and remained locked this way until they entered the homestretch.

The instructions to Sonny Workman on Whichone had been to take the lead immediately and run Gallant Fox off his feet. Figuring the middle of the track had better footing, Workman ran his race there, some thirty feet or more away from the rail, with Gallant Fox on his outside. The other two horses chose to stay on the rail. As they hit the near turn, Whichone bore out even more, carrying "The Fox" with him. It was at this point, explained "Roamer," that Workman's colt broke down; his near foreleg gave way and "he naturally flinched away to his right and, as the Fox of Belair was lapped upon him, he too was carried out." Jim Dandy, meanwhile, still hugging the rail, saving lengths thereby and staying close to the leaders, suddenly shot forward past the floundering two, moving from third to first within a hundred yards. Sande saw what had happened, tried to rouse his colt, but realized all too late that the duel with Whichone in the sticky mud had sapped his strength, making it impossible to give chase. Therefore, he eased Gallant Fox and was content to come in second, six lengths behind the leader. "It was like a transformation scene in a stage spectacle and left the entire assemblage, one of the largest in the history of racing at Saratoga, gasping in amazement," wrote John Hervey. "The famous favorites, to intents and purposes, stuck in the mud," is the way John Kiernan saw it. The result supported once again the axiom of backstretch people and track aficionados that Saratoga is "the graveyard of favorites." It also marked the end of a brilliant career for the crippled Whichone, and only the third win in thirty starts for the Californian, Jim Dandy. Moving out of the park, a fan was heard to mutter to himself: "I know that Jim Dandy. He did the same thing last year in the Grand Union," when he was only 50-1.

100-1 shot Jim Dandy stuns Saratoga throng with upset victory over Gallant Fox in the Travers. It was only the third win in thirty starts for the California colt.

"The Fox," showing no lasting effects from the loss, came out two weeks later and won the Saratoga Cup as he pleased, negotiating the mile and three quarters in 2:56, just a second slower than Reigh Count's 1928 record. He reaffirmed his prowess on September 6, when he ran what is considered the greatest race of his career in the Lawrence Realization at Belmont Park. "When it was over, turf veterans who have seen many champions in thrilling finishes lowered their glasses, still trembling with excitement," said Bryan Field. Only four horses were entered, and this time Sonny Workman was gunning for Gallant Fox aboard Questionnaire, an outstanding colt who, after finishing third in the Belmont Stakes, had won seven straight races and had never allowed a horse to come from behind and pass him. Gallant Fox was rated at 3-5, carrying 126 pounds, and Questionnaire was at 8-5 under 123 pounds. The others were unimportant.

Workman used the same strategy as in the Travers. He moved out front and stayed there, trailed furiously by Gallant Fox, until they reached the stretch. "Workman waited until Sande and Gallant Fox were at his saddle girth on the outside and then he bore out—bore out so far that he left a hole along the rail through which a couple of hay wagons could be driven," commented Bryan Field. When they straightened out, however, Sande moved to the rail, to pick up momentum from the slight inward sloping of the track and to shut off any of the other horses that might have designs for slipping through. There would be no Jim Dandy this time to steal a race. "The Fox" came on, ran head and head, with Questionnaire just a nose in front. Both jockeys went to the whip, Workman reputedly the best with the bat, Sande the worst. "Then Sande dropped his bat and put up one of the hand rides that made him the king pin on the American turf," and in a bitter, fighting struggle in the last two hundred yards won by a head.

There were statistics galore to gloat over after the race. The time for the mile and five-eighths was 2:41$\frac{1}{5}$, only $\frac{2}{5}$ second behind Man o' War's world's record, which never before had been so nearly reached. They ran the mile and a half in 2:28$\frac{2}{5}$, surpassing the American record for that distance by $\frac{1}{5}$ second. Gallant Fox won $29,610, which made him the country's greatest winning horse, with a total of $317,865, surpassing Zev's mark of $313,639. He was now second in world ranks only to the French horse Ksar, who had earned $335,340. In summing up, "Roamer" wrote of Gallant Fox: "He coupled the speed of a thoroughbred with the heart of a lion. After this race it was the general opinion that he was the best horse bred in this country since Man o' War."

All was anti-climax from here on. In the two-mile Jockey Club Gold Cup at Belmont on September 16, only the three-year-old maiden Yarn came out against him. "A battle between these two was like a battle between a spurred cock and a new-hatched chick," was the opinion of "Roamer." Therefore, in a wan effort to reduce the ridiculous, Belair Farm also sent out their Frisius, and the entry was rated at 1-30. But Frisius showed up heavily bandaged and looking on the verge of a

Earl Sande rides Gallant Fox to a bitter, fighting victory by only a head over Questionnaire (barely seen on rail) in the Lawrence Realization, considered the greatest race of his career.

breakdown. He was taken in hand after a mile, and just did manage to hobble over the finish line. Gallant Fox, in the easiest win of all his races, came in three lengths to the good in the rather slow time of 3:24²/₅. He won $10,300, to push his total to $328,165, and his earnings for just 1930 to $308,275, the first time a Thoroughbred had ever won over $300,000 in a single year.

"The Fox" suddenly developed a fever and cough after the race. Therefore, William Woodward, who had all the money he needed and all of the glory he could expect from a horse, announced that he was retiring him to stud. The colt arrived at Claiborne Farm on October 28. His stud fee was set at $3,000, with no return if a foal was not produced, and his book was filled for his first season as a stallion in the spring of 1931. Woodward had also arranged for Gallant Fox's measurements to be authenticated by the New York Museum of Natural History, and to be preserved on a plaque that was placed next to the skeleton of the great Sysonby that was on display in the venerable institution.

The stud career of "The Fox of Belair" was short. He was successful for only a few years, siring the next Triple Crown champion, Omaha, and Flares and Granville, both of whom won the Ascot Gold Cup in England. In twenty years, from 1934 to 1953, his get earned $1,788,648 in North America and £25,957 in England. One reason attributed to the poor showing in stud is that there were so few good mares sent to him that he had little chance to gain a place among the leading sires. He was finally retired from stud in 1952. Death came to him at about one p.m. on November 13, 1954, at the age of twenty-seven, an hour before the running of two important stakes races whose names reflected his fame. They were the Gallant Fox Handicap at Jamaica, N.Y., and the Marguerite Stakes at Pimlico, Baltimore. He was buried alongside his sire and dam on a hill overlooking the stallion barns at Claiborne Farm. A "Roamer" comment was his epitaph: "Since the retirement of Man o' War no horse has captured the imagination of the American public as has Gallant Fox. After a relatively light campaign as a two-year-old, he swept like a meteor across the racing sky in 1930 and when he was retired for all times after his bloodless triumph in the Jockey Club Gold Cup he was more than a race horse—he was an institution."

OMAHA

OMAHA
(Chestnut Colt)
{
Gallant Fox {
*Sir Gallahad III

Marguerite
}

Flambino {
*Wrack

*Flambette
}
}

Omaha

3

The career of the third horse to wear the Triple Crown in the United States could best be summed up in a word as "erratic." For every soaring peak that it reached, there was a valley of despair into which it plummeted. It was a thoroughly frustrating experience to his owner, William Woodward, his trainer, "Mr. Fitz," and the fans who backed him with hard-earned cash at the betting windows.

Woodward was the master of Belair Stud in Maryland, and had long espoused the theory that excellent breeding results could be attained through a blending of the best French and American Thoroughbred blood strains. A notable example of this, of course, was Gallant Fox, whose sire had been imported from France by a syndicate which Woodward helped form. It was with understandable anticipation, therefore, that he awaited the first crop of Gallant Fox, in 1932. On March 24, at Arthur Hancock's Claiborne Stud, one of these was foaled out of the mare Flambino. He was a bright-golden chestnut colt, slashed with a blaze, and he was named Omaha. It was soon apparent that he had inherited his sire's early lazy racing habits, for he, too, was a slow starter. He made his debut as a two-year-old on June 18, 1934, at Aqueduct, and finished second by a nose to Sir Lamorah, among a field of maidens. Five days later, be broke his maiden in a five-furlong dash, which was it for him for the rest of the year. He started in seven more races, failing to win any. However, he ran well, coming in second in the Sanford, Champagne, and Junior Champion stakes, while displaying sufficient talent to convince many that he was a potential three-year-old champion.

"That Omaha was a comparatively unpretentious two-year-old," recorded "Salvator," "was largely due to the fact that he was so big, lathy and as yet needing time to develop and grow together." He did just that, for as a three-year-old he was built on heroic lines, standing sixteen and a half hands tall and very long. Coming out of his winter at Aqueduct, in April 1935, he won his first race easily, an allowance event of a mile and seventy yards. The following week, he had his first big test, in the Wood Memorial. Although he finished third, he ran strong at the end, which convinced his owner and trainer that he was a Kentucky Derby prospect.

The public took to him as well, and made him a pre-race choice until May 4 dawned. Churchill Downs was enshrouded in a steady drizzle, which turned the track into a sea of mud and made an estimated 50,000 spectators miserable as they waited impatiently for the march to the post. Suddenly, the odds swung away from Omaha to the filly Nellie Flag, who became the favorite of the eighteen-horse field, at nearly 4 to 1. St. Bernard took the early lead, followed closely by Shut Eye and Nellie Flag. Jockey Willie Saunders bided his time until the backstretch, when he guided Omaha to the outside and charged into the lead. They were ahead by two lengths at the top of the homestretch, as a challenge by Roman Soldier materialized. It was shortlived, for, despite the heavy footing, Omaha closed fast in the last half-mile to beat out Roman Soldier by a length and a half, in 2:05.

For some reason, the victory failed to impress the railbirds, a situation which had also confronted Sir Barton and Gallant Fox. The win, nevertheless, was not without a significant sidelight to intrigue turf historians. It was only the third time in sixty-one Derbies that a father-son double had been completed—Gallant Fox and Omaha. The others were Halma (1895) and Alan-a-Dale (1902), and Bubbling Over (1926) and Burgoo King (1932).

Willie Saunders rides Omaha through the mud of Churchill Downs to a length-and-a-half win over Roman Soldier in the 1935 Kentucky Derby. It was only the third time in Derby history that a father-son double had been completed—Gallant Fox and Omaha.

SIXTH RACE
09640
May-4-35-C.D

1 1-4 MILES (Out of Chute). (Twenty Grand, May 16, 1931—2:01⅘—3—126.) Sixty-First Running KENTUCKY DERBY. $40,000 Added. 3-year-olds.

Net value to winner $39,525; second, $6,000; third, $3,000; fourth, $1,000.

Index	Horses	Eq't A Wt PP St	½	¾	1	Str	Fin	Jockeys	Owners	Equiv. Odds Str't
09312³	OMAHA	wʙ 126 10 12	9½	5¹	1²	1¹½	1¹½	SaundersW	Belair Stud Stable	400-100
(09170)	ROMAN SOLDIER	wʙ 126 3 10	11¹	8¹½	4ʰ	2²	2⁴	BalaskiL	Sachsenmaier & Reuter	620-100
(09434)	WHISKOLO	w 126 8 15	12½	10¹½	2¹	3²	3¹½	WrightWD	Milky Way Farms Stable	†840-100
(09328)	NELLIE FLAG	w 121 9 1	8¹½	7½	5³	4³	4ʰ	ArcaroE	Calumet Farm Stable	380-100
09327²	BLACKBIRDER	wʙ 126 13 14	14¹	11¹	11²	5¹	5²	GarnerW	Mrs C Hainsworth	†
09312	PSYCHIC BID	wʙ 126 7 11	4ʰ	4¹	7¹	6³	6⁴	JonesR	Brookmeade Stable	4920-100
09312	MORPLUCK	wsʙ 126 11 16	16¹	13²	12²	7ʰ	7ʰ	GarnerM	J H Louchheim	†
09312²	PLAT EYE	w 126 15 4	1½	1½	3¹	8¹	8¹	CoucciS	Greentree Stable	1640-100
09170	McCARTHY	wʙ 126 4 18	18	15¹	14⁴	14¹	9³	FinnertyR	Morrison & Keating	†
09163³	COMMONWEALTH	wʙ 126 17 17	17⁴	12¹	9ʰ	10²	10²	WoolfG	Mrs W M Jeffords	950-100
09163²	SUN FAIRPLAY	wʙ 126 5 3	10¹	9¹½	13³	11¹	11³	RenickJ	Fair Fields Stable	5230-100
(09312)	TODAY	wʙ 126 16 6	6¹	6½	8¹	9²	12⁶	Workm'nR	C V Whitney	840-100
09434³	WHOPPER	wsʙ 126 2 9	5½	3½	6½	12¹	13¹½	LandoltC	H P Headley	†
09434	BLUEBEARD	wʙ 126 6 2	7¹	14¹½	15¹	15¹	14¹½	SchutteH	Mrs R B Fairbanks	†
09318	TUTTICURIO	wʙ 126 18 13	13ʰ	16⁴	16³	16⁴	15¹	CorbettC	Brandon Stable	†
02596	BOXTHORN	wʙ 126 12 8	3¹½	2¹	10ʰ	13¹	16²	MeadeD	E R Bradley	500-100
01724	ST. BERNARD	w 126 1 5	2ʰ	18	18	18	17½	KeesterP	E G Shaffer	†
09434	WESTON	wʙ 126 14 7	15ʰ	17¹	17¹	17¹	18	YoungS	Braedalbane Stable	†

†Mutuel field.   Time, :23, :47⅗, 1:13⅖, 1:38⅗, 2:05. Track good.

	—$2 MUTUELS PAID—			— OFFICIAL BOOKING ODDS—			
OMAHA	$10.00	$5.00	$3.80	400—100	150—100	90—100
ROMAN SOLDIER		6.40	4.20		220—100	110—100
WHISKOLO (Field)			3.40			70—100

Winner—Ch. c, by Gallant Fox—Flambino, by Wrack (trained by J. Fitzsimmons; bred by Belair Stud).
WENT TO POST—5:13. AT POST—2½ minutes.
Start good and slow. Won easily; second and third driving.

OMAHA, much the best but lucky to escape interference in the early crowding, was taken to the outside after the first quarter, raced to the lead gradually after reaching the half-mile post and, upon taking command, held sway easily thereafter, winning with something left. ROMAN SOLDIER also enjoyed room in the early stages, worked his way to the outside after reaching the back stretch, responded well when called upon and stood severe pressure gamely in the final quarter, but could not menace the winner. WHISKOLO raced to a contending position with a rush, lost ground on the far turn and tired in the last three-sixteenths, but held the others safe. NELLIE FLAG suffered sharp interference from PLAT EYE soon after the start, was again impeded on the first turn, lacked room throughout the back stretch run and could not improve her position when clear in the last five-sixteenths. BLACKBIRDER came from far back and finished boldly. PSYCHIC BID raced well. MORPLUCK also showed good form. PLAT EYE caused much interference soon after the start, had speed, but quit badly after a mile. McCARTHY made up ground. COMMONWEALTH was never prominent, failing to respond to pressure. TODAY was in close quarters on the back stretch, but failed to respond when clear and tired in the stretch. BOXTHORN quit badly. ST. BERNARD was cut off after reaching the back stretch.

Scratched—02435 Color Bearer, 126; 09478³Chanceview, 126; 09434 Prince Splendor, 126; 09434 Calumet Dick, 126.

Official chart of Kentucky Derby.

There were an estimated 45,000 fans at Pimlico a week later, on Saturday, May 11, the largest crowd in the history of the track, as Omaha went up against seven other starters in the Preakness, at less than even money. This time the track was lightning-fast. Once again, Saunders lay back until they reached the backstretch, at which point he gave the horse his head on the outside. It was no contest thereafter, for Omaha "completely smothered his field," stifled any potential threat, and coasted home to a six-length victory. Actually, his cruise around the track was nothing more than a workout for the "Belair Bullet." In taking the race, he became only the fourth horse in history to win both the Kentucky Derby and the Preakness, as a result of which he brought back to him some hesitant fans and a bit more respect.

Omaha smothers the field as he coasts to a six-length victory over Roman Soldier in the Preakness.

Official chart of Preakness.

SIXTH RACE
09965
May-11-35-Pim

1 3-16 MILES. (Gallant Knight, May 7, 1932—1:58—5—121.) Forty-Fifth Running PREAKNESS STAKES. $25,000 Added. 3-year-olds. Scale-weights.
Net value to winner $25,325; second, $2,500; third, $1,500; fourth, $500.

Index	Horses	Eq't	A	Wt	PP	St	½	¾	1	Str	Fin	Jockeys	Owners	Equ'v. Odds Str t
(09640)	OMAHA	wB		126	6	6	6^5	4^5	$1\frac{1}{2}$	1^6	1^6	SaundersW	Belair Stud Stable	95-100
(09702)	FIRETHORN	w		126	5	8	7^6	7^{12}	4^1	2^2	2^6	WrightWD	W M Jeffords	†355-100
09640	PSYCHIC BID	wB		126	7	4	3^4	3^2	2^3	3^4	3^2	WoolfG	Brookmeade Stable	1985-100
09312	MANTAGNA	w		126	3	5	5^h	$6\frac{1}{2}$	6^2	4^4	4^5	McCrossenC	Maemere Farm Stable	2460-100
09640	COMMONWEALTH	wB		126	1	7	8	8	8	6^h	5^1	Ros'gart'nC	Mrs W M Jeffords	†
09383^3	BRANNON	w		126	8	1	1^2	1^3	3^h	$5^1\frac{1}{2}$	6^{nk}	MerrittR	Mrs C S Bromley	8400-100
09640	NELLIE FLAG	wB		121	2	3	$4^1\frac{1}{2}$	$5\frac{1}{2}$	7^5	7^2	7^5	ArcaroE	Calumet Farm Stable	495-100
09640	BOXTHORN	wB		126	4	2	$2^1\frac{1}{2}$	2^h	$5^1\frac{1}{2}$	8	8	WorkmanR	E R Bradley	925-100

†Coupled as Mr. and Mrs. W. M. Jeffords entry.

Time, :23⅖, :47⅗, 1:12⅖, 1:38, 1:58⅖. Track fast.

	┌─ $2 MUTUELS PAID ─┐			┌─ OFFICIAL BOOKING ODDS ─┐		
OMAHA	$ 3.90	$ 3.10	$ 2.60	95—100	55—100	30—100
MR. AND MRS. W. M. JEFFORDS						
ENTRY		3.40	2.80		70—100	40—100
PSYCHIC BID			4.60			130—100

Winner—Ch. c, by Gallant Fox—Flambino, by Wrack (trained by J. Fitzsimmons; bred by Belair Stud).
WENT TO POST—5:56. AT POST—3½ minutes.
Start good and slow. Won easily; second and third driving.
OMAHA, kept clear going to the first turn, bettered his position readily after going seven-eighths, swung to the outside of the leaders when moving to the front midway of the final turn, then drew out at will during the stretch drive to win with much to spare. FIRETHORN, placed to a determined drive in the last five-eighths, was forced to circle his field when reaching contention, then closed willingly in the final drive. PSYCHIC BID raced strongly in the early running on the outside of the leaders, saved much ground during the stretch drive, but tired steadily. MANTAGNA raced under pressure from the beginning and passed tiring horses during the closing stages. COMMONWEALTH dropped far out of contention and was unable to threaten. BRANNON had much speed while setting the pace, but was unable to hold command when vigorously urged. NELLIE FLAG had clear racing room from the beginning, but failed to rally at any stage of the journey. BOXTHORN raced strongly for seven-eighths, then tired.
Scratched—09702³ Furfiber, 126; 09702 Legume, 126; (09318) Bloodroot, 121.

Then, on May 25, he lost the Withers by a length and a half, after going off as a 1 to 2 favorite. The reaction was bitter, even acrimonious, and he lost favor once more by the time June 8 rolled around for the Belmont Stakes. It was a rainy day, the track was sloppy, there were five starters, and he came in for a rough battle. It was not until the turn into the homestretch was reached that he caught up with the leader, Firethorn, who was running a strong race on the rail. The two engaged in a pulsating duel down the stretch, until Omaha proved his class by drawing away to a length-and-a-half dramatic victory and the Triple Crown.

The smiles were back, until he came in third to Discovery and King

Omaha passes Firethorn in a pulsating duel down the homestretch on a gray, rainy day and sloppy track, to take the Belmont Stakes.

Official chart of Belmont Stakes.

FIFTH RACE
11843
June-8-35-Bel

1 1-2 MILES. (Man o' War, Sept. 11, 1920—2:28⅕—3—118.) Sixty-Seventh Running BELMONT STAKES. $25,000 Added. 3-year-olds. Scale weights.

Net value to winner $35,480; second, $5,000; third, $2,500; fourth, $1,000.

Index	Horses	Eq't A Wt	PP	St	½	¾	1	Str	Fin	Jockeys	Owners	O	H	C	P	S
10733²	OMAHA	wB 126	3	5	3½	3¹	4¹²	2⁴	1¹½	S'undersW	Belair Stud S	†4-5	4-5	7-10	1-6	out
09965²	FIRETHORN	wB 126	2	2	2¹½	2ʰ	3½	1ⁿᵏ	2⁸	WorkmanR	W M Jeffords	5	6	6	7-5	1-4
(10733)	ROSEMONT	wB 126	5	3	5	4⁴	2ʰ	3²	3¹	WrightWD	Foxcatcher F S	13-5	14-5	13-5	1-2	out
11072³	COLD SHOULDER	wB 126	1	1	1³	1⁵	1³	4¹⁵	4¹⁵	RenickS	A G Vanderbilt	8	10	10	2½	4-5
11072	SIR BEVERLEY	w 126	4	4	4²	5	5	5	5	MalleyT	Belair S Sta	†4-5	4-5	7-10	1-6	out

†Coupled as Belair Stud Stable entry.

Time, :24⅕, :48⅖, 1:13⅗, 1:39, 1:52, 2:05, 2:18, 2:30⅗. Track sloppy.

Winner—Ch. c, by Gallant Fox—Flambino, by Wrack (trained by J. Fitzsimmons; bred by Belair Stud).

WENT TO POST—4:22. AT POST—1 minute.

Start good and slow. Won easily; second and third the same.

OMAHA was shuffled back after the break, recovered quickly and, allowed to settle in his stride, came to the outside of the leaders entering the stretch, finished fast and was drawing away at the end. FIRETHORN was rated along steadily, saved ground entering the stretch and finished well. ROSEMONT was forced wide rounding the first turn and dropped back. He moved up stoutly on the back stretch when called upon, but faltered badly in the stretch run. COLD SHOULDER was rushed into command going to the first turn, was rated along steadily and had no mishaps. SIR BEVERLEY was not persevered with when he faltered.

Scratched—(11394)Gold Foam. 126

Saxon in the Brooklyn Handicap, but he rebounded to take the Dwyer Handicap, on June 29, while equaling Man o' War's record time for the mile and an eighth, 1:49⅕, in the process.

By this time, Omaha had the public coming and going with his up-and-down performances. Consequently, he was written off as just the best of a bad three-year-old lot. Omaha, however, had a big surprise in store for everyone. On July 20, he flashed away from the starting barrier in the esteemed Arlington Classic, in Chicago, carrying scale weight of 126 pounds, and clocked the fastest mile and a quarter ever run by a three-year old in the country. The time was 2:01⅖. It was an electrifying win, which made him into a national hero as he traveled east to prepare for the Travers and Saratoga Cup races.

The joy was momentary, for soon after his arrival at the upstate New York track, the racing world was stunned by an announcement that Omaha had come up lame. Although the ailment subsided quickly, the champion was withdrawn from further competition for the balance of

Omaha blazes to electrifying, record-breaking victory in Arlington Classic. The time of 2:01²/₅ was the fastest mile and a quarter ever run by a three-year-old in the country. St. Bernard finished second, Bloodroot third. This race was the last for "The Belair Bullet" in the United States.

the year as a precautionary measure. There was no way of foretelling it then, but Omaha had run his last race in the United States. " . . . it was like the extinction of a great light," wrote "Salvator."

William Woodward was not that easily discouraged. He had an interesting notion. Coincident with his theory of breeding foreign and native horses, he nurtured the hope of developing an American Thoroughbred who could cross the Atlantic and take the English classics, notably the Ascot Gold Cup. Why not Omaha? There were enough compelling reasons, which dictated that he could be the one to do it. First, the horse had recovered rather well from his lameness. Then, his obvious strength suggested that he might well be suited for coping with racing on turf. Finally, the records showed that after his juvenile season the Triple Crown champion had never won except at distances beyond a mile, and since all of the major classics in Britain were between a mile and a half and two miles and a half, they might just be his cup of tea.

Once his resolve was firmed up, Woodward proceeded to make sure of the colt's condition for turf racing. He brought to America Captain Cecil Boyd-Rochfort, one of the most successful of English trainers, to pass judgment on the horse. It was favorable, and on January 8, 1936, Omaha was shipped out aboard the *Aquetania,* arriving in England seven days later. He sailed not without the good wishes of everyone, including a former worthy adversary, who sent him the following telegram:

> Roll on, roll on, O Omaha the great.
> Be sure you make the British late,
> And I will try to fill your place.
> You'll bet they'll know they had a race.
> Signed: FIRETHORN

Omaha is led aboard the liner Aquitania *on January 8, 1936, for the voyage to England to race in the Ascot Gold Cup.*

He made his English debut in the spring, on May 9, in the Victor Wild Stakes at Kempton Park, Middlesex, just fourteen miles from London. His reputation had come along with him, for he was soon the focal point of interest and popularity with the English racing fans. Omaha carried 129 pounds and won the mile-and-a-half race. On May 30, he took the Queens Plate by a neck, at the same distance but, this time, carrying 130 pounds. Both races were tuneups for the Ascot Gold Cup, on June 18. It was the 125th running of the race, and an estimated 150,000 excited fans jammed the Royal Ascot Track. Nine horses started, with Omaha rated the favorite at 11 to 8. The track was very heavy from rain, and he lost to the filly Quashed, to whom he had given a sex allowance of 3 pounds, at 123. It was a thrilling battle over the two-and-a-half-mile course, reported *The Blood-Horse*. "The two had engaged each other a half-mile from the finish, at the bottom of the uphill stretch, and had run head-to-head to the finish line, where the filly got the decision by a nose."

Filly Quashed (left) noses out Omaha at the finish line of the Ascot Gold Cup classic, after a head-to-head duel in the uphill stretch.

Omaha raced once more in England, in the mile-and-a-half Prince of Wales Stakes, at Newmarket. He carried top weight of 138 pounds, under severe conditions. The track was rain-soaked; he seemed ill at ease, sweated profusely in the paddock, and, as one reporter was heard to say, must have lost 7 pounds before going out on the course. Nevertheless, he was up with the leaders throughout the race. In the last quarter of a mile, he battled eye to eye with Taj Akbar, who carried only 120 pounds, and lost to the three-year-old by a neck. It was disappointing, but many blamed the loss on his handling by the jockey in the last moments of the race. It was also his last race of the season. Yet, in spite of the losses in the two stakes events, Omaha had captured the hearts of the British. The thrilling battles that he had put up caused them to proclaim him one of the best horses seen in England in years.

Woodward decided to keep him in the country for another crack at the Ascot Gold Cup in 1937. However, in mid-June he injured a tendon of the left fore leg, and was returned to the United States. Once again, the valley had replaced the golden peak. This time, there was no recourse but to retire him to Claiborne Farm, where he had been foaled. This time, there were to be no more peaks to climb. By 1943, it had become obvious that the colt was unsuccessful as a stallion. At least, he was not likely to produce anything approaching his own class. As a result, his owner leased him to the Jockey Club's Lookover Stallion Station, at Avon, in upstate New York. He remained there until 1950, when he was passed on to a group of breeders in Omaha, Nebraska.

Omaha, twenty-five years old, stands in pasture of the Nebraska City farm of Grove Porter, Nebraska racing commissioner. With him is Porter's son, Morton. The Triple Crown champion died two years later in 1959.

Final resting place for Omaha at the Ak-Sar-Ben race track near Omaha.

The colt finally stood in retirement at the Grove Porter Farm, Nebraska City, where he also was a popular tourist attraction. In the meantime, a monument in his honor, as a fitting tribute to the fame he had brought to the city and state, was erected at Ak-Sar-Ben (Nebraska spelled backwards), near Omaha, site of the race track and world-famous annual fair of that name. It was here that he was buried on his death in 1959.

Omaha's record was not the most distinguished of the Triple Crown winners. In his three seasons, he had come in first in only nine of twenty-two starts, second in seven, and third in two. He had won a total of $154,755. But he had been something to behold on the track. "In action he was a glorious sight; few thoroughbreds have exhibited such a magnificent, sweeping, space-annihilating stride, or carried it with such strength and precision. His place is among the Titans of the American turf," was "Salvator's" final tribute to him.

WAR ADMIRAL
and jockey Charley Kurtsinger.

WAR ADMIRAL
(Brown Colt)
{ Man o' War { Fair Play
Mahubah
Brushup { Sweep
Annette K.

War Admiral

4

A fan will be hard-pressed to name two back-to-back years in American Thoroughbred racing, which produced more absorbing drama and color than did 1937 and 1938. These were the years of the "Admiral" and the "Biscuit," two magnificent colts who streaked across the racing spectrum in a shower of speed, stamina, courage, and color. War Admiral was the fourth Triple Crown champion and "Horse of the Year" in 1937, a dynamic horse with an inbred spirit to win. Seabiscuit was the Handicap champion and leading money-winner of 1937 and "Horse of the Year" in 1938, one of the greatest campaigners who criss-crossed the country to race any and all comers. It was inevitable that these two fantastic steeds should clash in head-to-head combat. When they did, the race captured the attention of the public to such an extent that it even impelled the President of the United States to pause in his day's work and tune in on the action.

The careers of both horses also brought into the brilliant spotlight of publicity some of the most important figures of the turf at that time. First, there was Man o' War, the "giant stallion" who had made it all possible. He looked on with justifiable paternal pride, from his Kentucky retirement farm, at the accomplishments of his son, War Admiral, his most distinguished get, and his grandson, Seabiscuit. Then there were Samuel D. Riddle, owner of both Man o' War and War Admiral, who had already been to the well of success with a champion horse; Charles S. Howard, a San Francisco auto magnate and owner of Seabiscuit, who was making his first heady trip there; Cornelius V. "Sonny" Whitney, principal stockholder of Belmont Park and vice president of the Westchester Racing Association; Herbert Bayard Swope, chairman of the New York Racing Commission; Joseph E. Widener, president of Belmont Park, which was owned by the Westchester Racing Association; William Woodward, chairman of the Jockey Club; and Alfred G. Vanderbilt, president of Pimlico Race Course.

61

Seabiscuit and jockey Red Pollard.

War Admiral was foaled at the Riddle Faraway Farm, near Lexington, in 1934. He was out of Brushup, and it could be said that in many respects he was a mama's boy. He was on the small side, reaching a maximum growth of 15.3 hands, one hand shorter than his sire; and was brown, rather than red chestnut. When it came to racing, though, he took after his sire without question. Like his Triple Crown predecessors, he too was a late bloomer. His brief two-year-old season was promising: three wins in six starts, and never out of the money. At the end of the year he was sent to the Glen Riddle Farm in Maryland for the winter, and then shipped to Havre de Grace in the spring of 1937. His first race then was the mile-and-a-sixteenth Chesapeake Stakes, which he won with ease and because of which the Squire of Riddle was motivated to make an unprecedented decision.

For years, he had had a phobia against entering any of his horses in the Kentucky Derby. It was his contention that the race was only an interloper, trying to crack the orbit of renown of the Eastern turf centers. He also detested racing in the "West," as he considered Churchill Downs, because it was away from the stomping grounds of high society. Finally, and perhaps his most cogent reason, he felt that the Derby came too early in the year, before a Thoroughbred had developed to his full maturity. All of these reasons had kept the great Man o' War from the Triple Crown in 1920.

However, in 1937 Riddle decided to let War Admiral take a shot at the Derby, and sent him to Churchill Downs late in April to prepare for it. On May 4, the colt was given a full-blown tryout at the mile-and-a-quarter distance, in an allowance race. It was only four days before the Derby, and the "Admiral" breezed home in front in 2:08³/₅, an exhibition that immediately sent tremors through his opposition and caused him to become a strong favorite for the "Run for the Roses."

Churchill Downs, on May 8, saw one of the biggest crowds in attendance, 75,000, which included "princes and paupers, movie queens, captains of industry, statesmen—leaders from all walks of life." The weather was pleasant, the track good, even though it had been muddy all week. A field of twenty started, with War Admiral at 8 to 5. His strongest competition was Pompoon, the horse his handlers feared the most. The race was held up for eight minutes, when the "Admiral" acted up in a display of his aversion to the starting gate. It was a trait that could not be broken throughout his career.

War Admiral shot out from his number-one position at the start, with jockey Charley Kurtsinger in the irons, and was in front immediately and stayed there, wire to wire. He won by almost two lengths, came out of the race in excellent shape, and was shipped that same night to Baltimore to prepare for the Preakness the following Saturday. The second leg of the Triple Crown, on May 15, was a race of another sort. Pompoon was not easily denied, and it turned out to be the most exciting race of the year. The two horses took charge from the top. The Pimlico track is noted for its sharp turns, and the "Admiral" went wide on each of them. As they approached the last turn, with Pompoon a length and a half behind but gaining, he bore out once more and jockey Wayne Wright shot Pompoon to the rail and into the lead,

War Admiral, out in front wire-to-wire, wins the 1937 Kentucky Derby by almost two lengths over Pompoon.

SIXTH RACE
40796
May-8-37-C.D

1 1-4 MILES. (Twenty Grand, May 16, 1931—2:01⅘—3—126.) Sixty-third Running KENTUCKY DERBY. $50,000 Added. 3-year-olds. Scale weights.
Net value to winner $52,050; second, $6,000; third, $3,000; fourth, $1,000.

Index	Horses	Eq't A Wt	PP	St	½	¾	1	Str	Fin	Jockeys	Owners	Equiv. Odds Str't
(40297)	WAR ADMIRAL	w 126	1	2	1¹½	1¹	1¹½	1³	1¹¾	Kurts'gerC	Glen Riddle Farms	160-100
40490	POMPOON	w 126	14	6	5²	4¹	2²	2⁵	2⁸	RichardsH	J H Louchheim	800-100
40614²	REAPING REWARD	wb 126	17	7	8½	6¼	8³	5³	3³	Rob'tsonA	Milky Way Farm	‡460-100
(40490)	MELODIST	w 126	3	10	6ʰ	5¹	5ʰ	4ʰ	4¹	LongdenJ	Wheatley Stable	1510-100
(38966)	SCENESHIFTER	wb 126	12	13	10½	12½	11ʰ	7½	5²	StoutJ	M Howard	§1120-100
40127²	HEELFLY	w 126	10	1	3¹½	2½	3³	3½	6ʰ	WrightWD	Three D's Stock Farm	1620-100
(40614)	DELLOR	wb 126	2	4	7¹½	9½	6½	6¼	7½	JamesB	J W Parrish	1370-100
(40282)	BURNING STAR	wb 126	15	15	14¹	13¹	13¹	10¹	8ʰ	ParkeC	Shandon Farm	†930-100
40297²	COURT SCANDAL	wb 126	6	11	12½	8ʰ	9³	12¹	9¹	SteffenE	T B Martin	†
40490	CLODION	wb 126	13	14	13²	14½	12²	9ʰ	10¹	AndersonI	W A Carter	†
40297	FAIRY HILL	wb 126	4	3	2¹½	3³	4½	8¹½	11¹½	PetersM	Foxcatcher Farms	4460-100
40490	MERRY MAKER	wb 126	7	19	17²	11¹	10½	11½	12½	DabsonH	Miss E G Rand	†
40614	NO SIR	wb 126	19	17	16ʰ	17¹	17½	13¹½	13ʰ	LeBlancH	Miss M Hirsch	†
40349³	GREY GOLD	wb 126	11	18	19²	19¹½	18¹	14½	14¹	RosenJ	E W Duffy	†
40614	MILITARY	wsb 126	5	9	15¹½	15¹	15¹	15¹	15½	CorbettC	Milky Way Farm	‡
(39858)	SUNSET TRAIL II.	wb 126	18	20	20	20	20	16¹½	16²	DotterR	R Walsh	†
(40445)	FENCING	wsb 126	8	12	9½	10½	16ʰ	17²	17⁵	WestropeJ	M Howard	§
40614³	BERNARD F.	w 126	16	16	18⁵	18³	19½	18³	18¹	HardyL	I J Collins	†
40490²	SIR DAMION	wb 126	20	8	11½	16ʰ	14³	19⁴	19¹²	YagerE	Marshall Field	†
40445²	BILLIONAIRE	wb 126	9	5	4ʰ	7½	7²	20	20	WoolfG	E R Bradley	1650-100

†Mutuel field. ‡Coupled as Milky Way Farm entry; §M. Howard entry.

Time, :23⅕, :46⅘, 1:12⅖, 1:37⅖, 2:03⅕. Track fast.

	—$2 MUTUELS PAID—			—OFFICIAL BOOKING ODDS—		
WAR ADMIRAL	$ 5.20	$ 4.20	$ 3.40	160—100	110—100	70—100
POMPOON		9.40	6.00		370—100	200—100
MILKY WAY FARM ENTRY........			3.80			90—100

Winner—Br. c, by Man o' War—Brushup, by Sweep (trained by G. Conway; bred by Mr. S. D. Riddle)
WENT TO POST—4:42. AT POST—8½ minutes.
Start good and slow. Won easily; second and third driving.

WAR ADMIRAL, fractious at the post but away fast and sent clear of his company under brisk urging, was taken under steadying restraint after racing a quarter mile, set the pace easily to the final half mile, increased his advantage gradually following a brisk shaking up on the stretch turn and, continuing well to the end, won in hand. POMPOON, forced wide throughout and a contender from the start, was reserved off the pace, offered good response when called upon and held on with fine courage, though he did not seriously threaten the winner. REAPING REWARD, in close quarters briefly approaching the first turn, dropped back slightly on the stretch turn, but came again, only to tire in the late stakes. MELODIST, a factor from the start, tired when the real test came. SCENESHIFTER, jostled about on the first turn and eased back in several futile attempts to secure racing room between horses, lost much ground on the final turn, then closed well in a splendid effort. HEELFLY, fractious at the post but away fast, had to be taken back slightly on the first turn as FAIRY HILL came over, saved ground during the final three-quarters, but tired in the stretch. DELLOR lost ground much of the race. BURNING STAR could not get up. COURT SCANDAL tired. CLODION was in close quarters on the inside in the back stretch. FAIRY HILL had speed, but was through after racing a mile. MILITARY was far back throughout. FENCING quit. BILLIONAIRE was through early.

Official chart of Kentucky Derby.

In the most exciting race of the year, War Admiral (on outside) beats Pompoon by a nose in the Preakness.

SIXTH RACE
41058
May-15-37-Pim

1 3-16 MILES. (Dark Hope, May 9, 1936—1:58—7—113.) **Forty-seventh Running PREAKNESS STAKES. $50,000 Added. 3-year-olds. Scale weights.**
Net value to winner $45,600; second, $5,000; third, $3,000; fourth, $2,000.

Index	Horses	Eq't A Wt	PP	St	½	¾	1	Str	Fin	Jockeys	Owners	Equiv. Odds Str't
(40796)	WAR ADMIRAL	w 126	1	2	1^1	1^1	11^1_2	1^h	1^h	Kurts'gerC	Glen Riddle Farms	35-100
40796²	POMPOON	w 126	7	3	5^3	2^1	2^2	2^2	2^8	WrightWD	J H Louchheim	480-100
(40583)	FLYING SCOT	w 126	3	5	2^1_2	3^h	3^h	3^1_2	3^2	GilbertJ	J H Whitney	3830-100
(40421)	MOSAWTRE	wb 126	8	4	4^1_2	5^2	4^2	4^2	4^1	LeBlancH	J M Loft	4995-100
40297³	OVER THE TOP	wb 126	5	6	6^h	7^1	5^h	5^1	5^2	WestropeJ	Mrs W H Furst	5895-100
(40726)	MATEY	wb 126	4	8	7^2	6^h	6^1	6^1	6^2	RichardsH	W M Jeffords	1395-100
40796	MERRY MAKER	wb 126	6	7	8	8	8	7^2	7^6	WoolfG	Miss E G Rand	2635-100
40890³	JEWELL DORSETT	wb 121	2	1	3^1_2	4^1	7^1	8	8	DuboisD	J W Brown	11935-100

Time, :23⅕, :47, 1:12⅖, 1:37⅗, 1:58⅖. Track good.

	—$2 MUTUELS PAID—			—OFFICIAL BOOKING ODDS—		
WAR ADMIRAL	$ 2.70	$ 2.30	$ 2.40	35—100	15—100	20—100
POMPOON		2.40	2.70		20—100	35—100
FLYING SCOT			6.00			200—100

Winner—Br. c, by Man o' War—Brushup, by Sweep (trained by G. Conway; bred by Mr. S. D. Riddle).
WENT TO POST—5:25. AT POST—3½ minutes.
Start good and slow. Won driving; second and third the same.
WAR ADMIRAL, fractious as usual at the post, broke forwardly to take command in the opening eighth, was permitted to drift out after getting to the front, took a wide course at the first turn, then settled into his stride on reaching the back stretch, was steadied out in the firmer footing, rallied to a severe drive when POMPOON came to him on the inside entering the stretch, withstood a long drive willingly and was holding his own at the end. POMPOON stole through between horses after being slightly bothered at the break when MOSAWTRE came over, rallied strongly to engage the winner at the stretch turn, came through on the inside and fought it out determinedly after getting on even terms with the winner in the last sixteenth. FLYING SCOT held a forward position under good handling, made his challenge in the last five-sixteenths and continued gamely to prove best of the others. MOSAWTRE broke swiftly and toward the inside at the start, was straightened out quickly to follow close up on the outside, but failed to engage the leaders when the real test came. OVER THE TOP was kept under strong urging after getting into his best stride, but failed to enter contention. MATEY began slowly, saved ground, but could not reach a forward position. MERRY MAKER was outrun. JEWELL DORSETT showed speed for the first three-quarters, then retired.

Official chart of Preakness.

working hard and whipping his horse. Kurtsinger "sat tight and never did more with his whip than wave it once or twice alongside [his mount's] eyes." It was as stirring a stretch duel as had ever been witnessed on an American track, with the outcome in doubt to the very end, when the "Admiral" scored by only the margin of a nose. Although the track was not fast, War Admiral won in the excellent time of 1:58²/₅, within 1/5 second of the 1934 record time of High Quest.

There were three weeks to go until the Belmont Stakes, on June 5, and both horses were saved, being held out of the Withers or any other races. Once again War Admiral was favored, at 4 to 5, and once again he had trouble at the post, breaking out and delaying the start for five minutes. He even almost ruined himself as the race got under way, for he stumbled and, according to Robert Kelley, chronicler for the Jockey Club, "grabbed himself badly, shearing off a piece of the wall of his right forefoot. . . . He recovered with the agility of a dancer, however, and blazed the first quarter in :24 flat, to be nearly three lengths on top." A couple of horses made a go at him, but he would have nothing of that, finishing the mile and a half completely alone, in 2:28³/₅, the new Triple Crown champion. His time was outstanding in that it was ¹/₅ second faster than Man o' War's 1920 track record and equaled Handy Mandy's 1927 American record. The fact is, the Belmont was the "Admiral's" easiest of his three "jewel" victories, but it also was al-

War Admiral (bottom) stumbles at the start of the Belmont Stakes, injuring his right forefoot.

"The Admiral" cruises to an easy victory and the Triple Crown as he beats Sceneshifter. Foot injury put him out of action until October.

Trainer George Conway leads War Admiral and Charley Kurtsinger to the winner's circle.

Official chart of Belmont Stakes.

FIFTH RACE
42410
June-5-37-Bel

1 1-2 MILES. (Man o' War, Sept. 11, 1920—2:28⅘—3—118.) Sixty-ninth Running BELMONT STAKES. $25,000 Added. 3-year-olds. Scale weights.

Net value to winner $38,020; second, $5,000; third, $2,500; fourth, $1,000.

Index	Horses	Eq't	A	Wt	PP	St	¾	1⅛	1¼	Str	Fin	Jockeys	Owners	O	H	C	P	S
(41058)	WAR ADMIRAL	w		126	7	2	1³	1⁴	1⁴	1³	1³	Kurts'gerC	Glen Riddle Fms	4-5	1		9-10	1-3 1-8
(41486)	SCENESHIFTER	w		126	6	7	3⁴	2²	2⁵	2⁵	2¹⁰	StoutJ	M Howard	8	10	8	2½	1
41409	VAMOOSE	wв		126	1	5	4⁴	4¹	3¹½	3³	3²	WorkmanR	Falaise Stable	60	100	60	20	10
40445³	BROOKLYN	wв		126	4	4	7	5ʰ	6⁶	4ʰ	4³	WrightWD	E R Bradley	6	7	6	2	1
(41409)	FLYING SCOT	w		126	5	1	2ʰ	3³	5¹½	6¹⁰	5ʰ	GilbertJ	J H Whitney	12	15	12	4	7-5
41058²	POMPOON	w		126	3	3	5¹½	6⁴	4ⁿᵏ	5¹	6¹²	RichardsH	J H Louchheim	3	18-5	3½	4-5 1-3
41814	MELODIST	wв		126	2	6	6½	7	7	7	7	LongdenJ	Wheatley Stable	30	30	20	7	3

Time, :24, :48, 1:12⅕, 1:37⅛, 1:49⅘, 2:02⅕, 2:15⅖, 2:28⅜ (new track record; equals American record)
Track fast.

Winner—Br. c, by Man o' War—Brushup, by Sweep (trained by G. Conway; bred by Mr. S. D. Riddle)
WENT TO POST—4:22. AT POST—7½ minutes.
Start good and slow. Won easily; second and third the same.

WAR ADMIRAL, fractious at the post, began fast and, moving into command with a rush, was rated along steadily while saving ground and won with speed to spare. SCENESHIFTER raced forwardly from the start, was placed under severe pressure in the stretch, but was not good enough. VAMOOSE was restrained when outrun early, then moved up fast under urging in the stretch and held BROOKLYN safe. The latter was outrun early, but moved up gamely on the far turn, only to tire, but came again near the end. FLYING SCOT broke well and raced under restraint the first part, he was placed under pressure nearing the far turn, but could not menace the leaders and tired badly thereafter. POMPOON, sluggish in the early stages, failed to improve his position when called upon and tired. MELODIST was outrun and was never a factor.

most disastrous. He trailed blood from his injury on the way to the winner's circle, and wound up out of action until October. Still, he had made his own indelible mark in all of racing. No other three-year-old had caused so much talk since Man o' War. Here was a horse who loved to run, and "once away from the hated gate, seemed to enjoy himself."

It was in autumn of the year that a new excitement arose. Suddenly, every track fan began to stir in anticipation of a meeting between War Admiral and Seabiscuit, when it was learned that both had been named for the Washington Handicap, at Laurel, Md., on October 30. While the "Admiral" had been busy reeling off one victory after the other in the three-year-old classics, the "Biscuit" had been defying the norm for Thoroughbreds by first coming into his own in his fourth year and racking up the handicaps.

Seabiscuit was bred in 1933, at the Claiborne Farm, by Mrs. Henry Carnegie Phipps and her statesman-financier brother, Ogden Mills. He was by Hard Tack, owned by Mrs. Phipps, out of Swing On. Since his sire was a son of Man o' War, that made him a grandson of "Big Red." The "Biscuit," like the "Admiral," also took after his dam. He was a bay, on the small side, unlike his sire, who more closely resembled grandpa. When fully grown, he topped out at a fraction over fifteen hands, three inches. Size, though, was misleading, for he was a sturdy horse. When the time came, he was put in the care of "Mr. Fitz," who was then somewhat more preoccupied with the training of a rather more promising colt, Omaha.

He made his two-year-old debut at Hialeah, Fla., on January 19, 1935, and finished fourth. The consensus was that, although not striking, Seabiscuit could still be a useful performer. From then through November he made thirty-five starts, to wind up with the unimpressive record of five wins, while failing to place in eighteen and earning only $12,510. His three-year-old season was equally inauspicious, commencing in April at Jamaica. Perhaps all of this racing and attendant failure was getting through to the horse, because early in the year he became careless, even lazy. It was no surprise, therefore, that by August, at the end of the Saratoga meet and after some forty-six uninspired races spread over two years, his owners gave up and entered him in a claiming race for $6,000. He won the event, only to suffer the indignity of not being claimed by anyone.

Seated in the stands was a relatively new face in Thoroughbred racing, Charles S. Howard, a millionaire Buick distributor from San Francisco who hoped to establish racing on a grand scale on the West Coast. He was looking to add to his string. With him was his trainer, Tom Smith, a former cattle rancher, bronco buster, rodeo rider, and blacksmith who had a penchant and skill for rejuvenating discarded horses. Both men were attracted to Seabiscuit, possibly by the tremendous strength he seemed to possess, judging from the number of times he had raced in the past two years. Smith even discounted a left knee that was dangerously sprung. He had first seen the colt run at Suffolk Downs in June. After watching him take the Mohawk Claiming Stakes at Saratoga, he urged his employer to buy him for the $7,500 asking price.

Seabiscuit then made the first of a number of cross-country trips. After some preliminary training by Smith in California, the colt began to race. He seemed to come alive suddenly, and began to finish in the money. By the year's end, he had raced twenty-three times, scored nine wins, and earned $28,995, most of which winnings came in the last few months under the Howard colors.

In 1937, he became a "consistent and frequently brilliant performer." It was a rare occasion when he had to inhale the dust of front-runners. After two preliminary races, he was entered in the Santa Anita Handicap on February 27, at the time the world's richest race with a purse of $100,000. He was caught at the wire by Rosemont, losing by a nose. On March 6, he won the San Juan Capistrano at the same track, then polished off six more consecutive wins at California's Tanforan and Bay Meadows and New York's Aqueduct and Empire City tracks. His attempt to equal Discovery's record of eight straight wins came a cropper, when he finished third in the Narragansett Special, on September 11, on a sloppy track. The race proved conclusively that the "Biscuit" had developed a distaste for mud, so from then on his handlers avoided the goo whenever possible. The loss did not interfere with the colt's winning ways; he came back with three straight wins.

These set the stage for the "confrontation." It was October, and the leading three-year-old and the leading four-year-old were named for the Washington Handicap, a weight-for-age event. War Admiral was assigned 126 pounds and Seabiscuit 130. The tension rose acutely as the date approached, for this obviously had to be the race of the year, or years. "During 1937," wrote "Salvator," "the American public was privileged to behold in action two of the most remarkable Thoroughbreds that have ornamented the turf in recent times."

Unfortunately, it was not to be. Rain began to fall during the week of the race, causing the track to be heavy. It interfered with Seabiscuit's workouts, so he was withdrawn. War Admiral, on the other hand, stayed in and won handily. The racing fans were sadly disappointed, but their clamor for a meeting of the two horses continued at an octave higher and several decibels louder.

As the year finally drew to a close, both were in a struggle of another sort. Which of them would be the top money-winner of 1937? The final result was in doubt until the last weeks, when Seabiscuit took the honors with a total of $168,580, after fifteen starts that included eleven firsts, two seconds, and two thirds, to War Admiral's $166,500, from eight wins out of eight starts, six of which were in stakes. It was the first time since 1915 that an older horse had beat out a three-year-old.

In another respect, both horses did right well for their owners. Seabiscuit enabled the Howard stable to be the leader in point of money won, with $212,859, while Triple Crown champion War Admiral helped to raise the Glen Riddle Farm to third place, with earnings of $176,140. It was truly a good year for all concerned.

January 1938 rolled around and the public's call for a meeting of the two horses continued apace. At the time, though, the prospects seemed somewhat dim. War Admiral had been shipped to Hialeah, from the Riddle Farm in Berlin, Md., for the Widener Handicap in February. Seabiscuit was three thousand miles away, preparing for his second shot at the Santa Anita Handicap, also in February. There had been some speculation that the "Admiral" would be entered in the Santa Anita race, but Riddle quickly scotched this.

The "Mighty Atom"—another appellation hung on Man o' War's son—continued to show his class with an easy win of the McLennon Memorial Handicap on February 19, in a tuneup for the Widener. In fact, jockey Charley Kurtsinger was so confident of the result that he did not carry a whip. A week later, on February 26, both the "Admiral" and the "Biscuit" were in action on the same day. War Admiral, carrying top weight of 130 pounds, which caused Riddle to erupt in anger at the racing secretaries for setting such a heavy load on such a small horse, waltzed to his tenth consecutive victory in the Widener. Seabiscuit, on the other hand, lost by a nose to Aneroid, in the San Antonio Handicap. He was nosed out again on March 5, by Stagehand, in the Santa Anita Handicap, his second loss of the big race by a nose.

Of more importance to the owners, the three races pushed the earnings of both horses over the $200,000 mark. War Admiral thus became the second son of Man o' War to reach this goal, the other having been Crusader. Taking it back a step further, Fair Play could boast of five descendants who had hit the figure: his sons Man o' War and Display and Crusader, War Admiral, and Seabiscuit.

When Seabiscuit won the Agua Caliente Handicap on March 27, also carrying the top weight of 130 pounds, the die was cast, and there was no getting away from a match race with War Admiral. Unbeknown to the public, however, the wheels had started to move slowly toward this. One afternoon early in March in New York, Herbert Swope and Charles Howard discussed the idea for the race. The New York State Racing Commission chairman suggested that the horses be entered in the Suburban Handicap of the Belmont Park spring meeting. He also said that he would try to have the added value of the race increased from $20,000 to $50,000. Howard reacted by voicing a desire for a match race "so that there would be no other horses to cause interference." He also preferred the autumn, obviously aware of the fact that in September the scale weights for the four-year-old War Admiral and the five-year-old Seabiscuit would be the same—126 pounds. Finally, he asked for a purse of $100,000, saying that a Western track was willing to go that high, and that "Belmont Park, the country's leading race track, although not the most prosperous because of the sporting way in which it is run, should be willing at least to meet that figure."

It could be said that the tail was wagging the dog. Howard was a newcomer in racing circles, and he was bucking the conservative, ultra-dignified Eastern establishment. They needed him, he felt, and so he could lay down his conditions. Finally, in early April, Swope wired Howard that he thought something could be worked out. Although he still acted somewhat standoffish, Howard was anxious for the race to come off. He called Swope to say that he was amenable to the meeting.

As a result, the press was advised on April 5 that the race was in the offing, and that plans were proceeding to set a specific date. Joseph Widener, on behalf of the Westchester Racing Association, informed the commission that he would take immediate steps to arrange for the purse and the other details. The announcement was greeted immediately with loud hurrahs and a torrent of telegrams to the commission from appreciative fans all over the country. Riddle also wired in, to say that he would make a special trip to New York in a few days, after he had supervised the shipment of War Admiral and seven vanloads of his horses to Belmont for the spring season.

The newspaper columnists, in the meantime, began to warm up to the subject with a little acid in their typewriters. They had been championing the event for the better part of a year, and were tired of the slow pace at which things were moving. On April 7, David Alexander wrote in the *Morning Telegraph:* "There is about as much chance of China and Japan agreeing, or Franco and the Loyalists agreeing, as there is of Howard and Riddle agreeing in the matter of weight." That same day, Bill Corum opined sarcastically in the New York *Journal-American:* "If War Admiral had been a prizefighter and Seabiscuit had been a prizefighter, Mike Jacobs would have had them fighting in Yankee Stadium last September." He said the race was a "natural," and Jacobs, the successor to Tex Rickard as the nation's top boxing promoter, was "red hot after 'naturals.'"

Things really came to a boil when, suddenly, John D. Hertz, chairman of Arlington Park and the Arlington Park Jockey Club, offered to put up $100,000 if the race was held in Chicago in July. His deal, though, called for a three-horse event that would include Stagehand, who had beaten Seabiscuit in the Santa Anita Handicap and was favored to win the Kentucky Derby. Riddle greeted this with his own facetious suggestion, that of holding two match races, one in New York and the other in Chicago, so that everyone would be pleased.

Swope, in the meantime, was having his problems. Widener was ill in Palm Beach, but authorized him to negotiate with Riddle. However, C. V. Whitney, whose approval would be needed before the Westchester Racing Association could authorize the $100,000 purse, was at sea fishing and could not be reached. Still, it was reported that New York had the veto power over the race, and that no other city would be allowed to move in on it. "This race was originally our idea," boasted Swope, "regardless of what the Chicago people claim. Belmont is the cradle of American racing. Where else does such a race belong?" The following day, April 7, he reported that the proposed race had attracted so much worldwide interest that William S. Paley, head of the Columbia Broadcasting System, had offered to broadcast it internationally as well as in America.

Any doubts about New York's self-esteem in the racing world were set to rest when Mr. Swope further stated that "a meeting of the two horses in New York would give the occurrence added importance, as foreign turf bodies, notably the English Jockey Club, recognized only the New York Jockey Club as the governing body in this country." He went on to say that "Mr. Whitney has always been in favor of those steps which benefit New York racing and which bring honor to the Thoroughbred horse." It was all there. No intruders would be allowed to move in on what already was being hailed as "the race of the century."

On April 8, Riddle finally met with the racing chairman to work out the details. When the conference was over, the race was virtually set, to the amazement of most of the reporters. Normally a very obstinate man, he gave in to almost all of Howard's conditions. He agreed to the scale weights of 126 pounds, the distance of a mile and a quarter, postponement if the track was not fast or if muddy, and even offered the post position to Seabiscuit. His only demand was that there should be a walkup start, because "War Admiral has never taken kindly to the stall gate," but he even relented on this. He agreed with Howard on a $100,000 purse, largely because each was anxious for his horse to surpass Sun Beau as the greatest money-winner in the world. It was William Woodward, of the Jockey Club, who approved of the suggestion to use scale weights, because it "would lend a classic touch to the event."

Handlers have War Admiral practice race start in 1938 in an effort to break his aversion to the stall gate.

At this stage in the negotiations, Chicago was definitely ruled out. Aside from New York's control over the matter, neither owner was particularly keen to run in the blistering heat usually on hand in that city in July. Furthermore, War Admiral had already been entered in the $50,000 Massachusetts Handicap at Suffolk Downs, and Seabiscuit in the $50,000 added Hollywood Gold Cup at Inglewood, both of which occurred at that time. They even ruled out a last-minute proposal by Charles F. Adams, chairman of the board of Suffolk Downs in Boston, to stage a $100,000 race. This would have included six to twelve starters, made up of winners of the Kentucky Derby, Preakness, and Massachusetts Handicap, as well as outstanding older horses to be selected by a board of leading handicappers and racing secretaries.

The press was advised, on April 10, that Howard had sent in his acceptance of the conditions for the race. All that remained was receipt of approval from Whitney, who was known to be against match races with big purses, because they tended to commercialize Thoroughbred racing. Two days later, Whitney arrived for the board meeting of the Westchester Racing Association, and the vote was unanimous in favor of the race and the purse. However, they insisted that it be held on Memorial Day, May 30, rejecting a fall date on the grounds that there was no assurance of the physical condition of either horse then, that the possibility existed that one or the other might be defeated in other races which would reduce the value of the match race, and, most important, that they did not wish to detract from other traditional stakes races during the year. Whitney summed it up when he said: "We are offering this race because public interest is high and the two horses are sound and at the top of their form." He then added pointedly: "Why wait for one of them to break down?"

A few days later, both Riddle and Howard put the icing on the cake by agreeing that the winner would take the whole purse. This, in effect, would make it the largest purse ever offered in any race in the world.

Almost immediately, the experts began to send out a stream of assessments of the respective horses. The supposition seemed to be that War Admiral would outrun Seabiscuit and grind him to pieces, as he had done to his other opponents. For example, David Alexander, in the *Morning Telegraph,* checked the records and found that Seabiscuit had never won at a mile and a quarter. He also reasoned that since he had lost by a nose twice at Santa Anita at that distance his "nose isn't long enough to win." The New York *Times'* Bryan Field said: "The race seems likely to develop into an East-West controversy as to the respective merits of the horses, as there appears one corporal's guard in this area willing to concede Seabiscuit any chance. From Herbert Bayard Swope through the ranks of officials who desired not to be quoted, and down to the ordinary horse player, there was a surprising unanimity for War Admiral." Charley Kurtsinger, War Admiral's jockey, was very confident. "It won't be close. How can Seabiscuit get close to War Admiral?" John "Red" Pollard, Seabiscuit's jockey, on the other hand, had some interesting observations. "If the race comes off, and somehow

I'm skeptical about it coming off, I think the Biscuit will fool 'em all by showing as much early speed as the Admiral. From what I've seen of the Admiral, he's a horse that wins his races in the first eighth of a mile. When he takes his first step out of the gate he's already in stride. But what would you say if I told you that all I have to do is give Seabiscuit a couple of whacks on the flanks at the start to make him run the first three-eighths in :33?" At the time, the world's record for an official three-eighths of a mile was :32$^4/_5$.

His statement was remarkable, for it proved to be prophetic on both counts. The colt gave added dimension to these words a few days later, when he won the Bay Meadows Handicap, at San Mateo, Calif., carrying 133 pounds "as lightly as a feather" for the mile and a furlong in the track record time of 1:49. It was a performance sufficiently impressive to impel an imaginative Associated Press sportswriter to call him the "black bullet of the American turf."

After the race, George Woolf, who rode him, was quoted as saying: "He hasn't a single bad habit. Riding Seabiscuit is just as easy as resting in a cradle." This was hotly disputed by Joe Palmer in *The Blood-Horse*. "Seabiscuit has a perfectly maddening habit," he wrote, "of having his nose just behind Rosemont or Aneroid or Stagehand or Esposa at the finish of important races. The record further shows that War Admiral does not have this habit or anything resembling it. Seabiscuit is unquestionably a very high-class horse, and there have not been a dozen like him in the last twenty years. But how many years has it been since we have had a genuine stayer which did his staying from two to three lengths in front of his field? If you don't remember, Man o' War was retired after his race with Sir Barton at Kenilworth Park, October 12, 1920."

The tension mounted fiercely with the arrival of Seabiscuit at Belmont Park, on April 25, after his train trip from California. He arrived in excellent condition, which was no surprise to Murray Tynan, of the New York *Herald Tribune,* because he was "an accomplished traveler, who has made almost as many trips from coast to coast as the average film star." War Admiral was already at the track, and the sportswriters continued to size up the colts. Burris Jenkins, Jr., the noted cartoonist of the New York *Journal-American,* captioned his drawings of the two with: "Like Dempsey, the Admiral is fiery, nervous, eager, emotional—a flaming, fighting spirit that wants to let everything go from the start. Like Tunney, the Biscuit is steady, quiet, determined, intelligent, courageous—'races with his head' and has a bulldog tenacity. The Admiral would run his eyes out in the first furlong if Kurtsinger gave him his head or his temper. While the Admiral is a bad boy at the barrier, the Biscuit is a scholarly gentleman who never neglects his lessons."

The bomb dropped on May 24. Charles Howard called the race off because Seabiscuit's legs were bothering him; they looked sore and puffy. There were reports that "Seabiscuit was high in flesh and wobbly in the knees." To experienced turfmen, the announcement came as no surprise, because they had wondered all along about the horse's lack of speed in his workouts. Furthermore, the early odds indicated an easy win for War Admiral, which added to the suspicion. The disappointment was tremendous, but accepted in good faith.. According to Joe Williams, in the New York *World-Telegram:* " . . . the 'Race of the Century' turned out to be the 'Sporting Gesture of the Century.' For once the public got a break. All parties concerned got together and decided this would not be fair. If it couldn't be a real good race, there would be no race at all." Samuel Riddle came up with another sporting gesture, when he announced that War Admiral would start in the Suburban Handicap on May 28, against his old rival, Pompoon, to ease the disappointment and enable New York track fans to see the "Mighty Atom" in action once more.

The second bomb dropped on the day of this race, when War Admiral was scratched at the last moment. The reason given was the condition of the track, but the sportswriters disputed this, reporting that it was fast. More realistically, they wrote, it was because he was being asked to carry 4 more pounds than Pompoon, 132 to 128, which was too much in view of the fact that Pompoon had won his last ten races. " . . . Riddle repeatedly had declared," wrote Bill Corum, "that his champion would never carry more than 130 pounds." The net result was extreme anger by the 25,000 fans present, who hissed and booed and jeered the announcement for several minutes, and the mortification of track officials. Whitney called it an outrage. When asked about setting up another match race, he exploded: "Not if I could buy them for a dime a dozen . . . I'll never again consent to such a thing." The public assumed Riddle was afraid to run War Admiral and had backed out as soon as a tough race came up, and was furious with Riddle for wanting everything letter-perfect. There was even speculation that this was why War Admiral had such a fine track record. As Murray Tynan put it, "The turf believes there was only one reason War Admiral was scratched. It feels certain that the Riddle stables feared a defeat and simply could not take it." A defeat, it was assumed, might tend to lessen War Admiral's importance as a sire.

Within one week in May 1938, therefore, the King of Sports had suffered two successive black eyes. While the first had been tolerable at the outset, it took on a different significance with the advent of the second. *Newsweek* magazine wrote: "Turf fans soured on their sport last week. What promised to be one of the most glorious events in horse-racing history faded to mediocrity, then to washout."

Ironically, Riddle's concern about the outcome of the Suburban was ill-founded. The joke was really on him, for Pompoon lost by a nose to Snark, a 6 to 1 outsider who ran the race in record time, 2:01$^2/_5$. So, the big excitement subsided going into the summer racing season. There was another flurry in July, when both War Admiral and Seabiscuit were entered in the Massachusetts Handicap at Suffolk Downs, but the "Biscuit" was withdrawn a half-hour before post time with a "fever-wracked tendon" in his leg. The track was also muddy. War Admiral finished a bad fourth, after having cut his right forefoot by a sharp edge of his rear hoof plate. He had also given away 23 pounds to the winner, Menow. The race proved, too, that he was not a particularly good mudder. It was his first loss in twelve starts, and the first time that he had ever finished out of the money. Thereafter, in July, August, and into September, Seabiscuit campaigned in California, while War Admiral continued to race in the East. It looked for sure as though the two would never meet.

In mid-September, Seabiscuit returned to New York to run in the Manhattan Handicap, at Belmont Park, for his first appearance there since he was withdrawn from the match race. It was at this juncture that a new racing personality entered the picture in the history of the two horses. He was Alfred Gwynne Vanderbilt, the twenty-six-year-old scion of a distinguished family. His father had lost his life in the sinking of the *Lusitania* and, at the age of twenty-one, he had taken over the management of the family estate. It included his mother's Sagamore Stable of horses and the 400-acre Sagamore Farm, near Glyndon, Md. By 1935, he had become America's leading money-winning owner, with a total of $303,605 and a top horse, Discovery. Two years later, he acquired a large interest in the Pimlico Race Course, was elected a director of the Maryland Jockey Club, and shortly thereafter was named president of the track. Early in 1938, while racing at Santa Anita, he was introduced by Charles Howard to his wife's niece, Manuela Maria Hudson. The chance meeting blossomed into a romance, and the two were married during the summer. It was in September, after returning from his honeymoon, that Vanderbilt caught up with War Admiral and Seabiscuit.

The Pimlico track, in 1938, was a poor business risk. It was drawing weak attendances and losing money. Something was needed desperately to instill new life and interest in it. Why not the match race between War Admiral and Seabiscuit? After all, the public would still like to see it come off, and this was the opportune time, what with both horses racing in the East. So, much against the advice of his elders, who said it was an impossible dream, and with the zeal and fearless determination of youth, Vanderbilt tackled both owners in New York late in September. It took two weeks of endless telephone calls, meetings, cajoling, flattering, and reasoning before he was able to work out a viable agreement. First, he got both owners to agree in principle to the race. With Howard, he pressed the point that this would be the last chance for Seabiscuit to meet War Admiral, since the year was coming to a close and Riddle had already announced plans to retire his horse to stud. With Riddle, he voiced confidence that War Admiral would have no trouble in beating the Western colt, playing up to the elderly gent's enjoyment at hearing nice things said about his horses. Vanderbilt then recommended a purse of only $15,000, plus a gold cup, winner take all, as a concrete gesture to the turf fans that this would be strictly a sporting venture by the owners and not a money-making deal. As further proof that they meant business, he even asked each to put up a $5,000 forfeit bond in case of a "no show." This, too, would indicate to the fans that every effort was being made to avoid a repetition of the previous fiasco.

November 1 was selected as the date of the race, with November 3 the alternate date in the event of rain, and the track would have to be judged fast on the morning of the race. The distance of a mile and three sixteenths would seem to be acceptable, since War Admiral had won the Preakness and Seabiscuit had run the distance in winning the Riggs Handicap, also at Pimlico, the previous year. The proposed terms were acceptable to both owners, and then Riddle added a few of his own. He insisted on his own starter, George Cassidy, from New York's tracks, in place of Pimlico's Jim Milton, with whom he apparently had a disagreement. He demanded a walk-up start with the drop of a flag and the ringing of a bell. Finally, each horse would carry 120 pounds, instead of the 126-pound scale weight.

Vanderbilt relayed this to Howard with bated breath, but the Westerner did not demur. He even signed a contract stipulating all of the terms. The young track executive then made a mad taxi dash through midtown Manhattan to Pennsylvania Station, where he caught up with Riddle as he prepared to board a train for Philadelphia. Shoving the contract into Riddle's hands, Vanderbilt refused to let him board the train until he had signed it. The following day, October 5, a formal announcement of the race was made to the press. It was regarded as a turf coup to rival all others on record.

At eight a.m., November 1, a brilliant sun was rising in a cloudless sky, giving promise of a beautiful Indian-summer day. Two lonely figures walked slowly on the dirt of the Pimlico track, carefully examining the surface and underlying soil. One was Maryland State Racing Commission chairman Jervis Spencer, Jr., and the other was Pimlico steward A. G. Weston. They made a complete circle of the track in half an hour, after which they joined Alfred Vanderbilt at the winner's circle. Spencer nodded and Vanderbilt stepped to a microphone and said: "In my opinion, there is no question but that the track will be fast this afternoon. The race is on." The gates were opened to the public at ten a.m., and more than 40,000 people swarmed in, 10,000 alone standing in the infield. It was the largest crowd in the history of the track.

There was no turning back now. The two titans of the turf were on the threshold of their long-sought, much-discussed adventure. It could truly be the race of the century, pitting two Thoroughbreds with distinctly different styles of racing. The "Admiral" liked to start with a burst of speed, sustain it until the end, and kill off his opposition early. Seabiscuit, the more phlegmatic of the two, preferred to come from behind, charging down the stretch with a terrific rush, frequently winning races at the wire. Their records attested to their phenomenal success. War Admiral, four years old and Triple Crown champion of 1937, had been in twenty-two starts, winning eighteen and finishing second in two, third in one, and out of the money once. His total earnings to date were $257,050, surpassing those of his great sire, Man o' War. Seabiscuit, five years old and "Handicap Champion" of 1937, had raced eighty-three times, winning thirty-one, coming in second in twelve and third in thirteen, and winning $331,405.

Theirs was the seventh race on the program. War Admiral was a 1 to 4 favorite; Seabiscuit was at 22 to 10. The fans poured out $78,811 in bets on the race. The "Admiral" won the toss and pole position, and as recounted by "Salvator," came out on the track first at four p.m., his seal-brown satin coat "gleaming and shimmering in sunlight." Charley Kurtsinger was his jockey. The "Biscuit" followed, his hard bay coat, with black points, also glistening as his "full-made coat of flesh . . . gave him an almost gladiatorial aspect . . . [in] contrast to the Admiral's slim elegance." George Woolf was up, in place of "Red" Pollard, who had broken a leg while exercising a horse as a favor for a friend. It had happened at Narragansett Park, in Rhode Island, when the horse bolted into the fence.

Two false starts kept the multitude on edge. First War Admiral broke, and then Seabiscuit. On the third try, George Cassidy sent them off and running for keeps. At the drop of the flag, Woolf whacked the "Biscuit" hard on his flanks, and he shot out in front with a great burst of speed as he was guided to the rail in front of the "Admiral." They passed the stands, with Seabiscuit leading by an open length after one-sixteenth of a mile. "He was running cheerfully and boldly," wrote "Salvator," "with his legs and feet well under him and his stride in perfect control. War Admiral, following directly in his wake, was also under a snug hold . . . "

It was an unexpected development, which shocked the crowd that had come to expect the "Admiral" to be in front at this stage of the race. "They raced around the turn with Seabiscuit nicely in front and the stage was set for one of the most thrilling scenes ever enacted in racing," reported Murray Tynan. "Kurtsinger called on the Admiral and in a half-dozen jumps he was at the Biscuit's head. . . . For a delicious half-mile the two went on as a team. No quarter was asked and certainly none was given. One heart had to break, one horse had to give up. As they rounded the turn still locked together, matching stride for stride, Kurtsinger brought his whip down sharply. The crowd knew that he was finished. If he needed the whip, then he couldn't last much longer. He didn't. The Biscuit was cracking him then and he split him wide open when they reached the stretch. War Admiral was losing ground slightly when they straightened out for the terrific run to the finish, but he was still in hot contention. If he had it this was his golden opportunity. Kurtsinger lashed him savagely, but the Admiral was through. As he began to wilt, the relentless Seabiscuit went on, seemingly faster. Racing was never presented a finer sight than Seabiscuit charging down the stretch to his clean-cut victory." Seabiscuit won by four lengths, in 1:56^3/$_5$, beating Pompoon's track record by ^{1}/$_5$ second.

A whole chorus of top turf correspondents waxed enthusiastic over the race. Bill Corum called it "undoubtedly the greatest match race of all times" and went on to say, "Seabiscuit proved himself the champion race horse of America. . . . the grand old veteran from over the Rockies made the vaunted little horse walk the plank every step of the furious mile and three-sixteenths. . . . Men will grow old and their beards will be longer than the bearded lady's in the circus before they see another such race as this." As to the furious backstretch duel, he wrote: "Foot by foot, War Admiral cut down the distance. He caught the leader and, for a few strides as they moved by the regular half-mile post, the Riddle colt was in front. The pair ran the next furlong like two wrestlers locked together, but War Admiral couldn't get by, couldn't wrest the advantage from the other." The horses then turned into the homestretch. "Kurtsinger SOS'd the first faint signal of doubt and probably sent a tremor of fear through the hearts of the Admiral's backers, when he reached back and cut sharply at the brown colt's straining flank. It was only one swipe and it produced no result. . . . as Woolf swung the pacemaker into the home lane, he also plied the lash vigorously. Then, as he glanced fearfully back over his shoulders, the Montana cowboy caught a fleeting glimpse of the little Admiral's eyes. 'All I could see was white,' George said afterward, 'and I knew the race was over. I stuck my bat in my boot, and set down to ride my horse out with my hands, hoping we might break the record. You see, I knew we had been going pretty fast all the way round.' "

Grantland Rice, in the Baltimore *Sun*, reported: "A little horse with the heart of a lion and the flying feet of a gazelle proved his place as the gamest Thoroughbred that ever raced over an American track. . . . The Admiral looked Seabiscuit in the eye at the three-quarters—but Seabiscuit never got the look." "Red" Pollard, Seabiscuit's regular jockey and the man who had predicted the result as early as the previous May, exulted: "Once a horse gives Seabiscuit the old look in the eye, he begins to run to parts unknown. He might loaf sometimes when he's in front and think he's got the race in the bag. But he gets gamer and gamer, the tougher it gets."

After the race, some interesting sidelights became known:

George Cassidy, the starter, had to pay his way into the track. Somebody had failed to notify the guard at the jockey gate. He did not know Cassidy and refused to let him enter. . . . The crowd at the paddock was so great before the start of the race that NBC's famous race announcer, Clem McCarthy, was unable to get back to the broadcast booth, and wound up calling the action while roosting on the fence at the finish line. . . . The bell used to start the race was the one Seabiscuit's trainer, Tom Smith, had used during practice sessions. Smith had made it himself, and offered it for the race when no other bell was available. . . . It was reported that Tom Smith had trained his horse secretly at getting away to a fast start. Smith had trained quarter horses in the West, and that is the way they usually start a race. Both Howard and Smith had settled on the strategy of trying to beat the "Admiral" at his own game, by sending the "Biscuit" off with a flying start. . . . Mrs. Henry Carnegie Phipps, the original owner of Seabiscuit, was present, as was actor Pat O'Brien, making his second cross-country trip

War Admiral (1), with Charley Kurtsinger up, leads Seabiscuit (2), ridden by George Woolf, in march to starting line for their match race at Pimlico.

Seabiscuit (on outside) leaps into the lead at the start of the race.

"The Biscuit" widens his lead as horses pass the second turn.

War Admiral (on outside) moves up on Seabiscuit as they round the third turn.

Heading into the stretch, Seabiscuit pours it on and begins to move away from War Admiral.

Seabiscuit relentlessly drives to finish line and four-length win over trailing War Admiral, in what is regarded as the greatest match race of the century.

Left to right: owner Charles Howard, jockey George Woolf, trainer Tom Smith, and Pimlico president Alfred Vanderbilt hold winner's cup after Seabiscuit's victory over War Admiral.

from Hollywood for the race. He had also come east in May. . . . President Franklin D. Roosevelt arrived a few minutes late for a White House press conference. He explained to the reporters that he had been listening to the race on the radio. . . . Mrs. Howard, a devout Catholic, pinned a medal of St. Christopher, the patron saint of travelers, on the saddle blanket of Seabiscuit before the race. A month earlier, Commander R. B. Irving had docked the mammoth liner *Queen Mary* in New York Harbor without assistance from tugs because of a strike. He credited his success for the unprecedented feat on the St. Christopher medal he carried, causing a boom in the market for the lucky piece. . . .

Howard increased his colt's insurance from $100,000 to $200,000 after the victory. . . . Vanderbilt had scheduled the race for a Tuesday, because he feared the track could not handle a Saturday crowd. . . . Charles Hatton, in the *Morning Telegraph,* gave Seabiscuit perhaps the kindest bow of all when he said: "From a rather cheaply held stallion, he had become fashionable."

The race saw the curtain descending on a spectacular career for America's fourth Triple Crown champion. War Admiral ran once more that year, eleven days later when he won the Rhode Island Handicap, and once as a five-year-old before he was retired to stud. As a sire, he again showed his Thoroughbred class. In 1945, his progeny made him the leading stallion of the year, with twenty winners piling up purses amounting to $591,352. His stakes-winner get included Busher, War Jeep, Blue Peter, Busonda, and Navy Page. He died in 1959.

Seabiscuit, on the other hand, did not race again in 1938, but his victory over War Admiral earned for him "Horse of the Year" honors. He returned to the West Coast to rest, before running once in 1939 at Santa Anita. He bowed a tendon and was retired to stud at the Howard Ridgewood Ranch, some 200 miles north of San Francisco. The "Biscuit's" stud record was not particularly good. Through 1946, his get won $261,313. Actually, Howard refused to ship him to a stud farm in Kentucky, where he might have had a better stud record, because he wanted to keep him "at home."

Seabiscuit came out of retirement on February 9, 1940, just short of a year after his last race. There was one more goal to attain—the Santa Anita Handicap, which he had lost twice by a nose. This time, he prevailed, winning in the record time of $2:01^1/_5$, the second-fastest mile and a quarter ever run in American turf history. The win boosted his earnings to $437,730, the most ever won by a Thoroughbred anywhere in the world. In six years, he had been in eighty-nine races, and he had won thirty-three of them. On May 17, 1947, he died in his stall of a heart attack.

WHIRLAWAY

WHIRLAWAY (Chestnut Colt)	*Blenheim II	Blandford
		Malva
	Dustwhirl	Sweep
		Ormonda

Whirlaway

5

He was colorful. He was controversial. He generated more charisma than is likely to be found in a whole herd of thundering Thoroughbreds, much of it due to some rather unique traits. To begin with, he had an inordinately long tail, reaching to just about an inch from the ground. Naturally, it became a focal point for imaginative sportswriters, who promptly nicknamed him "Mr. Longtail" and "The Flying Tail." David Alexander commented sardonically that he was "a horse with a tail that resembled the beard of the Smith Brother on the right-hand side of the cough drop box." Conversely, he was middle-sized, a modest 15.2 hands tall. Nevertheless, he was a graceful, powerful, courageous racer, who drove his fans into frenzies with a pulse-quickening propensity for coming from behind to win in the last quarter-mile.

He was also one of the fittest Thoroughbreds ever to campaign in America. In a little over three years on the track, he started in sixty races, and failed to finish in the money in only four of them. This remarkable feat of stamina made it all too obvious halfway through his career that he was on a collision course with a record set by Seabiscuit, who was winding up his illustrious turf days as the greatest money-winning horse in the world the very same year the young chestnut colt was embarking on his own spectacular racing career.

The other side of the coin presented a somewhat less heroic picture of the colt. Dumb, half-witted, willful, knuckleheaded, stubborn, unmanageable—these and similar adjectives were sprinkled in the reams of copy written about him. But for his winning ways, it was difficult to dispute the barbs. At one time or another during his career, each could be applied with some justification, and it is a wonder that he ever made it to the track, let alone won the Triple Crown. This study in contrast is what makes the story of Whirlaway one of the most fascinating chapters in American turf lore.

Warren Wright, Sr., in the late 1920s, inherited two thriving enterprises. One was the Calumet Baking Powder Company of Chicago, and the other was the Calumet Farm at Lexington, Ky. His father had purchased the 1,000-acre spread in 1924 to raise Standardbred horses (trotters). When he died, his son converted the facility to breeding Thoroughbreds. Wright's first horses raced in 1932, and within the next quarter-century the Calumet colors were carried across the finish line by some of America's greatest equine stars.

It was on July 7, 1936, that a syndicate of ten breeders, formed by Wright, consummated a deal in London for the purchase of a nine-year-old stallion, Blenheim II, from His Highness, Prince Aga Khan. During his racing days, the horse had won the Epsom Derby and later had sired the Derby winner Mahmoud. In stud, he was reported as perhaps the best revenue producer among European stallions. His price tag was in the neighborhood of $250,000, and he arrived in America from the Aga Khan's stud, Marly la Ville, near Paris, on July 21, aboard the liner *Berengaria*. He was immediately shipped to the Claiborne Farm in Kentucky, where his stud mate was Sir Gallahad III, sire of the great Gallant Fox.

One of the Calumet mares sent to Blenheim II in the mating shed at Claiborne was the twelve-year-old Dustwhirl. She had been bred by Joseph E. Widener and had shown good speed. However, according to *The Blood-Horse,* she was "marked by a distinct willfullness, which may have been the cause of her failure to race and for her retirement to stud as a three-year-old." As a broodmare, though, she was eminently more successful, producing stakes winners Feudal Lord for Widener and Reaping Reward for A. B. Hancock, her next owner, before she was sold to Warren Wright in 1936. Then on April 2, 1938, at Calumet Farm, she dropped a blaze-faced, chestnut colt, who was named Whirlaway. His lineage was indeed one from which champions are made. Not only could he draw from the racing prowess of his sire, but his dam had a fine bloodline. She was a daughter of Sweep, who had sired Brushup, the dam of War Admiral, who, in turn, was a son of Man o' War.

In his second year, Whirlaway was turned over to the talented Ben Jones for training, and made his successful racing debut on June 3, 1940, at Lincoln Fields, winning by a nose over Beau Brannon. The next five races produced one victory and four defeats, ranging from a fourth-place finish to a loss by a neck. More significant than the outcomes for trainer and racing fan, however, were the colt's long tail and his peculiar style of racing, both of which became conversation pieces. He displayed a great kick in the stretch, but also a zany habit of running out from the rail on the turn into the stretch. It was only his remarkable speed that saved him from disastrous defeats. Consequently, his performance in the six-furlong, winner-take-all Saratoga Special on August 10 seemed to cast the die on what could be expected from the colt in the future. Although he was the favorite, he almost went down at the start, and ran last in a field of eight at the far turn. According to Arthur Daley, of the New York *Times,* it was Whirlaway's supreme race as a two-year-old, "where he was at his knuckleheaded worst." He was running so hard that he never did make the turn but, instead, ran straight into the outside rail. By the time jockey Johnny Longdon straightened him out, he was in last place. "Did he win? Don't be silly," exclaimed Daley. "Of course he won. He came like the whirlwind he was to triumph in the very last twenty-five yards" by a length over New World.

The story by now was out; Whirlaway at age two had become acutely unmanageable. At times it took several men to saddle him. "He jumped, he reared, he developed a habit of bearing out on the track as if headed for the rail. It was feared he might become an 'outlaw' or go completely to pieces and never be able to race again," was Anita Brenner's analysis of him in the *Times Magazine.* It was as though the genes of his equally temperamental dam had taken control over his personality and senses. His behavior caused an exasperated Ben Jones to expostulate at one point: "Dumbest horse I've ever trained." He claimed the colt learned everything very slowly, and that he would "have to give him plenty of races" to try to get the message through. His performances for the rest of the year were virtually carbon copies of each other. He lost his next race, the Grand Union Stakes, and then smashed to a smart win in the Hopeful Stakes in the mud, each finding him trailing at first and making up the distance at the very end. By September 28, with the advent of the prestigious Belmont Futurity, he was one of the leading money-winners among the two-year-olds, which gave him stature among his peers against whom he was to run. They included King Cole, New World, Attention, Swain, Porter's Cap, and Bushwacker, in a field of thirteen colts and one filly. The race was likely to determine the champion of the juveniles.

Whirlaway was in trouble from the start. He shuffled back as was his wont, and the crowd anticipated his late rush. Jockey Eddie Arcaro, on Our Boots, thought otherwise and kept his mount moving. As a result, Whirlaway "cracked and King Cole put him away near the sixteenth pole." The chestnut colt with the long tail was not about to do his usual thing and wound up third.

He brushed off the defeat to take the Breeder's Futurity at Keeneland, Ky., in the last seventy yards, but failed in the Pimlico Futurity on November 2, when he bore out in the stretch and blew a race he seemingly had sewn up. With all of his ups and downs, he kept piling up purse money, so that by the time he ran his last race of the year, the Walden Stakes, on November 14, he was breathing down the neck of the leader, Our Boots. Whirlaway took care of this, when jockey George Woolf rode him to victory and pushed his earnings to a handsome $77,275, or about $5,000 ahead of the year's total for Our Boots. All in all, therefore, despite his problems the colt had had a rather successful year, with wins in three stakes events, the Saratoga Special, the

Hopeful Stakes, and the Breeder's Futurity. The sportswriters acknowl-
edged this by voting him "Best Two-Year-Old," 425 votes to 345 over
Our Boots. It marked the first time in the history of the poll that a
horse beaten in the Belmont Futurity had been chosen leader of the
two-year-old colts. He also was the first of Blenheim II's offspring to
win an American stakes race.

Whirlaway's first start as a three-year-old, in 1941, was on February
8, in an allowance race at Hialeah. Ridden by Wendell Eads, he continued to display his old tendency to run in the middle of the track, as
well as his ability to "run down his field" in the final quarter-mile as he
won the race by a head. Then, he finished third in his next race, was
held off until March, and came in third and second by a neck in two
events at Tropical Park. His first real pre-Derby test was in the Blue
Grass Stakes, on April 24, at Keeneland, in fact the first important
challenge of the year for him. The evil habit continued to plague him.
He ran so far out that he had to make up too much ground in the
stretch, weakened, and lost to Our Boots by six lengths.

With each race, it appeared that Whirlaway's Derby chances grew
dimmer. The final test was the Derby Trial, on April 29. He began
slowly, in fifth position, for the first half-mile, at which point he was
sent with a rush around the far turn, a drive which some track buffs
said was the fastest they had ever seen. He was leading by a half-length
going into the stretch but bore out. Before Eads could get him straightened out, Blue Pair caught him and went on to win by three-quarters
of a length.

The spring had turned into a nightmare for Ben Jones. He was at his
wits' end. How to cure this miserable habit was the big question. The
sportswriters were hardly helpful. Early in the season, the eminent
Grantland Rice had needled the trainer. "They tell me that your horse
is a halfwit," he said. "I don't know about that," replied Jones. "But
he's making a halfwit out of me." The patience of Jones was shored up
only by an abiding faith in Whirlaway. "Plain Ben loved Whirly just
as a father grows to love a child who almost drives him to distraction.
That's what Mr. Longtail did to Jones," is the way another writer saw
it. The trainer, on the other hand, thought of himself as a friend, convinced Whirlaway would be a great horse if only he could smooth out
the things that were bothering him. He realized the horse was filled
with fears and tried to dissolve them. He spent most of the day with
him, riding alongside of him on his white pony. He repeated over and
over things that appeared to excite Whirlaway at the track, but under
quiet, reassuring conditions. He even worked out a sort of therapy routine. One day he would have the colt run as fast as he could, and on
another he would keep him on grass. Some days the colt was saddled
and unsaddled over and over again. Groups of people were even
moved around him, in an effort to make him feel comfortable in a
crowd. It was, indeed, a rather unorthodox training program for a
Thoroughbred.

Trainer Ben Jones, on white horse, walks slowly down the track at Hialeah next to Whirlaway, ridden by exercise boy Pinky Brown, in ritual devised to help dissolve the colt's fears on the track.

Only two other people had the same confidence in the horse as did Jones, reported Frank Graham in the New York *Journal-American*. One was Pinky Brown, his exercise boy, a "mild-mannered feller" who would "kill anybody that harmed Whirlaway," and who "believed that his darling, with whom he lived day and night, could beat anything on four legs." The other was Hearst columnist Bill Corum, who in July of 1940, at Arlington Park, had made the rash prediction that Whirlaway would win the Hopeful, Futurity, and Triple Crown. As of now, Corum was batting .500.

Just four days remained before the Kentucky Derby, and Jones made a last-ditch effort to resolve his problem. Following the defeats in the Blue Grass Stakes and Derby Trial, he reasoned that Wendell Eads was not the jockey for Whirlaway in the big race. Once before he had made a similar decision, in Florida, when he put Eads up in place of Basil James. Now, Jones went for hard experience, for a man he hoped would be able to control his horse and keep him on course. It was Eddie Arcaro, the "Kentucky Italian," who happened to be without a Derby mount. Arcaro had been riding for ten years, had been in eight thousand races, and was known as a strong jockey with a light touch, "good hands." This was important, since Whirlaway was known to have an extremely sensitive mouth. Furthermore, the jockey had won his first Derby with Lawrin, in 1938, for Jones, so they understood each other.

The trainer then planned another special exercise. He would sit on his white pony at the bend of the track, leaving just enough room for a horse to get through on the rail, and would have Arcaro drive the colt into this narrow opening. It was a somewhat hairy maneuver, but the jockey was not one to question the wisdom of the boss. Finally, after one such workout, when the horse still veered out, Jones stomped toward him, pulled a knife out, and muttered: "I'll get that so-and-so." Arcaro blanched for a moment at what he thought was about to happen, but calmed down as he saw the trainer cut away the inside blinker on the horse, leaving him with a broader vision out of his left eye. He hoped this would help keep the colt's attention drawn to the inner part of the track.

The sixty-seventh running of the Kentucky Derby took place on May 3, 1941, on a bright day and a fast track. A crowd of 100,000 turned out, the first time the attendance had reached that figure at Churchill Downs. A field of eleven horses went to the post, making it the richest running of the classic, worth $61,275 to the winner. Except for the losses in the Blue Grass and Derby Trial, Whirlaway should have been quoted at the shortest odds. "What was going on in Whirlaway's head and whether 'something' was hurting him became matters for nationwide speculation," opined *The Blood-Horse* in its report on the race. Yet, for all his straying problems, he was still the public's choice, albeit a lukewarm choice, with Porter's Cap and Our Boots next in line. Starting from the fourth stall in the gate, the chestnut "flying tail" got off slowly, but Arcaro was in no hurry as he moved quickly to the inside and let Whirlaway take his time to the first turn. The colt was still among the tailenders at the three-quarter pole, when he began to plow through the pack. With only a quarter-mile to go, he had moved up to fourth place behind the pacesetter, Dispose. It was then that the one-eyed blinker, Arcaro, the horse's adrenalin, and all the tender loving care that had been heaped on him for months seemed to join forces for the supreme effort. "Whirlaway came between horses on the turn, went to the front in a cyclonic burst of speed, and the colts which had been fighting for the lead ceased to be contenders." He ran faster the farther he went. The others just gave up. As the fans looked on in disbelief, Whirlaway streaked over the last quarter in :23³/₅ seconds to win by an amazing eight lengths. It was a record-breaking performance, 2:01²/₅, clipping ²/₅ second from Twenty Grand's 1931 track mark. It was also perhaps the fastest last quarter ever run in a ten-furlong race. Although the official time for the quarter was :24 seconds, Whirlaway's was less, since he had to come from behind to win.

Bill Corum was ecstatic. "Oh Whirlaway, Oh Whirlaway, that you made me feel so good today," he crowed in his column. "One instant they had all been there on the bend together, the next, and only the bright and red blouse and the blue cap were where the race was supposed to be going on." Arcaro was hailed as a "miracle man," for hav-

"The Flying Tail" streaks across the finish line eight lengths ahead of Staretor, to take the Kentucky Derby in the record time of 2:01²/₅. He ran the last quarter in :23³/₅ seconds.

Official chart of Kentucky Derby.

SEVENTH RACE 1 1-4 MILES. (Twenty Grand, May 16, 1931—2:01⅘—3—126.) Sixty-Seventh Running **KENTUCKY DERBY**. **$75,000 Added. 3-year-olds.** Special weights. Trainers of the winner, second and third horses to receive $3,000, $2,000 and $1,000, respectively. Breeders of the winner, second and third horses to receive $2,000, $1,000 and $500, respectively.

06306
May-3 41-C.D

Net value to winner $61,275; second, $8,000; third, $3,000; fourth, $1,000.

Index	Horses	Eq't A Wt	PP	St	½	¾	1	Str	Fin	Jockeys	Owners	Odds $1 Str't
06106²	WHIRLAWAY	w B 126	4	6	8¹	6¹½	4¹	1³	1⁸	ArcaroE	Calumet Farm	2.90
04709²	STARETOR	w 126	2	1	7²	4¹½	5³	2½	2nk	WoolfG	H S Nesbitt	36.00
(05979)	MARKET WISE	w B 126	7	5	6²	8⁴	6³	5³	3²	AndersonI	L Tufano	19.10
(05760)	PORTER'S CAP	w B 126	0	4	2ʰ	3⁵	2¹½	3ʰ	4¹	HaasL	C S Howard	3.30
05760²	LITTLE BEANS	w B 126	5	10	10¹²	9⁵	8⁵	7²	5¹	MooreG	Mrs L Palladino	12.10
05751	DISPOSE	w 126	11	2	1²	1²	1ʰ	4ʰ	6¹½	BiermanC	King Ranch	7.20
(06106)	BLUE PAIR	w B 126	3	3	3⁵	2ʰ	3½	6½	7½	JamesB	Mrs V S Bragg	20.60
(05922)	OUR BOOTS	w 126	10	9	4³	5½	7²	8⁵	8³	McCrearyC	Woodvale Farm	3.90
(05752)	ROBERT MORRIS	w 126	8	8	5¹½	7¹	9⁶	9⁸	9¹²	RichardsH	J F Byers	13.90
05922³	VALDINA PAUL	w B 126	6	7	9³	10¹⁵	10¹⁵	10¹⁵	10¹²	LemmonsH	Valdina Farm	†24.30
(05906)	SWAIN	w B 126	1	11	11	11	11	11	11	AdamsJ	C Putnam	†

(Complete finish confirmed by Kuprion Camera.)

†Mutuel field. Time, :23⅘, :46⅘, 1:11⅘, 1:37⅘, 2:01⅘ (new track record). Track fast.

	$2 Mutuels Paid			Odds to $1		
WHIRLAWAY	7.80	5.00	4.40	2.90	1.50	1.20
STARETOR		35.20	17.00		16.60	7.50
MARKET WISE			10.80			4.40

Winner—Ch. c, by Blenheim II.—Dustwhirl, by Sweep (trained by B. A. Jones; bred by Calumet Farm).
WENT TO POST—5:53. AT POST—1½ minutes.
Start good and slow. Won easily; second and third driving.
WHIRLAWAY, eased back when blocked in the first eighth and taken to the inside approaching the first turn, started up after reaching the final half mile, was taken between horses on the final turn, responded with much energy to take command with a rush and, continuing with much power, drew out fast in the final eighth. STARETOR, away slowly and allowed to remain well back the first five eighths, made his move gradually, drifted out slightly before straightening up in the stretch and held on well in the final drive. MARKET WISE, also well back early, was slow to respond to pressure, but rallied after reaching the last five sixteenths and, finishing with courage, was wearing down STARETOR. PORTER'S CAP, a strong factor from the start and always clear as he raced on the outside, responded to strong urging when rounding the final turn, but tired after reaching the last three sixteenths. LITTLE BEANS raced well from a very sluggish beginning, then closed courageously to pass tired horses in the stretch. DISPOSE took command easily, was allowed to run along well within himself through the back stretch, was under pressure after three quarters and held on fairly well to the closing three sixteenths, where he faltered badly. BLUE PAIR quit after showing speed for a mile. OUR BOOTS could not go with the early leaders under urging and failed to keep up after reaching the last half mile. ROBERT MORRIS began well, but dropped out of contention after a half mile and was far back thereafter.

ing ridden a perfect race, for having held the colt thoroughly in check until the final stages of the race. It was later revealed that this was all part of a carefully mapped-out plan. Jones and his jockey had prepared an exact schedule of points on the track where the colt would be let out. "He was a 'one run' horse," claimed Arcaro, "and if he was to win his speed had to be preserved for that part of the race where they pay off." Other unusual precautions were also taken. Before he was to be saddled, Whirlaway had been walked around the track, hemmed in between the inner rail and a Calumet lead pony. Then he was marched back and forth in front of the grandstands, to get him used to the noise of the crowd. The public was unaware that this was the favorite of the race, because he wore no identifying number or colors. Finally, just before he was to go out onto the track for the race, the trainer gave his jockey last-minute instructions. "Eddie, don't take the lead until you're headin' for home. This horse can pass any livin' horse. Jes' wait for the straight part of the track, 'cause when he's got horses to pass he won't run wide." He did not. He had hugged the rail for the entire race.

The spectacular result notwithstanding, ugly rumors and whispers suddenly cropped up, relating Whirlaway's incredible late bursts of speed to the use of drugs. On May 8, New York *Daily Mirror* columnist Dan Parker wrote of how the colt had been given a saliva test after a winter race at Hialeah and the results proved to be positive. He complained that nothing had been done about this, that the entire matter had been written off as medicine for a cold. He seemed to imply that the prestige of Warren Wright had prevented further inquiries. Then, he reported, Whirlaway lost the next race and the public lost its shirt. "Whirlaway's imitation of a streak of lightning at the Derby last Saturday has set tongues wagging," he continued. "One trainer came back with the story that Whirlaway had such a bad cold on Derby Day he had to have a triple dose of medicine." He even questioned whether the horse had been given a saliva test after the race.

This brought Bill Corum to the rescue, in a high state of dudgeon. He led off his column on May 9 with a verse:

> "No, Dan, it wasn't the cough medicine
>   that carried 'em off;
> It was the coffin, they should have
>   carried the rest of those horses in,
> When he left 'em for dead at the
>   head of the stretch."

"He could scarcely be expected to set a mile-and-a-quarter record in a five-and-one-half furlong dash," he concluded.

Even the normally placid Southern gentleman from Parnell, Mo., Ben Jones, had his ire worked up. "I will, if Mr. Wright approves, match Whirlaway against any three-year-old anywhere," he cried. "I would like to bring Whirlaway out of the stable at midnight, high noon, or any time, and without any notice whatsoever throw a saddle and rider on him and let him show you what he can do to any horse of his age at any distance and under any conditions." Parker apparently

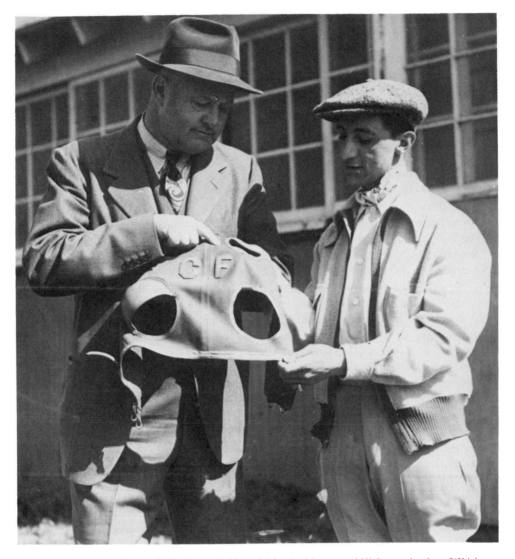

Trainer Ben Jones and jockey Eddie Arcaro hold special hood with one-eyed blinker used to keep Whirlaway from running wide on the turns.

realized he had made an error, for he recanted the story, and on May 11 reported that he had received assurances from Louis F. McNeely, sports editor of the Louisville *Times,* that Whirlaway had indeed been given the saliva test after the Derby, under proper conditions and control, and that the results had been negative.

This rumor having been scotched, others cropped up in what seemed to be an effort to discredit the victory. There was the claim that Churchill Downs had been rolled until it was a "pasteboard track," that it had been packed deliberately to ensure a spectacular time for the benefit of the huge crowd. Some even speculated about the long tail, claiming it was indicative of a "good doer," a good eater in track parlance. Others claimed that it served to prevent trailing steeds from closing in on the flying colt.

The net result of the controversy was to create doubts in the minds of the public. "Eastern fans just couldn't conceive another such performance in the Preakness, particularly after hearing ugly rumors about Kentucky's saliva test," observed *The Blood-Horse*. Although betting at the Pimlico track during the day was brisk, it fell off noticeably for the Preakness. Thus, on May 10, just a week after the Derby, "Mr. Longtail" went to the post, in a field of eight at even money. Again, he was in no hurry to get going. "Whirlaway walks out of the gate counting the house," was the way Ed Thorgersen described the start for Movietone News. When the field passed the grandstands for the first time, "Whirlaway was so far last that he wasn't bothered by the dust the other horses were raising," reported Joe Palmer. Coming into the backstretch, he was six or seven lengths behind the last horse. In fact, the bulk of the field was already going into the last turn when Whirlaway first passed the half-mile mark. That was when Arcaro gave him the green light. The colt responded. He gouged huge chunks out of space in front of him with devastating strides and, quite suddenly, it appeared as though the seven other horses had slowed to a crawl. Down the backstretch, Arcaro took Whirlaway to the outside, and charged the leaders, King Cole and Our Boots. He caught them at the quarter pole, having passed seven horses in a matter of twenty seconds. "Somebody suggested afterward that maybe they didn't see him go past" . . . "A small horse, as to height, he seemingly disappeared from sight as he went on the outside of the field, which was fairly well bunched" . . . "Arcaro sent Whirlaway well out, perhaps fifteen feet from the rail, and then tightened his inside rein. Whirlaway straightened out as if he were on a trolley, and the race was virtually over," was the way Joe Palmer and Joe Estes called the race for *The Blood-Horse*. The high-stepping Thoroughbred showed his heels to the field, waved his high-flying tail goodbye to them all, and blazed to a five-and-a-half-length victory.

The convincing win proved conclusively that the results of the Derby a week earlier had been no accident. Joe Palmer put his finger on the reason. "He carries in his armament the deadliest weapon a Thoroughbred can have—an annihilating burst of speed which he can apparently turn on at any stage of a race." Ben Jones exulted, "He's like an old ham getting better with age." In the jockey room, Eddie Arcaro's fellow riders marveled. "Boy, what a horse that is you were riding. We'd sure like to get a good look at him some time." "That's all right, pals," Arcaro replied, grinning. "Just hand me a towel. I want to wipe the jam off my lips. This is too easy and you said it when you said he was a whirlwind. I was just gunning you all the way. It was just as well that my horse propped a little on the break and walked out of the box. I'd have had to run over horses because he certainly swings when he gets ready to roll."

"Whirlaway walks out of the gate counting the house" and dead last in a field of eight at the start of the Preakness.

Despite poor start, Whirlaway smashes to a six-length victory in the Preakness. King Cole finishes second, followed by Our Boots.

SIXTH RACE
06600
May-10-41-Pim

1 3-16 MILES. (Seabiscuit, Nov. 1, 1938—1:56⅗—5—120.) **Fifty-First Running PREAKNESS STAKES.** $50,000 Added. 3-year-olds. Weight-for-age. Nominator of the winner to receive $1,500, nominator of the second horse $750, and the nominator of the third horse $250 of the added money. Net value to winner $49,365; second, $10,000; third, $5,000; third, $2,000.

Index	Horses	Eq't A Wt	PP	St	½	¾	1	Str	Fin	Jockeys	Owners	Odds $1 Str't
(06336)	WHIRLAWAY	wв 126	1	8	8	7^5	$11\frac{1}{2}$	1^5	$15\frac{1}{2}$	ArcaroE	Calumet Farm	1.15
05979³	KING COLE	wв 126	5	2	1^1	1^1	2^2	$21\frac{1}{2}$	2^2	GilbertJ	O Phipps	25.75
06336	OUR BOOTS	w 126	8	6	$4\frac{1}{2}$	$51\frac{1}{2}$	$3\frac{1}{2}$	3^h	3^{nk}	McCrearyC	Woodvale Farm	3.85
06336	PORTER'S CAP	wв 126	3	3	$6\frac{1}{2}$	6^h	4^h	4^5	4^9	HaasL	C S Howard	5.40
06392³	KANSAS	wв 126	6	7	$51\frac{1}{2}$	3^h	5^3	$52\frac{1}{2}$	$52\frac{1}{2}$	HarrellJ	Millsdale Stable	45.10
06336	DISPOSE	w 126	7	4	2^h	4^h	7^6	6^2	6^3	BiermanC	King Ranch	13.60
05979²	CURIOUS COIN	wв 126	4	5	$3\frac{1}{2}$	2^h	6^h	7^{10}	7^{15}	AndersonI	Coldstream Stable	15.55
(06392)	OCEAN BLUE	wв 126	2	1	7^5	8	8	8	8	HanfordI	C Oglebay	8.65

(Complete finish confirmed by Photochart Camera.)
Time, :23⅗, :47⅗, 1:12⅗, 1:39⅕, 1:58⅘. Track good.

	┌─$2 Mutuels Paid─┐			┌──Odds to $1──┐		
WHIRLAWAY	4.30	4.40	3.30	1.15	1.20	.65
KING COLE		16.30	7.80		7.15	2.90
OUR BOOTS			3.60			.80

Winner—Ch. c, by Blenheim II.—Dustwhirl, by Sweep (trained by B. A. Jones; bred by Calumet Farm).
WENT TO POST—4:58. AT POST—1 minute.
Start good and slow. Won easily, second and third driving.
WHIRLAWAY, slow to begin, was some distance back of the field passing the stand the first time around, but improved his position after entering the back stretch while saving ground, then came to the outside of KING COLE nearing the stretch turn to dash to the front and, easily opening up on his opposition in the stretch, won with speed in reserve. KING COLE headed the field early and set a good pace to hold DISPOSE, CURIOUS COIN and OUR BOOTS down the back stretch, but was no match for WHIRLAWAY when the latter challenged, although easily best of the others. OUR BOOTS, close to the pace early while racing on the outside of DISPOSE and CURIOUS COIN, dropped back in the stretch, but was not good enough to withstand PORTER'S CAP. The latter, under restraint not far from the leaders in the first half mile, made a mild move nearing the stretch while racing rather wide and continued wide in the stretch to falter near the finish. KANSAS raced up strongly in the back stretch and was impressive for seven-eighths, then faded. DISPOSE had good early speed, but tired in the stretch. CURIOUS COIN was used up keeping up with the early leaders and tired after going seven eighths. OCEAN BLUE was off well, but was unable to keep up after going a half mile and was badly beaten at the end.

Official chart of Preakness.

Confidence and joy reigned supreme at Calumet. This was the first Preakness victory for Warren Wright, Ben Jones, and Eddie Arcaro. It also meant another $49,365 added to the colt's winnings. The payoff to his betting backers, however, was rather slim, a mere $1.15 to the dollar. The winning time, too, was 1:58⁴/₅, which hardly approached Seabiscuit's 1938 track record of 1:56³/₅. After the race, it was learned that Ben Jones had once more walked the colt around the track "almost within splinter distance of the inside rail." This, plus the outcome of the Preakness, may have caused turf reporter Norris Royden to conclude: "The dumbest horse Ben Jones ever encountered finally has learned . . . how to negotiate left-handed turns."

The pressure was now off, as they prepared for the final leg of the Triple Crown. However, Ben Jones refused to let up, and had his mount run in a tuneup on May 20. He might have saved himself the effort. The seventy-third Belmont Stakes on June 7 was hardly a contest, virtually a walkover for Whirlaway. Few doubted the end result, even among the Thoroughbreds, as only three showed up to oppose "The Flying Tail," the smallest field since Twenty Grand had run in the race ten years earlier. At the outset, Robert Morris, Yankee Chance, and Itabo set a very slow pace, hoping to upset the timing of the favorite. But Eddie Arcaro would have nothing of this nonsense. They had gone a half-mile when he turned to Alfred Robertson on Robert Morris and Basil James on Yankee Chance and yelled: "The hell with this, fellas, I'm leaving." He then gave Whirlaway his head, and within the next quarter-mile moved out to a seven-length lead. To all intents and purposes, the race was won at that point. The colt had beaten the field, and had nothing else to do. Therefore, he was eased to finish in an easy gallop and in the rather unimpressive time of 2:31, nearly three seconds off the track record set by Sorteado in 1939.

Owner Warren Wright missed the glory of the Triple Crown achievement. He was attending his son's graduation from the University of Denver. However, he had listened to the radio broadcast of the race, and then had been interviewed by reporters. He was quick to give

Whirlaway coasts to an easy victory in the Belmont Stakes. Robert Morris finished second and Yankee Chance third.

Trainer Ben Jones holds flower-bedecked Whirlaway, the new Triple Crown champion, in the winner's circle after the Belmont victory. Eddie Arcaro is in the saddle.

Official chart of Belmont Stakes.

SIXTH RACE
08106
June-7-41-Bel

1 1-2 MILES. (Sorteado, Sept. 23, 1939—2:28⅖—4—112.) Seventy-Third Running BELMONT STAKES. $25,000 Added. 3-year-olds. Weight-for-age.

Net value to winner $39,770; second, $5,000; third, $2,500; fourth, $1,000.

Index	Horses	Eq't	A	Wt	PP	St	½	¾	1	Str	Fin	Jockeys	Owners	Odds $1 Str't
(07004)	WHIRLAWAY	wB		126	3	3	3¹½	1⁷	1³	1²	1²½	ArcaroE	Calumet Farm	.25
(07176)	ROBERT MORRIS	w		126	4	4	2½	2⁶	2⁷	2²	2⁵	RobertsonA	J F Byers	4.30
07725³	YANKEE CHANCE	w		126	1	2	4	4	4	3³	3⁵	JamesB	C V Whitney	36.05
(07279)	ITABO	w		126	2	1	1¹	3²	3³	4	4	BiermanC	King Ranch	7.70

(Complete finish confirmed by James J. Jones Photo Finish Camera.)
Time, :25⅖, :49⅗, 1:13⅘, 1:39⅛, 2:05, 2:31. Track fast.

	$2 Mutuels Paid			Odds to $1	
WHIRLAWAY	2.50	2.10	No show prices.	.25	.05
ROBERT MORRIS		2.40			.20

Winner—Ch. c, by Blenheim II.—Dustwhirl, by Sweep (trained by B. A. Jones; bred by Calumet Farm).
WENT TO POST—4:56. AT POST—1 minute.
Start good and slow. Won easily; second and third the same.
WHIRLAWAY was under restraint for a quarter and, when settled rounding the first turn, moved into command with a rush, then drew away into an easy lead and was rated along steadily, came a trifle wide rounding the stretch and finished in the middle of the track with speed in reserve. ROBERT MORRIS reared at the start and broke off stride, settled quickly and was kept close up throughout, improved his position rapidly rounding the far turn and, nearing the stretch turn, was placed under pressure, but could not menace the winner, yet held the others safe. YANKEE CHANCE was fractious at the post and was taken under restraint when outrun, then began to move up when settled in the stretch and hung at the finish. ITABO was sent into command to show the pace for the early stages under sufferance, then dropped back steadily when settled after the first mile and was never a factor thereafter.

Ben Jones credit for "making a great consistent racer out of a temperamental, willful two-year-old." He also offered a cogent analysis of
what Jones had done. "One doesn't employ a system in raising an unusual child," he said. "One studies the child, watches nervous reactions,
follows awakening interests, or, in other words, carefully bends the
twig." Wright, in addition to enjoying the thrill of winning the Triple
Crown, could also point to the fact that his remarkable horse had just
scored his thirteenth victory in twenty-six starts and had moved into
seventeenth place, behind Bimelech, as the leading money-winner.
Thus, he became only the second horse since Man o' War to lead his
age division in earnings at two and three, and the first leading two-
year-old since "Big Red" to have a better record at age three than at
two.

For the rest of the year, "The Flying Tail" literally terrorized his
competitors. His next victory was the Dwyer Stakes, which was his
eighth win of the year and fifth straight since the Derby. Other major
stakes victories included the Saranac, Travers, American Derby, and
Lawrence Realization. He did lose the Arlington Classic, Narragansett
Special, and Jockey Club Gold Cup, the last by a nose to Market Wise
in a sizzling finish down the stretch. Coming up to the Saranac, following his Arlington loss, a whole raft of excuses were voiced for the defeat. It was said that Jones did not give the colt enough strenuous work,
that only Arcaro raced him best, that he had been hit in the eye with a
clod of dirt, that the classic was a jinx for favorites.

The fact is, he won the Saranac with Alfred Robertson in the irons,
although only by a whisker in a three-horse photo finish. Some, including Samuel Riddle, owner of War Relic, refused to concede the win,
with Riddle displaying an uncontrolled anger before fans, swinging his
cane wildly and sending officials scurrying to right and left. In the
Travers, they sent Whirlaway out with his tail braided, to prevent him
from picking up mud in the soft going. All in all, the general consensus
was that there really was no telling just how good he was, simply because no three-year-old appeared capable of extending him. Whatever
losses he suffered were largely because of his ingrained habit of bearing
out in the stretch run. The prevalent theory was that Whirlaway could
go any distance which American racing called for and could carry
weight. In fact, he was asked to bear as much as 130 pounds. Furthermore, by the time he had put away the Realization in September, he
had pushed his earnings to $347,661, passing Challedon, Gallant Fox,
and Equipoise to become the third highest earner in history. He had
been in training since August 1, 1939, had started thirty-five times, and
had shipped a total of 12,500 miles, for which he was being touted as
the new "iron horse" of racing. Finally, never in the history of Thoroughbred racing had another horse racked up such a total of money
won prior to the end of his five-year-old season.

Late in October, Calumet Farm sent a string of its racers to Santa
Anita, Calif., for the winter season. There seemed little doubt that

Whirlaway, who was among them, would be able to top Seabiscuit's earnings record while participating in the stakes races there. Once again, severe precautions were taken to make the Triple Crown champion comfortable during and after his cross-country journey. At the West Coast track, a special screened-in stall was built, from which the colt could extend his head but not be annoyed or petted by onlookers. He was also accompanied by his pet pony, Silver King.

However, all plans were negated abruptly by the Pearl Harbor disaster on December 7 and the outbreak of World War II. Eight days later, the entire 1941–1942 Santa Anita season was canceled. Therefore, the year wound up in a state of suspended activity for Whirlaway, but not before he had been voted "Horse of the Year" by *Turf and Sport Digest*. He did just beat out a talented newcomer, Alsab, 96-90 votes, said rising star being voted best among the two-year-olds and destined to confront the older star the following year. Whirlaway also won the three-year-old honors, which made it only the second time that a leading two-year-old had also captured top honors the following year. The last Thoroughbred to do this was Bimelech in 1939 and 1940.

When the war broke out, all transportation facilities were mobilized, which stranded the Calumet horses on the West Coast. It was not until March of 1942 that they were able to ship east. Ben Jones claimed that Whirlaway had benefited from the rest, but that he was "crying to run."

As a four-year-old, "The Flying Tail" picked up where he had left off. He won twelve of twenty-two races, mostly handicaps, while carrying weights of up to 132 pounds. He was second in eight events and never failed to place. His victories included the Clark, Dixie, Brooklyn, Massachusetts, Garden State, Narragansett Special, Jockey Club Gold Cup, Washington, Pimlico Special, Governor Bowie, and Louisiana handicaps. There were some notable highlights in this skein. In the Suburban, at even money, $149,968 was bet on him, the most ever on a single horse, and he doubtless caused not a few heart seizures when he finished second after trailing by nearly twelve lengths at the final turn. Perhaps the biggest thrill for owner Warren Wright came at Suffolk Downs, Boston, on July 15, when the colt won the Massachusetts Handicap. It was worth $43,850, and brought Whirlaway's total winnings past Seabiscuit's record of $437,730 by $16,606. He was now the world's leading money-winner, and also the 1942 handicap leader, with his earnings from these races coming to $104,675 to date. Then, on October 3, he won $18,350 in the Jockey Club Gold Cup, which carried his total past the half-million-dollar mark, the first Thoroughbred ever to reach that pinnacle. In the Pimlico Special, on October 28, no other horse dared to come out against him, and he won the race in a walkover. He broke another Seabiscuit record on November 11 with his win in the Governor Bowie Handicap. The purse brought his total for the year to $198,810, which was some $30,000 higher than the previous mark for winnings by a four-year-old Thoroughbred. In fact, Whirlaway's achievements on the track also attracted glory to his dam,

Dustwhirl. Largely because of him, she set a record for earnings by her produce as three of them won a total of $641,479. This beat the record of Marguerite, the dam of Gallant Fox, five of whose get won $620,080.

The year 1942 was notable for Whirlaway in another respect. It marked the third time since 1920 that the gauntlet was thrown down at a Triple Crown champion in a challenge to a match race. The challenger was the very exciting three-year-old Alsab. He was a bay, with a white star, by God Goods, out of Wind Chant. His career had had a rather unassuming start, when he was included "in a consignment largely made up of foals of untried stallions" and wound up being bought for only $700 at the Saratoga Sales. He was purchased by Albert Sabath, of Chicago, and gratefully rewarded his new owner's confidence in him by amassing winnings of $110,000 by the end of his second year.

Alsab scored fifteen victories in twenty-two starts, finishing the season, in the opinion of John Hervey, with a "future more eagerly looked forward to than that of almost any horse since Man o' War." He had two notable races. One was a match with another two-year-old, Requested, a six-and-a-half-furlong sprint at Belmont Park, which he won in 1:16, a record for a juvenile horse as of that date. The other was the Champagne Stakes, which he took in 1:35^2/$_5$ seconds, the fastest mile run by any horse in 1941, and a new world's record for a two-year-old, breaking that set by Twenty Grand in 1930. Alsab was so good that his owner entered him for the following year's Kentucky Derby on October 14, the earliest registration ever for the classic. "In action," wrote "Salvator," "Alsab is not of the drum-roll stroke so common among precocious juveniles, neither had he their quickness away from the gate. He gets off, on the contrary, rather moderately, if not even slowly at times, and requires a bit of ground over which to extend himself before moving into high. . . . When at the very top of his flight, he never struggles or gives an effect of extreme exertion, rather everything he does appears easy and within his powers."

Alsab's third year was good and bad. He missed the Triple Crown, losing the Derby and Belmont to Shut Out, while winning the Preakness. He ran twenty-three times, winning nine, placing in seven, coming in third in three, and finishing out of the money four times. His total winnings were $234,565, not a bad year's pay for any horse. The fact is, he was an exciting performer, second only to Whirlaway, which made the match race a "natural." It took place on September 19, at Narragansett, with a $25,000 purse to the winner. The distance was a mile and three-sixteenths, at weight-for-age conditions, giving Alsab 119 pounds to Whirlaway's 126.

George Woolf, who had guided Seabiscuit to victory in the match race with War Admiral, was on Whirlaway, while Carroll Bierman rode Alsab. The crowd of 35,000 anticipated excitement, since both horses had reputations for coming from behind. The start saw Alsab jump out first to a half-length lead at the first quarter. Woolf, riding confidently, stayed behind, biding his time. He was never more than

Spectacular photo finish of match race between Whirlaway (on outside) and Alsab, at Narragansett Park on September 19, 1942.

Official photo showing Alsab winning the race by the tip of his nose.

two lengths off. At the mile, he was only a half-length away, as Whirlaway crept up on the outside and began one of his late surges. The two colts ran head to head in a savage, awe-inspiring stretch run, "a finish fought with exceptional bitterness and gameness on both sides." They crossed the finish line locked tightly, although Whirlaway was still moving up at the end and in fact was ahead by a few strides past the wire. It was a photo finish, of course, and the decision in favor of Alsab was made only after a magnifying-glass inspection of the film showed that he had won by the barest of possible margins, the tip of a nostril. The time was 1:56^2/$_5$. Ironically, the Narragansett Championship marked the third instance when a Triple Crown champion lost out in a match race. It was notable in another respect. Never before had two such top money-winners met in a special race. The pair subsequently raced against each other in two other stakes events, with Whirlaway avenging his defeat in one and succumbing again in another.

"Mr. Longtail" finished up his fourth year with a win in the Louisiana Handicap, at the Fair Grounds in New Orleans, on December 12. He also suffered his first real injury, a hurt foreleg which subsequently was diagnosed as a bowed tendon. Four days later, his hurt was eased somewhat when he was named "Horse of the Year" for the second successive time. He received 76 votes, to 45 for Alsab and 4 for Count Fleet. The honors would not quit, for he was also named "Best Four-Year-Old" and "Best Handicap Horse." It was the third year in a row that he had won top spot in his own division.

Ben Jones nursed Whirlaway carefully until the following spring, and then tried him out in two races. He lost both. The last was the Equipoise Mile, at Arlington Park, on June 26, in which he finished fifth and pulled up somewhat lame. The losses convinced Warren Wright that his marvelous horse had reached the end of his campaigning days, and had earned a life of ease in retirement. His last appearance was at Washington Park, Chicago, on July 5, when he paraded in silks before a cheering crowd.

Not since Man o' War had a horse made such a triumphant return to Kentucky. He arrived in Lexington on July 13, and on August 8, was honored with a "Whirlaway Day" celebration, replete with speeches from leading citizens and public officials, in a manner befitting the return of a conquering hero from battle. The colt then settled down at Claiborne Farm for stud duty, where he lived a regal life as choice mares were sent to him at $1,500 per breeding effort. His first get began to race in 1947, and through 1949 he had produced fifty-two winners out of seventy-one starters, including seven stakes winners—Dart By, Duchess Peg, Going Away, Scattered, Whirl Flower, Whirl Some, and Whirling Fox. His fillies had won, or were in the money, in just about every major stakes event for the distaff Thoroughbred. These achievements of his offspring resulted in his making the list of the twenty leading sires of 1949. Finally, through 1951, his 283 starters had earned $1,631,330, or some $5,764 per starter per year. It is somewhat noteworthy, in passing, that in September 1944, a mare which

Proud owner Warren Wright (left) and trainer Ben Jones hold Whirlaway as he makes the final public appearance of his racing career at Washington Park, Chicago, July 5, 1943. Devoted exercise boy Pinky Brown is astride him.

had been served to Whirlaway as part of his fertility tests late in 1943 produced a foal that was registered and became a winner. It was First Whirl.

Marcel Boussac, one of Europe's celebrated Thoroughbred breeders, owners, and turf personalities, visited Lexington in 1950, took one look at Whirlaway, and exclaimed: *"C'est pour moi."* The French textile magnate and industrialist had a keen eye for Thoroughbred stock, having produced such stars as Goya II, Adaris, Hierocles, Ardan, and Djeddak, all of whom subsequently were purchased and imported by American syndicates. He was not to be dissuaded, therefore, from negotiating a three-year lease for Whirlaway to stand in stud at his own farm. By now, Bull Lea had become the choice stallion at Calumet Farm, so Warren Wright was prevailed upon to send his prize champion to Boussac's Haras Fresvay-le-Bufford farm in southern Normandy. It was the first time that Calumet Farm had ever exported one of its Thoroughbreds. Before the contract had expired, though, Monsieur Boussac had become so enamored of his American stallion that he succeeded in convincing Wright to sell him outright. On the morning of

April 6, 1953, at the age of fifteen, Whirlaway died suddenly in his stall, ten minutes after he had been bred to a mare. The cause of death was said to have been a rupture of nerve tissue.

Years after Whirlaway had retired, Eddie Arcaro perhaps best crystalized just what it was that made the colt such a unique racer. "It never was any picnic to ride Whirlaway," he said. "Once he started to climb you just couldn't slow him down. It was like stepping on the accelerator of a big Cadillac. How he could pour it on!"

Ben Jones truly loved the eccentric colt, and could never reconcile himself to his eventual retirement. "If Whirlaway was my horse," he boasted early in 1943, "he would still be running when he was ten years old. He is the soundest horse I have ever seen." The day the colt had to be retired, however, he lamented: "It's like losin' an old friend."

COUNT FLEET

COUNT FLEET
(Brown Colt)
{
    Reigh Count
    {
        *Sunreigh
        *Contessina
    }
    Quickly
    {
        Haste
        Stephanie
    }
}

Count Fleet

6

Breeding Thoroughbred horses is a treacherous business. The odds for success are so stacked against the breeder, the wonder is that so many of them keep chasing the ever elusive prize at the end of the rainbow—another Man o' War or the next Triple Crown champion. Patience, perseverance, and unlimited ready cash are indispensable prerequisites. It is equally true that a rich lode of luck must also accompany the fat wallet. The history of Thoroughbred racing in America is replete with stories of champion heroes emerging from the pack of thousands of foals bred each year, largely because of a twist of fate. The saga of Count Fleet is one such chapter.

John D. Hertz was a self-made millionaire. He emigrated to America from Czechoslovakia as a youngster, settled in Chicago, and amassed his fortune when he founded the Yellow Cab Company and then proceeded to put Americans in the driver's seat with his car-rental operations. His interest in Thoroughbred racing and breeding began in the early '20s. He rose rapidly to prominence in the sport, eventually heading up the Arlington Race Track. It was he who in 1939 tried to woo the special race between War Admiral and Seabiscuit to Chicago, by offering to match the $100,000 Belmont Park was putting up as a purse.

In 1927, six years after he and his wife had joined the owner-breeder ranks, he saw a young colt catch up to the leader of a race, reach over, and bite him. The Hertzes were so taken with this remarkable display of fired determination that they made up their minds then and there to buy him. The following year, they wound up with their first Kentucky Derby trophy. The colt's name was Reigh Count, who went on to victory in other major stakes races in the United States and England. When he eventually was retired to stud he was among the top twenty leading sires for five consecutive years. But none of his get won a Futurity or Kentucky Derby, which convinced Hertz that he could not expect too much more success from him. However, he was not about to sell him, so he decided to breed him to no more than four mares a year for as long as he lived or remained active in stud. Considering that it is usual for a top stallion to receive between thirty and forty mares in a breeding season, the decision was hardly a vote of confidence in Reigh Count, more likely a sentimental gesture to the stallion. On the other hand, Hertz still had it in the back of his mind that he might yet bring off the long-tried breeding theory of mating a distance-running sire, like Reigh Count, with a flashy, speedy mare, to produce a son with the best qualities of both.

Such a mare did come along, but it took better than ten years, and it called for even more of the gambler's gambit to take a chance with her. She was Quickly, a shifty mare by Haste, out of a daughter by Stefan the Great. Hertz, in buying her for only $2,500, was bucking the wisdom of breeders, who distrust any mare that has run too much. The reasoning is that they have worn themselves out to be any good as a broodmare. On the surface, Quickly fit that theorem. She was seven years old, footsore, in poor physical condition, having raced eighty-five times in six seasons, winning thirty-two times and earning only $21,530. Most of her victories were at six furlongs; distance obviously was not her forte. Quickly's first mating was poor. The next year she was barren. Hertz still refused to concede, with the result that his luck, gambling instinct, and sheer stubbornness bore fruit on March 24, 1940. To the cover of Reigh Count at Hertz's Stoner Creek Farm in Kentucky, she produced an ugly duckling of a foal, "a gangling little brown chow-hound that was promptly named Count Fleet."

He was a disappointment as a yearling, showing signs of difficulty in handling. The combination of negatives nudged Hertz to offer the youngster for sale. Count Fleet, therefore, was shown to prospective yearling buyers, but the trainers shied away because of his dam. On the other hand, they snapped up two other yearlings by Reigh Count. About the only one who believed in the young Thoroughbred at the time was the stable boy, Sam Ramsen. He envisioned a great horse in the brown, gawky colt. He worked diligently with him and, when about to be inducted into the Army, he begged the manager of Stoner Creek Farm to tell Hertz not to sell Count Fleet, because "someday he is going to be one fine racer."

Hertz had little choice, when 1942 rolled around and still no buyer in sight. He simply shipped the fractious problem off to the races, placing him in the hands of his trainer, the big, quiet, florid-faced Scot, G. D. "Don" Cameron. It took until June 1 before Cameron was willing to chance his educational indoctrination of the horse in an outing at Belmont Park. "The Count" swerved at the start, banged into Vacuum Cleaner, and lost. He did the same two weeks later. A few days afterward, the colt's jockey, Johnny Longdon, chanced to visit Cameron's barn at Belmont and noticed a trainer examining Count Fleet. He jumped on his bicycle, pedaled furiously to a nearby telephone booth, and called Hertz. "That was the first time I knew that Mr. Hertz had put him up for sale," recalled Longdon. "The price, they told me, was $4,500. I felt it was a bad mistake to let him go. Just his love of running, if it could ever be properly controlled, had convinced me that he would be a good one." When he explained this to the owner, he was told: "The colt's dangerous. Someday, I'm afraid he'll do you serious injury." "I'm not afraid," countered Longdon. This, coming from a thirty-four-year-old jockey, one of the top riders of the American turf, convinced Hertz. "All right," he sighed, "if you're game enough to ride him, I'll keep him."

The tide took a dramatic turn almost immediately. He broke his maiden in a five-and-a-half-furlong sprint in 1:06, just $3/5$ second shy of the track record, and repeated on July 4 at the same distance, at $1/5$ second faster, in both as if the opposition had suddenly stopped running. He lost the next time out, in the East View Stakes on July 15, only to rebound in the Wakefield Stakes on July 22, when three horses came out with him and he "strung them out like the proverbial 'string of suckers,'" as one reporter called it. These performances convinced the railbirds that he was probably the best two-year-old in the East. The only one who could stack up to him was Occupation, a Westerner whose followers were touting him for juvenile champion honors and as unbeatable, coming off victories in the Arlington Park Futurity and other races. The showdown between the two was inevitable, slated for the Washington Park Futurity in Chicago, on August 15.

Eleven horses went to the post, with Occupation the favorite at 3-5. "The Count" trailed at the top of the stretch, following a troublesome start, and then Longdon sent him after the leader. As they approached the wire, "Count Fleet seemed . . . literally to be eating him up," recalled "Salvator." He failed by a neck. It was back to the drawing board once more, and two quick wins followed, as the colt was prepared for the upcoming Futurity Stakes at Belmont Park on October 3. Just before the big race, though, big news was made at a morning workout. Johnny Longdon was observed having his hands full trying to hold in the horse, as he rocketed through six furlongs, or three-quarters of a mile, in an unprecedented $1:08^1/5$. There were too many onlookers with stop watches for Cameron and Longdon, who said he thought it was more like 1:12, to discount the time. Although Count Fleet had always been considered a horse of competitive temperament and a stretch runner of ability, none had seriously thought of him as a speedster. The workout changed many minds, including that of the trainer, who, for the first time, was ready to concede that the colt had tremendous potential.

It came as a rather severe shock, therefore, that "The Fleet" ran third in the Futurity, five lengths behind Occupation and a neck back of Askmenow. Many felt that he had, in track parlance "left the race on the track in the trial"; the remarkable workout had simply drained him. There was a more practical explanation, after the dust had settled. For one thing, confusion was rampant at the outset of the race, when jockey Carroll Bierman was unseated in the gate by Askmenow, the only filly in the race. Then the two ran two-three for the six and a half furlongs, as the colt played "Romeo to his Juliet." Longdon later told reporters of his ordeal. "We broke all right, but Count Fleet grabbed his quarter [part of the hoof] right after the start. For the last three-eighths he laid on Askmenow, and I couldn't drag him off. Even after the finish neither of us could pull up." It was shades of the shenanigans his sire was guilty of as a two-year-old, and it was a tribute to his taste for the fairer sex. The little lass was worth the extra look, for she subsequently was named the year's "Best Two-Year-Old Filly."

Count Fleet (far left) comes in third behind winner Occupation and filly Askmenow (hidden) in the Futurity Stakes at Aqueduct. "The Fleet" played "Romeo to his Juliet" throughout the race.

A more cogent reason made the race noteworthy for turf historians. It marked the last time Count Fleet would ever again suffer defeat. He went on, in 1942, to take the one-mile Champagne Stakes in a breeze, 1:34⁴/₅, beating Alsab's record by ³/₅ second and Jack High's twelve-year-old track record by ¹/₅ second. It proved to be the fastest mile run by any horse that year, regardless of age, sex, or track. Three more victories followed, including the Pimlico Futurity, in which he equaled the track mark.

It was quite a year, considering the inauspicious beginning. Count Fleet had racked up ten wins in fifteen starts, including four stakes races, the largest number of victories by a two-year-old in 1942, and had earned $76,245. He easily captured "Best Two-Year-Old" honors, and his prowess on the turf was further acknowledged when he was assigned 132 pounds in the Experimental Free Handicap. This is a rating of the best two-year-olds of the previous season, with each assigned weights as a measuring device of their potential as three-year-olds. The mark had not been equaled by any horse as of 1974.

In reviewing the year, assistant trainer Charles Hewitt tried to explain the colt's success. "They fault his conformation but he can do the job . . . He doesn't pound the ground like most horses. He doesn't have to dig in and push, but sort of rocks along as if it were the easiest thing in the world." The stable boys had another way of assessing Count Fleet's power. Normally, after a tough race or workout, it takes about forty-five minutes of just walking about to cool out. With Count Fleet, the editors of the book *Call Me Horse* wrote, he "just couldn't seem to amble along in leisurely fashion as most horses do. He had to make a walking-race out of it. After about twenty minutes his handler would holler for relief, and The Fleet would have the second worn out and puffing audibly by the time the forty-five minutes were up."

They shipped Count Fleet to Stoner Creek Farm for the winter. Then, in late January, he went to Oaklawn Park, Hot Springs, Ark., where Don Cameron began to bring him back to racing form, finally taking him to Belmont in mid-March for the start of the racing season. By now, he was hardly the gaunt ghost of a horse; rather, he had grown into a handsome brown figure, having filled out at the rate of two pounds a day and improving his weight from 978 pounds in December to over 1,000 pounds within a month. He was, for sure, a good doer. Robert Kelley claimed that 1943 was "Count Fleet's Year," that his second year of racing was like a "skyrocket flaring across the sky." Unfortunately, like the rocket, the brilliant burst of flame and color was snuffed out just as it reached the zenith of its flight. He made six starts, and "demolished just about every other opponent that came along to challenge him." His first race at three was the St. James Purse, at New York's Jamaica track, on April 13. He won it without urging, the victory dropping the winter book odds on him for the Kentucky Derby from 2-5 to 4-5. However, he did come out of the race with a nicked foreleg, though Don Cameron discounted the injury. On April 17, he spurted through the mile-and-a-sixteenth Wood Memorial in 1:43, within $2/5$ second of the track record. What started out to be a two-horse affair wound up as a one-horse dash after six or seven furlongs. According to Arthur Daley of the New York *Times*: "If the Count had been a man instead of a horse, he would have yawned politely in the homestretch at the total lack of opposition. But being of decidedly equine ancestry, the Count merely kept his ears pinned down in strict attention to business—and thereby pinned the ears of all who were willing to challenge him. . . . It is a lead-pipe certainty now that the parallel between Count Fleet and Man o' War is going to be more sharply drawn."

The colt was such a favorite of the fans at the track that they had backed him almost to the exclusion of the other seven horses. Of the $310,112 bet on the race, $196,192 was on Count Fleet, the largest amount ever placed on a single horse in New York since the introduction of the pari-mutuel machines. The glee of victory was mutted somewhat when he trailed blood from a three-inch gash on a hind leg as he returned to the winner's circle. He apparently had sustained it when Modest Lad pushed Vincentive into him on the breakaway and he cut himself with one of his own hoofs. They packed the wound with sulfa drugs and shipped him off at once to Churchill Downs. For Cameron, it meant a string of sleepless nights thereafter, filled with worry over whether or not the colt would be able to run in the Derby.

Blacksmith Stan Martin (right) and helpers bandage left hind foot of Count Fleet in his stall at Churchill Downs. The colt had cut himself with one of his own hoofs in Wood Memorial race.

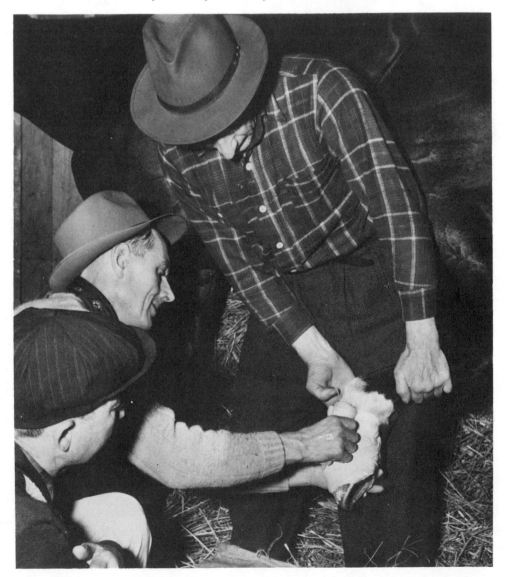

The 1943 Kentucky Derby was unique in that just three months before the date there was the possibility that it might not be staged at all. This was wartime, in the midst of World War II, and there were heavy restrictions on travel, accommodations and gasoline. Virtually everything was being rationed and in short supply, even bourbon. The threat caused Matt Winn, head of Churchill Downs, to "get his back up." He devised a plan that pledged "only neighbors and their children from greater Louisville would attend." He promised, further, to run it as a "street-car" affair, with only cars that had "A" gas-ration coupons admitted to the track grounds, and taxis not permitted to drop off passengers less than a mile from the entrance, all of which was dutifully spelled out in a New York *Times* editorial. As a result, the sixty-ninth running of the classic did in fact come to be nicknamed the "Street-Car Derby," and only 62,000 people made it to the track.

The word was "go" for Count Fleet on the day of the race. His handlers felt the wound was sufficiently under control and, for added protection, they covered the sulfa drugs with axle grease before he moved onto the track. As far as the fans were concerned, it made no difference. He was down to prohibitive 1-2 odds, the shortest price in the history of the race. The only colt that figured to give him trouble was Ocean Wave, a stablemate of Whirlaway and trained by Ben Jones, but he was scratched, so there was little opposition to anticipate. This had one reporter musing that "the Count figures to make a conga line out of this $82,750 classic like his daddy, Reigh Count, did fifteen years ago." He did just that. "The Fleet sailed into port . . . without even getting up a full head of steam," reported the Associated Press, ". . . broke out in full battle array after bouncing with some others in the field of ten for a half-mile, and from there on it was just a gallop." He scored by three lengths over Blue Swords. Finishing last was Burnt Cork, owned by Eddie "Rochester" Anderson, the radio sidekick of comedian Jack Benny.

Count Fleet cruises to a three-length victory over Blue Swords in the Kentucky Derby. Slide Rule is third.

SEVENTH RACE　1 1-4 MILES. (Whirlaway, May 3, 1941—2:01⅖—3—126.) **Sixty-Ninth Running KENTUCKY DERBY. $75,000 Added. 3-year-olds. Weight, the scale. (Owner of winner to receive a gold trophy.)**

3 9 9 6 7

May　1-43—C.D　Net value to winner $60,725; second, $8,000; third, $3,000; fourth, $1,000; trainers of the winner, second and third horses receive $3,000, $2,000 and $1,000, respectively; breeders of the winner, second and third horses receive $2,000, $1,000 and $500, respectively.

Index	Horses	Eq't	A	Wt	PP	St	½	¾	1	Str	Fin	Jockeys	Owners	Odds $1 Str't
(39413)	COUNT FLEET	WB		126	5	1	1^h	1^2	1^2	1^2	1^3	LongdenJ	Mrs J Hertz	.40
39413²	BLUE SWORDS	WB		126	1	2	$4^{1\!\!/_2}$	$4^{1\frac{1}{2}}$	$2^{1\frac{1}{2}}$	2^2	2^6	AdamsJ	Allen T Simmons	9.00
39761²	SLIDE RULE	WB		126	2	6	$6^{1\!\!/_2}$	3^h	$4^{1\frac{1}{2}}$	3^3	3^6	McCrearyC	W E Boeing	10.80
39546²	AMBER LIGHT	WB		126	7	5	$5^{1\frac{1}{2}}$	5^3	$3^{1\!\!/_2}$	4^2	$4^{1\!\!/_2}$	RobertsonA	Dixiana Farm	17.50
39761	BANKRUPT	W		126	6	9	9^3	9^1	$7^{1\!\!/_2}$	$6^{1\!\!/_2}$	$5^{1\frac{1}{2}}$	ZufeltF	T B Martin	†21.90
39761³	NO WRINKLES	W		126	10	7	8^3	$7^{1\!\!/_2}$	6^1	7^h	6^h	AdairR	Milky Way Farm	34.60
39546	DOVE PIE	WB		126	4	10	10	10	8^2	8^1	7^3	EadsW	J W Rodgers	86.50
39147	GOLD SHOWER	W		126	9	4	2^4	2^1	5^3	$5^{1\!\!/_2}$	8^{10}	AtkinsonT	Vera S Bragg	12.10
39761	MODEST LAD	WB		126	3	8	7^h	6^h	9^4	9^4	9^8	SwainC	Mrs H Finch	71.20
39761	BURNT CORK	WB		126	8	3	3^1	$8^{1\!\!/_2}$	10	10	10	GonzalezMN	E Anderson	†21.90

†Mutuel field.

Time, :12⅖, :23⅕, :34⅖, :46¾, :59⅖, 1:12¾, 1:25, 1:37¾, 1:50⅖, 2:04. Track fast.

Mutuel Prices {

		—$2 Mutuels Paid—			—Odds to $1—		
COUNT FLEET	....	2.80	2.40	2.20	.40	.20	.10
BLUE SWORDS	....		3.40	3.00		.70	.50
SLIDE RULE	....			3.20			.60

Winner—Br. c, by Reigh Count—Quickly, by Haste, trained by G. D. Cameron; bred by Mrs. J. Hertz. **WENT TO POST—5:30½. OFF AT 5:31½ CENTRAL WAR TIME.**

Start good from stall gate. Won handily; second and third driving. COUNT FLEET began fast, was hustled along until reaching the stretch, shook off the bid of GOLD SHOWER and, responding to a shaking up, won handily. BLUE SWORDS, away well, was in hand until reaching the last half, came determinedly when subjected to punishment, but was not good enough for the winner, although easily best of the others. SLIDE RULE saved ground while outrun to the final half, was blocked when moving up approaching the final turn and, taken out for the drive, could not reach the leaders when subjected to punishment. AMBER LIGHT raced evenly under restraint until reaching the final half, made a game bid entering the stretch, but tired. BANKRUPT, outrun until the final quarter, failed to respond when called upon in the stretch. NO WRINKLES, on the outside throughout, could not better his posiiion and had no excuses. DOVE PIE swerved to the inside after the start and was never a serious contender. GOLD SHOWER, much used engaging COUNT FLEET in the first three-quarters, gave way badly thereafter. MODEST LAD, bothered slightly after the start by DOVE PIE, was always far back. BURNT CORK began fast, displayed good speed in the first half and then quit.

Scratched—39761 Twoses, 126; (39761) Ocean Wave, 126.

Official chart of Kentucky Derby.

Longdon, the British-born jockey, did recall a slight threat from Blue Swords. "Sure I saw him coming. I just gave the Count a little nudge and he gave out some more. That's all." He then observed that he had come to understand his horse's temperament, that the colt was bred to run and wanted to run. "Get him out on top, give him the race track, and let him run. It was what he loved to do more than anything else." He also commented that the colt had an abhorrence of defeat, "and if he didn't have racing room, he'd go to the outside or just climb over horses. If you were in close quarters with him you were in trouble." Naturally, the conversation turned to "Big Red." "I don't know the great horses like Man o' War," said Longdon, "because I wasn't around then. But the Count is the greatest I've ever ridden. Got everything, speed, heart—just everything." Although the general public "felt like nothing had happened because everything had happened as expected," many were disappointed in the slow time of 2:04. The gripes started the "He Ain't So Hot Club" going, as they questioned his greatness, and wondered if he was just lucky to come along when there was no competition to make him prove it. They were in agreement on one point, though, that Ocean Wave would have pushed him rather than allowed him to loaf through the last eighth of a mile. As one scribe put it, the "Count hardly could be put down as a P-38 on the prowl." It was also reported that he had nicked his left front foot, giving fits to his handlers. He was developing a very distressing habit.

The gripes notwithstanding, the Preakness on May 8 looked like it would be merely a fight for second, with only three other horses, Blue Swords, Vincentive, and New Moon, prepared to brave the debacle. It really was no contest, virtually a replay of the Derby. "With the serenity of an old gentleman in his rocking chair on the veranda, Johnny Longdon sat down on the famous back of Count Fleet . . . and rode a mile and three-sixteenths to fame and glory," said Robert Kelley. "Grim-faced and unemotional, Longdon sat still. Once rounding the turn into the stretch, he looked back over his shoulder to see what the rest of the world was doing, turned around again, sat down and came home," never using whip or heels. New Moon made an all too brief move to the front at the start, but Count Fleet was on top to stay by the time they reached the grandstands on the first pass-by. He led by five lengths at the three-quarter pole, and by eight over Blue Swords at the wire. It was a slow track, as was the time once more, a full second over the track record of 1:56^2/$_5$.

In analyzing the way he ran, Longdon told Emanuel Strauss of the New York *Times* that Count Fleet insisted on taking the lead early in every race, and could be controlled when he was kicking dust in the faces of his rivals, after which "it's like sitting behind the steering wheel of a Cadillac." Some interesting statistics showed up following the victory. He was the shortest-priced winner in the history of the classic, at 3-20, paying $2.30 for $2.00. When he started from the paddock, "The Count" was 1-5. By the time he reached the starting gate, he was 1-9. The purse of $43,190 brought his total winnings to $202,260, which moved him into twenty-sixth place among the all-time money-winners. For Blue Swords, it was the sixth time he had chased the "Hertz hurricane" across the finish line, eliciting the wry comment from *The Blood-Horse:* "If Count Fleet is the spectacular comet in the racing skies of 1943, then Blue Swords is the comet's tail."

The Withers, on May 22, was nothing more than a workout for Count Fleet, before the third jewel of the Triple Crown, the Belmont Stakes. Only three horses came out against him, and he waltzed over the finish line six lengths in front of Slide Rule. To most everyone, the race was close only at the starting gate.

They sent out two horses to be "slaughtered" on the track, for the running of the seventy-fifth Belmont Stakes on June 5, and the wonder is the ASPCA did not come to the rescue. The opposition to Count Fleet consisted of Fairy Manhurst, winner of only a maiden race and a Class C allowance, and Desorante, a rather unpretentious son of Man o' War, with only a maiden victory to his credit. When the farce was run, "The Fleet" had roared over the mile and a half to win by an incredible twenty-five lengths in 2:28^1/$_5$, beating War Admiral's stakes record by ^{2}/$_5$ second, but shy of Bolingbroke's track mark of 2:27^3/$_5$. "There was nothing to the race, the riders of Fairy Manhurst and

Count Fleet makes it look easy as he blasts to an eight-length win over Blue Swords in the Preakness. Vincentive is a distant third. Only three horses dared face "The Fleet" in the race.

Count Fleet, with Johnny Longdon in the saddle, receives honors in the winner's circle after the Preakness. At left is trainer Don Cameron.

SIXTH RACE

4 0 3 9 3

May 8-43—Pim

1 3-16 MILES. (Riverland, May 1, 1943—1:56⅖—5—123.) Fifty-Third Running PREAKNESS STAKES. $50,000 Added. 3-year-olds. Weight-for-age. By subscription of $10 each, which shall accompany the nomination, with the following payments to continue eligibility: $25 additional by Aug. 15, 1942, and a further payment of $100 on or before Jan. 15, 1943. Supplementary entries may be made on or before April 15, 1943, by payment of an eligibility fee of $1,500. Starters to pay $500 additional. All eligibility, entrance and starting fees to the winner, with $50,000 added, of which $10,000 to second, $5,000 to third and $2,000 to fourth. The nominator of the winner to receive $1,500; the nominator of the second horse $750, and the nominator of the third horse $250 of the added money.

Net value to winner $43,190; second, $10,000; third, $5,000; fourth, $2,000.

Index	Horses	Eq't	A	Wt	PP	St	½	¾	1	Str	Fin	Jockeys	Owners	Odds $1 Str't
(39967)	COUNT FLEET	w B		126	2	1	1^4	1^4	1^5	1^5	1^8	LongdenJ	Mrs J D Hertz	.15
39967²	BLUE SWORDS	w B		126	4	3	2^2	2^1	2^1	2^1	2^5	AdamsJ	Allen T Simmons	10.00
(40094)	VINCENTIVE	w B		126	1	4	3^1	3^{10}	3^{10}	3^{10}	3^{20}	WoolfG	W L Brann	6.15
40157²	NEW MOON	w B		126	3	2	4	4	4	4	4	WrightWD	H L Straus	48.65

Time, :23⅗, :47⅖, 1:11⅘, 1:38½, 1:57⅖. Track good.

Mutuel Prices

	⎯$2 Mutuels Paid⎯			⎯⎯Odds to $1⎯⎯	
COUNT FLEET	2.30	2.10	....	.15	.05	....
BLUE SWORDS		2.40	....		.20	....
NO SHOW MUTUELS SOLD.						

Winner—Br. c, by Reigh Count—Quickly, by Haste, trained by G. D. Cameron; bred by Mrs. J. Hertz. WENT TO POST—2:41. OFF AT 2:42½ EASTERN WAR TIME.

Start good from stall gate. Won easily; second and third the same. COUNT FLEET outran his field from the start, opened up a safe lead, came slightly wide entering the stretch and finished with speed in reserve. BLUE SWORDS was taken under restraint when outrun and steadied along to the stretch turn, where he shook off VINCENTIVE and finished well, but could not menace the winner, pulling up slightly sore. VINCENTIVE was under steady restraint, made a determined bid entering the stretch, but could not improve his position and was not unduly persevered with. NEW MOON swerved sharply after the start and was never a factor in the running and was not persevered with when hopelessly beaten.

Scratched—40316 Radio Morale, 126.

Official chart of Preakness.

Desorante giving up so far as winning was concerned after about six furlongs, even though they battled tooth and nail for the place money of $5,000. Fairy Manhurst . . . got that by a length," reported Bryan Field. Count Fleet was eight lengths in front at the half-mile, twenty after ten furlongs, from where he just galloped down the stretch. It was a spectacular run in that he drove for the record despite the lack of competition. When asked why he did not shoot for the track record, Longdon replied: "It's a long summer. We're trying to beat horses. Why run against the clock and risk injury, when the colt can breeze and sweep all before him?"

Practically everyone bet on the winner, $249,516 out of $261,787, thereby producing a legal minimum payoff of 1-20. America's new Triple Crown champion captured a $35,340 purse, bringing his total earnings to $250,300. The win also meant that he and Sir Barton were the only horses to add the Withers to the Triple Crown races, while he was the only Thoroughbred to win all five spring racing specials—the Wood, Derby, Preakness, Withers, and Belmont. They auctioned off his silks in the unsaddling enclosure for $50,000 in war bonds, which added a patriotic touch to the victory. Bryan Field could hardly be aware of how prophetic he was being when he also wrote: "Count Fleet achieved 21 . . . twenty-one races, the number run by Man o' War in his entire career." The tragic fact is, this was all for the colt, too—his

Only two horses dare to challenge Count Fleet (center) at the Belmont Stakes.

The Belmont turns into a rout as Count Fleet charges to an incredible twenty-five-length win. He beat War Admiral's stakes record by $^2/_5$ second.

Proud owner Mrs. John D. Hertz takes "The Fleet" in hand for the parade to the winner's circle. The Belmont race was the last of his career, because of the injury to his left fore ankle at the start of the race.

Official chart of Belmont.

SIXTH RACE	1 1-2 MILES (Main Course). (Bolingbroke, Sept. 26, 1942—2:27⅗											
4 1 8 4 7	—5—115.) Seventy-Fifth Running BELMONT STAKES. $25,000											
June 5-43—Bel	Added. 3-year-olds. Weight-for-age. (Geldings not eligible.)											
	Net value to winner $35,340; second, $5,000; third, $2,500.											

Index	Horses	Eq't	A	Wt	PP	St	½	1	1¼	Str	Fin	Jockeys	Owners	Odds $1 Str't
(40971)	COUNT FLEET	wʙ		126	2	1	1⁸	1¹²	1²⁰	1²⁰	1²⁵	LongdenJ	Mrs John Hertz	.05
(41475)	FAIRY MANHURST	w		126	1	2	2½	2¹	2¹½	2¹	2¾	GilbertJ	Foxcatcher Farm	28.85
41475²	DESERONTO	wʙ		126	3	3	3	3	3	3	3	StoutJ	Beverley Bogert	52.70

Time, :23⅗, :48, 1:12⅗, 1:37⅘, 2:03⅗, 2:28⅕. Track fast.

	⌐$2 Mutuels Paid⌐			⌐Odds to $1⌐	
Mutuel Prices { COUNT FLEET	2.10	....	....	.05	....	....
NO PLACE OR SHOW MUTUELS SOLD.						

Winner—Br. c, by Reigh Count—Quickly, by Haste, trained by G. D. Cameron; bred by Mrs. John Hertz.
WENT TO POST—4:18. OFF AT 4:19 EASTERN WAR TIME.

Start good from stall gate. Won easily; second and third driving. COUNT FLEET outran his opposition from the start, drew into a long lead, was steadied along and was galloping through the stretch run. FAIRY MANHURST was under restraint and, under urging, outfinished DESERONTO. The latter was under pressure in the late stages, but had no mishaps.

last hurrah. After the race, he was reported to have struck himself in the left fore ankle during the early running. He walked soundly, and an X-ray examination showed nothing more than a slight wrench. Later, the ankle filled slightly, but soon subsided. Nobody seemed terribly alarmed. The injury, however, stubbornly refused to respond completely to treatment, finally causing cancellation of all further racing in the remaining months of the year.

The unexpected turn of events did not diminish the heroic achievements of Count Fleet during the previous six months. Certainly, they were not lost sight of when the balloting for year-end honors was conducted. There never was a doubt, and he was named "Horse of the Year" and "Best Three-Year-Old." The tally was a testimonial of sorts in itself, for he received 135 out of a possible 143 votes from the sportswriters and broadcasters polled by *Turf and Sport Digest.* Confidence in his return to the track also remained high, especially with Hertz, who in January 1944 happily announced from Florida that "The Count" had recovered completely, that he would be entered "in enough handicaps to establish him further as a great horse" and that he would be retired in 1945. It was wishful thinking. July rolled around, and Don Cameron still had failed to bring the colt up to racing form. It was all too apparent that the injury sustained in the Belmont race had created a splint which affected his ankle. Any further racing could aggravate the injury and perhaps cause more serious harm. Consequently, the trainer sadly recommended that Count Fleet be retired from racing for all time. "The Fleet" was beached.

He was retired to Stoner Creek Farm, where the "skyrocket" flared up once more, this time to burn brightly for a long time. Count Fleet enjoyed a tremendously successful career as a stallion. Without solicitation or advertising upon his retirement, his stud book was filled with the names of thirty mares, and his stud fee was set at $1,500. The way things turned out, the price was a bargain. For example, in 1951 thirty-eight of his get were stakes winners, including "Horse of the Year" Counterpoint and "Best Three-Year-Old Filly' Kiss Me Kate. Interestingly enough, he dominated the 1951 Triple Crown races, as Count Turf, another of his standout sons, won the Kentucky Derby, while Counterpoint took the Belmont Stakes.

The 1951 Derby also marked another unusual achievement. It was the first three-generation sweep of the event—Reigh Count (1928), Count Fleet (1943), and Count Turf (1951). Another measure of his importance as a sire in 1951 was recorded, when John Hertz insured his prize stallion wth Lloyds of London for $550,000, the largest policy ever written on any horse. The following year, One Count was named "Horse of the Year," and by 1963 Count Fleet was acclaimed as the leading broodmare sire, as eighty-eight stakes winners from his daughters included Kelso, Lamb Chop, Lucky Debonair, Quill, Tompion, Prince John, Fleet Nasarullah, and Fur Sail. The fact is, through 1972 he had 1,095 year-starters, sons or daughters who actually went to the post. His last crop was foaled in 1967.

Stoner Creek Farm, in the mid-1960s, was converted from a Thoroughbred nursery to a Standardbred breeding farm. At the time, it was stipulated that Count Fleet would live out his remaining days on the farm, under the care of its manager, Charlie Kenney, and that he would be buried in the Stoner Creek graveyard. As the years went by, age seemed to embrace the great horse with grace. In the June issue of *Horsemen's Journal,* in 1971, Dave Hooper was able to write a glowing report from information provided by Kenney. "He's quite swaybacked as an equine senior citizen. But he's very, very active for thirty-one." Although he was retired from stud in 1966, he has "never lost his interest in the opposite sex. I guess he won't till he has all four feet in the grave. He still likes the girls very much. How do the French say it—he's still got that *joie de vivre.*" Kenney further revealed that the horse had retained a dislike for the dark. "Mr. Hertz wouldn't let him stay out at night when Count Fleet was much younger. . . . We keep him out in the daytime from seven-thirty until four. And he still attracts a lot of sightseers."

On December 3, 1973, Count Fleet died at Stoner Creek Farm. He was thirty-three years old. Said the *Times'* Red Smith: "Under the weight of years his front legs gave out; he tried for a day or two to get up and, failing, slipped quietly away. . . ."

ASSAULT

ASSAULT (Chestnut Colt)	Bold Venture	*St. Germans
		Possible
	Igual	Equipoise
		Incandescent

Assault

7

It had to happen sooner or later. It was inevitable that somewhere along the line a non-Kentucky-bred Thoroughbred would come along to challenge the three-year-old field for the Triple Crown. If he were to hail from a state other than Kentucky, it would have to be Texas, of course, where everything is proverbially bigger and better. The fact is, the state's first home-bred candidate for the Triple Crown was hardly that at the outset.

In the spring of 1943, on March 26, a chestnut colt was born to the mare Igual, a daughter of Equipoise, on the fabulous King Ranch, at Kingsville, Texas. His sire was Bold Venture, winner of the Kentucky Derby and the Preakness in 1936, and his grandam was a full sister of Man o' War. The foal was named Assault. It is remarkable that he ever was born. His dam, as a foal on the ranch, was so sickly and unpromising that serious consideration was given to having her destroyed. She was saved by the intercession of the ranch's veterinarian, Dr. J. K. Northway, who discovered an abscess under her stifle, which apparently affected her whole condition. He prevailed on owner Robert J. Kleberg, Jr., to allow him to treat the horse. The good doctor succeeded in curing her, but she never recovered to racing form, Instead, she was prepared for breeding.

Her first two foals were not much to brag about, hardly a recommendation for a bright future. On the third try, this time to the cover of Bold Venture, she produced Assault. Unlike his dam, the weanling displayed a frisky, frolicsome personality, which was almost his undoing. On one of his gambols around the ranch, he stepped on a sharp stake and ran it through the front wall of the hoof of his right foreleg, half crippling himself. Once more the doctor's skill was tested, and once again he succeeded. The injury, though, was like a damaged fingernail that heals but with a deformation. The foot never did grow to normal size, causing the colt to develop a peculiar walk. In fact, the wall of the hoof became so thin that it was difficult to find room enough to anchor a nail for shoeing, a ticklish problem that remained with the horse for the rest of his days. It was, in a sense, a reminder of Sir Barton, whose soft hooves made it difficult for him to keep his shoes on.

Closeup of Assault's forelegs, showing the malformation of his right hoof.

Trainer Max Hirsch was less than bullish on taking his first look at Assault and his game leg. "When he came up from Texas, I didn't think he'd train at all. When he walked and trotted you'd think he was going to fall down. It wasn't hurting him any more but he'd gotten in the habit of favoring and protecting it with an awkward gait." Some unsympathetic observers thought the horse was clubfooted, which accounts for why he later was nicknamed "The Clubfooted Comet." However, at this early point in his career, when Hirsch had to start preparing him for his two-year-old season, it must have been a rather disheartening prospect for the trainer, especially when he could look back a few years to the glory days of Bold Venture.

The old adages might well have been applied to Assault: "Looks are deceiving" and "If at first you fail, try, try again." The colt made his first start at Belmont Park, on June 4, 1945, and finished twelfth in a field of maidens. It was not until his fourth start, at Aqueduct on July 12, that he won his first race. In fact, he ran nine times that year, won only once more, finished in the money just three times, and wound up with total winnings of only $17,250. Most of this total was earned in his sixth race, the Flash Stakes, on August 6, when he won a purse of $11,505. Prior to then, he had chalked up only one victory in five starts, in an allowance event. In the Flash, which was one of the races of the Saratoga meet but was held at Belmont because of the restrictions on travel imposed by World War II, he went to the post for the five-and-a-half-furlong event as a ridiculous 70 to 1 shot. The track was muddy, which may have had some bearing on the outcome. It was an improbable four-horse photo finish, each just noses apart, and Assault was awarded the victory to the astonishment of owner, trainer, jockey, and fans. Mist o' Gold was placed second, and Mush Mush third. Anyone who had been brave enough to bet on the Texas colt wound up with a tidy $443.20 payoff for a $2 bet. About the only other factor that could be pointed to as noteworthy is that the victory came on the very day America dropped the first atom bomb on Japan, on the city of Hiroshima.

Assault's last race of the year was at Jamaica, on October 8, after which he was shipped to Columbia, South Carolina, to winter. The general appraisal for the year was that the horse, despite a rather uninspiring record, ran well enough to try again.

The first two starts of 1946 provided some hopeful rays. He took the six-furlong Experimental Handicap, at Jamaica, on April 9, by four and a half lengths, even though he was at 9 to 1 odds. Next, he captured the important mile-and-an-eighth Wood Memorial, on April 20, by two and a quarter lengths, this time going off at somewhat less than 9 to 1. Winning this race was particularly heartening, since it is the first big event for three-year-olds before the Kentucky Derby. The elation was quickly dampened, and his chances for the classic noticeably dimmed, when he followed with a loss in the Derby Trial, at Churchill Downs, by a four-length margin. Bandages and a muddy track were given as excuses for the poor showing. "Assault had a tendency to strike himself, and usually ran with small adhesive bandages inside his hocks, and a long one down his left cannon in front," commented Joe Palmer in *American Race Horses.* "For the Derby Trial Hirsch also added 'Oregon Boots' on Assault's hind legs, and once these got properly water-soaked and filled with mud, Assault had little chance."

The explanation failed to allay the apprehension of turf fans, and he went to the post on Derby Day at long odds, 8 to 1, behind the favorites, Lord Boswell, Knockdown, and Perfect Bahram. There was an extra measure of excitement in the air as the field came out on the track. This was the first Derby with a $100,000-added purse, making it the richest race of the series to date. With Warren Mehrtens in the saddle, Assault settled into fifth position among the seventeen straining horses at the first turn. In the backstretch, he moved up to third place, but only because some of the other horses had dropped back.

It was at the quarter pole that Mehrtens made his "Run for the Roses." He pushed his colt savagely on the rail, and he responded by moving to the lead at the one-eighth pole and continuing his drive until he crossed the finish line an astonishing eight lengths ahead of Spy Song. Lord Boswell ran well out of the picture. The classic come-from-behind run confounded everyone, including his backers, who were paid off handsomely, his owner, who picked up first-prize money of $96,400, and Warren Mehrtens, who chalked up his first Derby win. The slow track resulted in the unimpressive time of 2:06^3/$_5$, but the victory reversed a year-and-a-half-long trend in Assault's career. He had won not only one of the most prestigious classic races in turfdom, but also his biggest purse. Suddenly he was respectable.

The proof was all too clear at Pimlico, where he suddenly found himself the favorite, at 7 to 5, the first time in his life that he had been so honored. It was a particularly startling development since through most of the spring he had been going off at long odds. Lord Boswell, conversely, was cast as the runner-up, at a little less than 2 to 1. The 1946, seventy-first running of the Preakness, like the Derby, also had a new look as it, too, moved into the $100,000-added-purse bracket. Consequently, both new price and purse would appear to be sufficient motivation for greater efforts by the Texas Thoroughbred.

Assault leads sixteen straining opponents across the finish line at the end of the Kentucky Derby. An 8-1 underdog, he won by eight lengths over Spy Song in a classic come-from-behind run.

Trainer Max Hirsch with Assault and jockey Warren Mehrtens in the winner's circle at Churchill Downs.

Official chart of Kentucky Derby.

SEVENTH RACE

9 7 5 9 5

May   4-46—C.D

1 1-4 MILES. (Whirlaway, May 3, 1941—2:01²⁴—3—126.) Seventy Second Running KENTUCKY DERBY. $100,000 Added. 3-year-olds. Weight, the scale. (Owner of winner to receive a Gold Trophy. Trainers of the winner, second and third horses to receive $3,000, $2,000 and $1,000, respectively, of the added money, and the breeders of the winner, second and third horses to receive $2,000, $1,000 and $500, respectively, of the added money, whether or not they are the owners of the horses when the race is run.

Net value to winner $96,400; second, $10,000; third, $5,000; fourth, $2,500.   Mutuel Pool, $1,202,474.

Index	Horses	Eq't A Wt PP St	½	¾	1	Str	Fin	Jockeys	Owners	Odds to $1
97370	ASSAULT	wb 126 2 3	5½	4h	3½	12½	1⁸	W Mehrtens	King Ranch	8.20
97370²	SPY SONG	w 126 6 2	1²	1½	1½	2²	2h	J Longden	Dixiana	7.80
(97226)	HAMPDEN	wb 126 17 14	6¹	5h	42½	5²	3¹	J Jessop	Foxcatcher Farm	5.80
(97136)	LORD BOSWELL	w 126 3 1	9½	7½	91½	3½	41½	E Arcaro	Maine Chance Farm	a-1.10
95332	KNOCKDOWN	w 126 11 4	2½	2½	21½	4½	5⁴	R Permane	Maine Chance Farm	a-1.10
97370	ALAMOND	wb 126 7 8	11½	8½	11²	6¹	6¹	A Kirkland	A C Ernst	65.30
97136	BOB MURPHY	wb 126 13 16	13½	11½	6²	7½	7½	A Bodiou	D Ferguson	f-31.80
97136²	PELLICLE	wb 126 8 11	12²	9½	8h	8h	81½	G Hettinger	H P Headley	16.10
(97324)	PERFECT BAHRAM	w 126 5 12	15³	13²	10½	11½	9½	T Atkinson	Maine Chance Farm	a-1.10
(97370)	RIPPEY	w 126 14 7	4h	6¹	5h	9¹	10¹	F Zufelt	W Helis	10.20
97220	JOBAR	w 126 16 17	17	17	16⁴	10⁴	111½	J R Layton	H W Fielding	f-31.80
(97135)	DARK JUNGLE	wb 126 12 6	3½	3h	7½	10½	12²	A LoTurco	Lucas B Combs	60.70
97324³	ALWORTH	wb 126 4 10	10¹	12¹	13h	13³	13½	O Scurlock	Mrs R D Patterson	f-31.80
97370³	WITH PLEASURE	wb 126 10 9	7½	10¹	14²	14²	141½	C Wahler	Brolite Farm	48.30
97370	MARINE VICTORY	wb 126 15 15	14¹	14³	15³	15½	15¹	D Padgett	Bobanet Stable	45.00
97370	WEE ADMIRAL	wb 126 9 5	81½	16¹	12½	12²	16³	R Watson	R S McLaughlin	59.40
97136	KENDOR	wb 126 1 13	16⁶	15¹	17	17	17	W L J'nson	Mrs D M Hollingsworth	f-31.80

a-Coupled, Lord Boswell, Knockdown and Perfect Bahram.   f-Mutuel field.
Time, :12, :23⅖, :35⅖, :48, 1:01⅕, 1:14⅕, 1:27⅖, 1:40⅘, 1:53⅖, 2:06¾. **Track slow.**

Mutuel Prices		⌐$2 Mutuels Paid⌐			⌐Odds to $1⌐		
	ASSAULT	18.40	9.60	6.80	8.20	3.80	2.40
	SPY SONG		9.00	6.60		3.50	2.30
	HAMPDEN			5.20			1.60

Winner—Ch. c, by Bold Venture—Igual, by Equipoise, trained by M. Hirsch; bred by King Ranch.
WENT TO POST—5:17. OFF AT 5:20 CENTRAL DAYLIGHT TIME.

Start good from stall gate. Won driving; second and third the same. ASSAULT, forwardly placed and saving ground from the beginning, came through on the inside entering the stretch, quickly disposed of SPY SONG and drew out to win with little left. SPY SONG assumed command early, made the pace until reaching the stretch, then gave way to the winner, but continued resolutely to hold HAMPDEN. The latter, on the extreme outside at the beginning, raced in the middle of the track the entire trip, was pulled up sharply when his rider misjudged the finish, then came again when roused, but could not better his position. LORD BOSWELL, in hand for six furlongs, was blocked near the upper turn, came again when clear, but could not overhaul the leaders when hard ridden through the stretch. KNOCKDOWN forced the pace to the mile, then gave way. ALAMOND, on the outside for the drive, failed to rally under punishment. BOB MURPHY, also on the outside entering the stretch, could not threaten. PELLICLE raced evenly and had no excuse. PERFECT BAHRAM lacked his usual early speed and was never dangerous. RIPPEY could not keep up after displaying brief speed. JOBAR began slowly. DARK JUNGLE was through after six furlongs. ALWORTH was always far back. WITH PLEASURE could not threaten and tired badly. MARINE VICTORY was never a serious factor. WEE ADMIRAL had speed for a half mile, then gave way. KENDOR was overmatched.

They were, but the colt's performance was enough to give his backers fits. First, he was hampered through the first sixteenth of a mile, when Natchez veered in toward the rail. Then his jockey made him move too soon to recoup his position. "Mehrtens may have been a bit scared, and he made up the lost ground quickly. When he asked Assault for his run, a little earlier than in the Derby, the colt came with a burst which carried him four lengths out from the field at the furlong pole, but then he had nothing left," wrote Joe Palmer. Lord Boswell put on a "frightening display of finishing power" in the stretch. "When Mehrtens hit him, as the challenge materialized, Assault ducked in badly, so the jockey, afraid to hit him again, hand-rode and hoped for the finish line." He just barely won by a neck. The race was exciting; the time was not very good—2:01^2/$_5$; the purse was substantial—$96,620.

As for his admirers, a noticeable chill developed between him and them. According to many, the Preakness showed a chink in Assault's armor. They discounted his spectacular showing in the Derby, and allowed that the slow times in both races established the colt's inability to finish well at distance. Therefore, mindful of the grueling mile-and-a-half grind that faced him in the Belmont Stakes on June 1, they dropped him out of the favorite's spot, although not by much, and rated him at 7 to 5 behind Lord Boswell, who was at a little less than that.

Assault barely wins the Preakness by a neck over Lord Boswell. Hampden is third. This race was the first of Assault's career in which he was favored.

SIXTH RACE	1 3-16 MILES. (Riverland, May 1, 1943—1:56⅗—5—123.) Fifty-Sixth Running

98024

May 11-46—Pim

1 3-16 MILES. (Riverland, May 1, 1943—1:56⅗—5—123.) Fifty-Sixth Running PREAKNESS STAKES. $100,000 Added. 3-year-olds. Weight-for-age. (All eligibility, entrance and starting fees to the winner, with $100,000 added, of which $20,000 to second, $10,000 to third and $5,000 to fourth. The nominator of the winner to receive $2,500; the nominator of the second horse, $1,000; and the nominator of the third horse $500 of the added money.)

Net value to winner $96,620; second, $20,000; third, $10,000; fourth, $5,000. **Mutuel Pool, $446,140.**

Index	Horses	Eq't	A	Wt	PP	St	½	¾	1	Str	Fin	Jockeys	Owners	Odds to $1
(97595)	ASSAULT	wb		126	5	6	6¹½	3ʰ	11½	14	1ⁿᵏ	W Mehrtens	King Ranch	1.40
97595	LORD BOSWELL	w		126	2	7	9⁶	6½	4¹	2½	23½	D Dodson	Maine Chance Farm	a-2.25
97595³	HAMPDEN	wb		126	4	5	5¹	41½	3²	31½	34	E Arcaro	Foxcatcher Farm	3.00
97595	KNOCKDOWN	w		126	3	4	4¹	5²	5ʰ	5ʰ	41½	R Permane	Maine Chance Farm	a-2.25
97595	ALAMOND	wb		126	8	9	7½	84	6⁶	6⁵	5³	K Scawth'n	A C Ernst	67.35
97226²	NATCHEZ	wb		126	9	2	2¹	1ʰ	21½	42	6⁴	J Gilbert	Mrs W M Jeffords	22.60
97784²	LOVEMENOW	wb		126	6	8	8²	95	8²	72	73	A Snider	Cedar Farm	10.75
97595	WEE ADMIRAL	wb		126	1	1	3ʰ	7½	9⁶	84	8³	N Wall	R S McLaughlin	42.55
97595	MARINE VICT'RY	wb		126	7	10	10	10	10	10	9⁵	D Padgett	Bobanet Stable	30.15
97226	TIDY BID	wb		126	10	3	1²	2½	7½	9¹	10	S Clark	W Helis	34.75

a-Coupled, Lord Boswell and Knockdown.

Time, :12⅕, :23⅖, :35⅖, :48, 1:00¾, 1:13, 1:27⅖, 1:40, 1:54⅖, 2:01⅖. Track fast.

Mutuel Prices {
	—$2 Mutuels Paid—			—Odds to $1—		
ASSAULT	4.80	3.10	2.20	1.40	.55	.10
LORD BOSWELL (a-Entry)		3.10	2.20		.55	.10
HAMPDEN			2.30			.15

Winner—Ch. c, by Bold Venture—Igual, by Equipoise, trained by M. Hirsch; bred by King Ranch.

WENT TO POST—4:57. OFF AT 4:57½ EASTERN STANDARD TIME.

Start good from stall gate. Won ridden out, second and third driving. ASSAULT, well handled while escaping trouble soon after the start, rallied well when called upon, circled the leader while forging to the front leaving the backstretch, drew clear rapidly on the turn and was ridden out through the final sixteenth. LORD BOSWELL, sluggish early, worked way into contention gradually, drove between horses entering the stretch and closed with a late rush to be getting to the winner. HAMPDEN, always forwardly placed, was in close quarters briefly when ASSAULT moved on the outside of him, followed ASSAULT while moving into contention, then hung in the drive. KNOCKDOWN raced prominently placed throughout, but was not good enough. ALAMOND, shuffled back when NATCHEZ moved over at the break, took the overland route throughout and could not seriously threaten. NATCHEZ cut across sharply at the start, disposed of TIDY BID for the lead, then weakened. LOVEMENOW showed nothing. WEE ADMIRAL was pinched back at the first turn and failed to recover. MARINE VICTORY was outdistanced. TIDY BID had early speed, but quit.

Scratched—96393² Billy Bumps, 126.

Official chart of Preakness.

Six other starters went to the post, and Assault promptly made them all look good as he stumbled at the bell. But he righted himself quickly and Mehrtens, feeling him running with his old power, held him back, biding his time, refusing to fall into the same trap as in the Preakness. Down the backstretch, they held fourth position, some five lengths behind the front-running Natchez. Once again, at the one-eighth pole, Mehrtens called on the colt to show his mettle and, once more, the Thoroughbred responded in stirring fashion. Between the furlong pole and the finish line, he closed the gap and tacked on a three-length lead. Lord Boswell never challenged, coming in a poor fifth. It was another exciting race but, again, the time was unspectacular—2:30⁴/₅.

For trainer and owner, the win was all that mattered. Assault was the new Triple Crown champion, the first from Texas, had picked up another hefty purse, $75,400, and had run his total winnings from the "three jewels" to $268,420, an astronomical figure when compared to the $57,275 earned by Sir Barton in the same three races twenty-seven years earlier.

Two weeks later, on June 15, Assault ran his winning streak to four straight by taking the Dwyer Handicap, at Aqueduct, four and a half lengths to the good. He had been the odds-on favorite, at 2 to 5, and

Assault, on rail, stumbles at the start of the Belmont Stakes.

Assault beats Natchez by three lengths, after catching him at the furlong pole to win the Belmont.

Left to right: owner Robert Kleberg, Jr., jockey Warren Mehrtens, trainer Max Hirsch, and Mrs. Kleberg enjoy the savor of victory around the Belmont Stakes trophy. Assault was the first Texas-bred horse to win the Triple Crown.

Official chart of Belmont Stakes.

SIXTH RACE
9 9 5 3 0
June   1-46—Bel

1 1-2 MILES. (Bolingbroke, Sept 26, 1942—2:27⅗—5—115.) Seventy-Eighth Running BELMONT STAKES. $100,000 Added. 3-year-olds. Scale weight. Colts, 126 lbs.; fillies, 121 lbs. (Nominators of the winner, of the second and third horses to receive $2,000, $1,000 and $500, respectively. Geldings not eligible.)

Net value to winner $75,400; second, $20,000; thmird, $10,000; fourth, $5,000; owners of starters other than first four horses, $20 each. Mutuel Pool, $640,495.

Index	Horses	Eq't A Wt	PP	St	½	1	1¼	Str	Fin	Jockeys	Owners	Odds to $1
(98024)	ASSAULT	wb 126	1	7	4²	4h	3²	3¹½	1³	W Mehrtens	King Ranch	1.40
98390²	NATCHEZ	wb 126	6	3	2³	2²	2¹½	1²	2²	C McCreary	Mrs W M Jeffords	a-8.60
98850	CABLE	w 126	2	1	7	7	4h	4½	3h	T Atkinson	Mrs A Wichfeld	45.50
(98390)	HAMPDEN	wb 126	7	5	1nk	1²	1²	2h	4½	E Arcaro	Foxcatcher Farm	3.75
98850²	LORD BOSWELL	w 126	5	4	5¹	5²	5²	5⁸	5⁵	E Guerin	Maine Chance Farm	1.35
(98850)	MAHOUT	w 126	4	2	6h	6½	6⁴	6²	6h	J Longden	Mrs W M Jeffords	a-8.60
98850	WAR WATCH	wb 126	3	6	3²	3⁴	7	7	7	A Scotti	Mrs A Roberts	92.80

a-Coupled, Natchez and Mahout.

Time, :24⅘, :49⅗, 1:14⅕, 1:39⅖, 2:04, 2:30⅘. Track fast.

	—$2 Mutuels Paid—		—Odds to $1—		
ASSAULT	4.80	3.10	2.70	1.40	.55	.35
NATCHEZ (a-Entry)		5.70	4.10		1.85	1.05
CABLE			6.50			2.25

Mutuel Prices

Winner—Ch. c, by Bold Venture—Igual, by Equipoise, trained by M. Hirsch; bred by King Ranch.
WENT TO POST—4:40. OFF AT 4:40 EASTERN DAYLIGHT TIME.

Start good from stall gate. Won driving; second and third the same. ASSAULT stumbled at the start but recovered quickly, was sent up on the inside, was steadied along to the far turn, where he began to improve his position, came to the outside for the stretch run, swerved slightly, disposed of the leaders and drew away. NATCHEZ bore out slightly rounding the far turn, was straightened out, moved up entering the stretch turn, assumed command, but could not stave off the winner. CABLE was steadied along, was well up under pressure in the stretch run and closed with good courage. HAMPDEN was sent into command after the first quarter, was steadied along and had no mishap. LORD BOSWELL was taken under steady restraint in the early running, improved his position going to the far turn, but flattened out when placed under pressure in the final furlong. MAHOUT was unable to improve his position in the stretch run. WAR WATCH raced evenly and was never a formidable factor.

Scratched—98850 Cedar Creek, 126; 98850³ Manor Lad, 126; (99177) Windfields, 126.

had run his by now typical race, sitting back at the early stages and then making his charge. His time was still slow, $2:06^4/_5$, which prompted the experts to conclude that Assault was merely the best of another poor crop of three-year-olds. The appraisal gained substance on July 27, in Chicago, when he finished sixth and last in the Arlington Classic. He started fast and then went dull. Every time Mehrtens used his whip, the horse seemed to fall back. It was a puzzling performance that mystified everyone until he was back in the barn. Here, he was in obvious pain, so much so that he was forced to lie down in his stall. Medical tests soon pinpointed the cause. It was a kidney infection, which necessitated his withdrawal from action for a month.

The interruption of his training started an unfortunate chain reaction. For a while, he just could not win a race. Assault returned to the campaign trail on September 7, in the Discovery Handicap at Aqueduct. The Triple Crown champion was promptly ruled the favorite, at 7 to 10, and asked to give away weight. He carried 126 pounds, to 115 by Mighty Story and 112 by Mahout. Although he came in third, he ran with something of his old determination, so the loss was accepted as the result of his long layoff and the extra weight. The following week, though, he lost in the Jersey Handicap by a half-length as he gave Mahout 12 pounds.

In his next race, he moved out of his three-year-old division for the first time to run against older horses in the mile-and-a-half Manhattan Handicap, at Belmont Park, on September 25. His reputation followed along with him, for here too he was asked to give up weight to the field as he was burdened with 116 pounds, the equivalent of 124 pounds on older horses. The event marked the first of Assault's series of bitterly waged battles with the vaunted Stymie. It was won by Stymie, who carried 126 pounds, as Assault wound up in a dead heat for third. The losing streak continue l into the Roamer Handicap, on October 19, when the filly Bridal Flower, with an 8-pound advantage, beat him by half a length. On October 26, it was back to the older horses in the Gallant Fox Handicap, carrying 114 pounds, the equivalent of 121 pounds for those out of his division. Stymie, with 126 pounds, was his nemesis one more time, catching him in the stretch as he fell to third place.

This defeat, though, was blamed on the jockey. The verdict was that Mehrtens had lost faith in the horse by now, and was unwilling to ride him to his fullest capabilities. It convinced trainer Max Hirsch that a change of jockeys was imperative, and he called in Eddie Arcaro to ride in the important winner-take-all Pimlico Special, November 1. He made no bones about his determination and his confidence in the horse's ability to win. "This horse can beat Stymie at any distance . . . two miles . . . four miles." Then he spelled out just what Arcaro was to do. "You watch Stymie," he ordered. He then told him to hold up making any move with Assault, regardless of what the other horses in the field were doing, until he saw Stymie come up on him. Arcaro obeyed and, as soon as Stymie crept alongside, drove his mount and won the race. The result saw a regeneration of some of the lost faith in the horse. He ran once more in 1946, in the Westchester Handicap on November 9, won it by two lengths, and wound up the year with eight firsts out of fifteen starts.

As Assault retired for the winter, the racing experts scratched their heads in trying to evaluate him. There was no gainsaying that he had had a spectacular year. On the positive side, the colt had captured the Triple Crown against all odds, and had surpassed Gallant Fox's record of $308,275 by winning $424,195, the most ever by a Thoroughbred in one year. Yet, more than three-fourths of the total had been won in only three races with very large purses. His times were rather slow, and he was considered a poor risk in distance races. Then again, he had given away considerable weight advantages to older horses and had even mastered Stymie. Furthermore, as the year progressed his times improved. As Joe Palmer put it, he "was flying in the fall." Thus, in summing up, the writers found that the positives outweighed the negatives, and voted him "Horse of the Year." Still, he lacked charisma, failed to generate excitement. The consensus, again according to Palmer, was that against three-year-olds he was "Good, maybe, but not great." He would have to show a lot more next year.

Assault, himself, seemed to be aware of this, and was giving signs that he was doing something about the matter. Early in 1946, he was a sort of matter-of-fact horse, but appeared to gain more confidence as the year wore on and he won important races. Suddenly, he was all business when he went to the track. In the barn, however, it was another thing. He became a character, pulling off high jinks that dismayed his handlers and that would never have been tolerated with an ordinary horse. His enormous appetite was a case in point. "He's perpetually hungry," trainer Hirsch would lament. No groom would dare to enter his stall without first giving him a mouthful of grain out of a feed-tub. When he was particularly hungry, he would create such a commotion in the barn that he would force an earlier feeding to avoid the possibility of his injuring himself as he stomped about in his stall, let alone upsetting all of the other horses.

Then, too, he began to develop physically. Although not a big horse, standing just above fifteen hands, he looked to have grown over the winter from a rather plain but substantial three-year-old into a very handsome four-year-old. When the spring of 1947 rolled around, he gave the illusion of being taller than he really was. Most important of all, there was no mistaking that he was a more assured Thoroughbred.

Two factors dominated the thinking of racing fans as the 1947 turf campaign prepared to swing into action. It was apparent that, as a result of handicap purses becoming increasingly inflated, year-end honors would very likely be determined by the amount of money earned. It was equally obvious that the year would see this goal challenged by three Thoroughbreds—Robert Kleberg's four-year-old Assault, Warren

Wright's five-year-old gelding Armed, and Hirsch Jacobs' six-year-old Stymie, each of whose earnings gave him a clear shot at surpassing Whirlaway's world's record.

Assault began his junior year like a demon possessed, reeling off five straight victories, seven in all if his last two wins in 1946 are included. The first was in the mile-and-an-eighth Grey Lag Handicap, at Jamaica, on May 3, just one year after he had won the Kentucky Derby. Carrying 128 pounds and jockey Warren Mehrtens, he beat Let's Dance, with only 110 pounds, by a neck in 1:49⁴/₅. Stymie, with 126 pounds, did not even place. On May 9, it was the Dixie Handicap at Pimlico, with Eddie Arcaro up. His margin of victory was a half-length, as he bested Rico Monte, to whom he had given 9 pounds. The time for the mile and three-sixteenths was 1:57⁴/₅, an improvement over his winning time in the Preakness on the same track the year before. Two weeks later, he came out for the Suburban Handicap at Belmont, saddled with 130 pounds to Stymie's 126. It was a fantastic victory. With Arcaro riding, he reached the stretch in second place, some

Assault slashes across the finish line at Aqueduct two lengths in front of arch rival Stymie to take the Brooklyn Handicap. This victory was the fourth in a row at the start of his fourth year of racing. It also boosted his earnings past Whirlaway's world's record.

six lengths behind Natchez, yet he flashed over the last sixteenth of a mile to beat him by two lengths, and Stymie by eight. The fourth victory in the skein, the Brooklyn Handicap, on June 21, was a milestone for the colt. Forced to carry 133 pounds to Stymie's 124, he again waited for his arch rival to make his move before he streaked to a three-length win. The victor's purse was worth $38,100, which boosted Assault's total earnings to $576,670, thereby surpassing Whirlaway's existing world's record of $561,161.

Later on, the picture of Assault and Stymie charging one-two down the homestretch was to take on special significance. It was the first time in the history of Thoroughbred racing that a horse had ever crossed the finish line as "the world's leading money-winner hotly pursued by one who would displace him twice."

"By now, Assault looked like the best horse in training. He had given weight and beating to everything in the East, and if ever there was a horse to run with him it would have to be Calumet Farm's Armed," wrote Joe Palmer when reviewing the 1947 racing scene. Armed, since the beginning of the year, had been creating his own excitement. He had picked up purses totaling $100,000 in two races early in the year. These continued his brilliant record of 1946, when he had won eleven out of eighteen races, been unplaced in only one, and had earned $288,725. Overall, in his three years of racing through 1946, his winnings amounted to $385,175, making him the richest gelding in history. He was so good that in 1946, his fourth year, he had never failed to get part of the purse in thirty-six consecutive races. By the end of June 1947, he had run his total winnings to $487,775.

Stymie, on the other hand, had not been standing by idly. Through 1946, in four years of campaigning, he had amassed winnings of $546,285. After his loss to Assault in the Brooklyn Handicap, he went on to win two races, the second of which was the Sussex Handicap, on July 5, and which pushed him ahead of Assault as the new money-leader, with $595,500. The reign was short, only one week, as he lost to Assault in the $50,000-added Butler Handicap. The victory and loss were both tough, but for the winner it earned new respect. Coming into the homestretch, Assault was wedged between Stymie and Gallorette. It seemed for sure that he was trapped and slated to lose. However, jockey Arcaro touched his whip to him, and the colt bolted through a virtually impossible opening to win by a head over Stymie. This fifth consecutive triumph was all the more remarkable because the Texas colt carried the heaviest impost of his career, 135 pounds, as compared to Stymie's 126. First prize amounted to $36,700, and Assault moved back into first place as his total soared to $613,370.

It was the pinnacle of his career. A week later, the winning streak came to an end in the International Gold Cup, at Belmont Park. This time, his usual strategy against Stymie and Natchez failed. He waited for Stymie's move while Natchez was setting the pace, but ran out of steam in the stretch. Nevertheless, the third-place finish was good for $10,000, which narrowly preserved his money-winning position.

While all of the leap-frogging was going on between Assault and Stymie, the chant could be heard from the fans for a match race between Assault and Armed, obviously the two most exciting horses of the year. Negotiations began in the middle of July between Warren Wright and Robert Kleberg. The plan was to stage the match at Washington Park in Chicago, on August 30, for a purse of $100,000, which would enable either one of the horses to achieve top money-winning honors. The race was then called off, when Assault injured his right foreleg. It was rescheduled for September 27 at Belmont Park, under the auspices of Joseph E. Widener, who had figured so prominently in trying to set up the $100,000 match race between War Admiral and Seabiscuit in 1937.

However, it seemed destined for trouble. On September 22, after a workout, Assault suddenly walked lame. Trainer Hirsch suspected an old splint on the left foreleg was acting up, but the ailment seemingly wore off soon. They watched it carefully for three days. Because of the uncertainty, things reached a pass where all of the principals were unhappy about continuing with the race. However, they felt obligated to the public. Kleberg finally issued a candid statement. "Because of the great public interest and long preparation for the race, we have decided to run Assault and hope he will be at his best." He then told of the colt's miseries. "In an ordinary stakes or other race," he continued, "I doubt that I should start him." Then, Wright and Kleberg agreed that neither would hold the purse if their horse won. Rather, they would split it up between the Red Cross and the Damon Runyon Cancer Fund. Finally, it was decided that no betting would be allowed on the race, that it would be only an exhibition. There was so much confusion that even the ASPCA got into the act, showing up at the track on the morning of the race, to demand proof that Assault was in condition to run and was not being abused.

Armed was favored at 1 to 3, with Assault at 7 to 5. It was a hollow victory for the gelding, who won by eight lengths as Eddie Arcaro eased Assault when he found that his horse could not keep up with the winner. It was an equally sad ending to an otherwise glorious year for the Triple Crown champion. He did not race again in 1947, and lost out to Armed for "Horse of the Year" honors, to the bitter recriminations of his handlers. The gelding took the Sysonby Handicap on October 9, won $18,000, and became the leading money-winner of the year with $376,325. His grand total was $761,500. Stymie, on the other hand, cracked the world's mark with total earnings of $846,060. Assault's record for the year was equally respectable, including five victories in seven starts, one second, one third, and winnings of $181,925. His total at the end of the year was $623,370, and twice during the year he had been the world's leading money-winner. Max Hirsch was thoroughly disgusted by the voting. He was particularly angry because he felt that Assault had been penalized unjustly for having run two bad races at the end of the season. "You'd think my horse wasn't worth fifteen cents," he groused.

The gelding Armed beats Assault by eight lengths in their match race at Belmont Park, September 27, 1947. The loss was attributed to leg injury. Before the race, the ASPCA demanded proof that the colt was in condition to run.

Assault was shipped to Columbia, S.C., for rest and treatment of his leg splints. He made his first start in 1948 in the Widener Handicap, only to finish fifth. The result convinced his owner that the time for retirement had arrived, and the colt was sent to the King Ranch's Kentucky stud farm. A routine chemical analysis of his semen disclosed the sad fact that the horse was sterile. Two weeks later, a second check was made, which substantiated the first report, and the colt thereupon was returned to Texas.

By August, Assault showed sufficient improvement in his physical condition to prompt a return to racing. His preparation for this continued into the following spring, and his first start in 1949 was at Aqueduct, on June 24. He lost by a nose. On July 2, though, he raised some hopes by taking the Brooklyn Handicap and the $40,600 purse. Then, on August 13, he finished fourth in the Massachusetts Handicap and bleeding from a nostril. A brief rest healed the cause, enabling him to race in the Edgemere Handicap at Aqueduct on September 10. He came in third. It was after he ran seventh in the Manhattan Handicap on September 24 and eighth in the Grey Lag Handicap on October 15, bleeding again following the latter race, that the announcement went out that Assault would be retired for the second time.

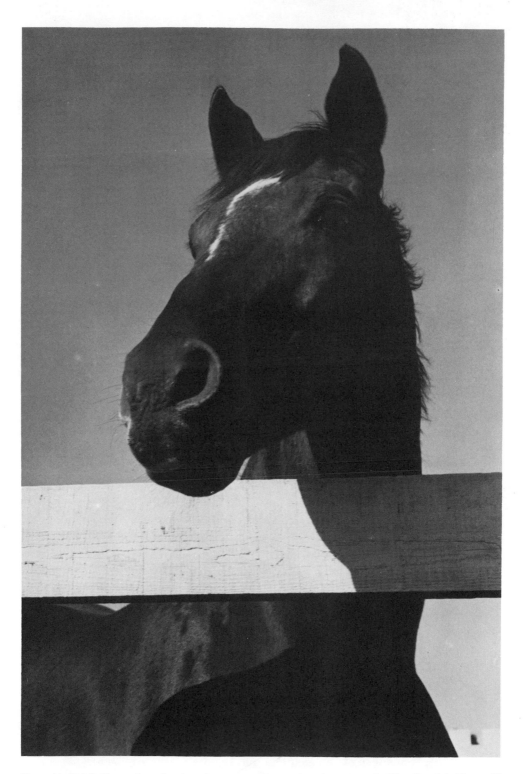

Venerable Triple Crown champion Assault at age twenty-two in retirement on the King Ranch in Texas. He was put to sleep six years later after fracturing a leg in a fall.

However, the story of America's seventh Triple Crown champion still had a few more interesting wrinkles. In 1950, he was allowed to run out with a band of young Quarter mares and got four of them in foal, which happening raised not a few eyebrows, especially among the breeders at the King Ranch. They felt so good about the news that they even brought out Assault for races in his seventh year. He ran in three, winning one, placing in another, and losing the third, while earning $2,950. These were his very final flings on the turf. He was retired for keeps thereafter.

Dr. Northway, in a letter dated August 2, 1971, explained what had happened. "As you know (and which is rather known throughout the Thoroughbred horse breeders) Assault did prove sterile, and has continued sterile to Thoroughbred mares and also to each examination of semen sent to many of the best veterinarians in the field. He was retired here and has remained sterile, with the exception (nobody knows from a genetic standpoint) when mated to young open Quarter mares, he did succeed in settling four out of eight from natural service in the pasture. We were very much elated over the outcome as he produced two fillies and two colts from these eight mares. We sent him to California to give him a chance to increase his winnings. . . . He is now definitely retired here on the ranch and is living happily and in good condition for his age. His appetite is good (he is fed twice a day) and he has a good pasture in which to exercise. He is quite a pet to all of the owners and to all who know him . . . this grand old champion horse."

Alas, the end came on September 2, 1971. The twenty-eight-year-old stallion stumbled and fractured his left front leg near the shoulder. Time had run out on him. The good Dr. Northway had no panacea for him this time, so he put him to sleep. The story of Assault thus ended almost the way it began.

CITATION
and trainer Jimmy Jones.

			*Bull Dog
	Bull Lea		Rose Leaves
CITATION (Bay Colt)			
	*Hydroplane II		Hyperion
			Toboggan

Citation

8

It could be said that the squire of Calumet Farm, Warren Wright, Sr., had a sixth sense for making the right buy at the right time. In 1936, while in the process of converting his breeding farm from trotters to Thoroughbreds, he was instrumental in organizing a syndicate that went to England for a top stallion and came home with Blenheim II. The result was Whirlaway. That same year, at the Saratoga Sales, he picked up a real buy when he paid $14,000 for the colt Bull Lea. By the time the horse entered stud, after a fairly successful racing career, Whirlaway was the number one stallion on the farm, enjoying the pick of the best mares. This created a need for a choice mare to accommodate Bull Lea.

To fill the void, Wright went to England once more and purchased Hydroplane II from Lord Derby's stable. It was the spring of 1941, and the British and Nazi Germany were at war. Wright wanted the mare badly, but did not want to see his investment lost because of a U-boat's torpedo. Therefore he arranged for the mare to be shipped to America via the safer Pacific route. She arrived in July. Her first two foals proved to be rather ordinary. On April 11, 1945, out of a mating with Bull Lea, she dropped her third foal, a bloodlike dark bay colt, who also was given somewhat short shrift at the outset. He was Citation, but unlike the previous offspring of the British mare, he was destined for top honors at Calumet Farm and in the racing world. Within three years, he would make Wright the proud owner of his second Triple Crown winner, a distinction enjoyed by only one other owner, William Woodward.

A sentimentalist could be pardoned if he were to claim that the colt was destined for great things in his lifetime if only because of the way he came by his name. Normally, Mrs. Wright, wife of the Chicago baking-powder magnate, enjoyed the honor of naming the Calumet foals. On this occasion, however, the pleasure was given to Mrs. Otto W. Lehmann, a close friend of the Wrights. "It was during the war, when you were hearing a lot about citations," said Mrs. Lehmann in retrospect. "It seemed like a good name for a good horse; an honorable mention for distinguished performance." She could not have been more clairvoyant.

On the way to the pinnacle in racing, Citation enveloped himself in a distinctive aura, joining a select group of Thoroughbreds who have been rated favorably with the twentieth century's turf touchstone, Man o' War. The fact is, racing experts reached the conclusion that Citation was equal to, if not better than, "Big Red." For example, noted trainer "Sunny Jim" Fitzsimmons stated unequivocally early in 1948, before the colt had even won the Kentucky Derby: "Up to this point Citation's done more than any horse I ever saw. And I saw Man o' War." By October, the rangy bay's trainer, Ben Jones, was unabashed to boast to the New York *Journal-American*'s Pat Lynch: "Citation is a better horse. . . . I think Citation shades him. Man o' War was an erratic sort and Citation has a perfect disposition. I've talked to a lot of men that saddled horses against Man o' War and they feel the same. . . . Two things make Citation a great horse. First he is far above average in intelligence. Secondly, he can run any kind of race. Come from behind or make his own pace . . . I've tried to fault him, but I just can't find any holes. He's the best. Maybe we'll never see his likes again in our time." From a jockey's viewpoint, Eddie Arcaro said: "Riding him is like driving a Cadillac. You get that chunk of speed whenever you ask for it." Finally, in the twilight of his career, other owners would sigh with envy at his earnings. Citation was the first millionaire in turf history, the first Thoroughbred to reach the exalted seven-figure mark.

He was remarkable in other respects. He was a horse who loved to run, and hardly cared where, when, or how. During his third year, he raced in Florida, Maryland, Kentucky, New Jersey, New York, Illinois, and California, on all kinds of tracks and handled by five different jockeys. As early as February, he gave up to 22 pounds to older horses on two occasions and beat the daylights out of them. So great was his stamina that in a period of seven weeks he won four races, at distances of six furlongs, a mile and a quarter, and two miles. He began the year with a $3,250 win in Florida, and closed it out in California with a total of $709,470, a record for earnings in one year. He was all horse.

The achievements at three were hardly a surprise, considering his sensational season at two, when he won eight of nine starts and $155,680. Ironically, for a while at the outset, it appeared as though he might never get the chance to prove his ability. That he succeeded at all is a credit to his tremendous racing power, which could not be denied, rather than to immediate recognition of this by his handlers. It was all because he had arrived at Calumet in the midst of a plethora of exceptional horses. Truly, the stable could crow that its cup runneth over. Its string had grown to such an extent that it had to be divided into two training camps, one handled by the boss, Ben Jones, in Florida, and the other by his son, H. A. "Jimmy" Jones, in Maryland. The luminaries of the pack included Armed, Coaltown, Bewitch, and Faultless, each of whom enjoyed distinguished careers. As far as young Citation was concerned at this stage of his life, he was in a spot you would hardly give to a dog, let alone a Thoroughbred. Actually, Calumet had so little need for a new top colt that there was no rush to get him going. This state of affairs prevented him from making his first stakes start until the end of July. Prior to then, he was "merely getting a race now and then to keep him sharp."

"Big Cy" made his debut on April 22, 1947, at Havre de Grace, in a four-and-a-half-furlong race for maiden colts and geldings, which he won by a length. He followed this with four consecutive wins, including a record-breaking :58 performance in a five-furlong sprint at Arlington Park on July 24, and his first stakes victory in the Elementary Stakes at Washington Park on July 30, in which he gave 12 pounds to the runner-up, Salmagundi. His next outing was in the rich Washington Park Futurity, on August 16, in a confrontation with two stablemates, the filly Bewitch and the colt Free America. The filly, also an offspring of Bull Lea, was the darling of Calumet. She boasted seven consecutive victories, was probably the fastest two-year-old in the country, and was well on her way to the title of the year's "Best Two-Year-Old Filly." Citation, on the other hand, had won "only" five in a row. Free America was the poor relation of the group, having lost once and won only his last three. Calumet wanted the race badly enough to go full blast by starting all three in it. However, in order to avoid a family donnybrook, in which his own horses might be punished by his own riders in their zeal to win, trainer Jimmy Jones ordered the jockeys to let whichever horse was leading win. He then sweetened the command by arranging for the winning purse to be split three ways. Everyone would be a winner.

Calumet scored a one-two-three finish—Bewitch, Citation, Free America—in a race that saw "Big Cy" make up a five-length deficit in the last furlong to lose by just a length. There were many, though, who felt that Citation could have caught Bewitch in the stretch had he been pushed hard enough, and that his second-place finish was a deliberate sacrifice to maintain Bewitch's unblemished record.

Thereafter, the colt went on to win Belmont's Futurity Trial and Futurity and Pimlico's Futurity. His three-length victory in the Belmont Futurity, America's outstanding race for two-year-olds, on October 4, was notable for several reasons. He won a purse of $78,450, and the win automatically assured his position as the "Best Two-Year-Old" of the year. It was also sweet revenge, for he beat Bewitch. In the Pimlico race, only four horses faced him. It was an easy win, worth $36,675, to close out a fantastic first year of campaigning. "Practically all of his victories found him going easily at the end, and once he gave evidence he could stay as well as sprint, he went into retirement as the winter favorite for the 1948 Kentucky Derby," said H. P. Robertson in reviewing the 1947 racing season. Citation's record also helped appreciably to make it a banner year for Calumet Farm, in its phenomenal 1947 sweep. Besides its two two-year-old stars, the stable could point to its Armed, who had prevailed over Assault and Stymie for "Horse of the Year" honors.

Citation started his third year in high style, with two impressive races at Hialeah. The first, a six-furlong allowance for three-year-olds and over, found him the only sophomore unafraid to show up. In fact, he even was asked to give away weight to his elders, so strong was his reputation from the previous year. He carried 113 pounds, equal to 129 on a four-year-old in February and 131 on older horses. Thus, Armed, with 130 pounds, had a one-pound advantage, while four other entries had upwards of 22 pounds. With it all, he won the race by a length. The second start was in the Seminole Handicap, on February 11, and once more he beat Armed. Both victories represented an unusual coup, since it is rare for a Thoroughbred to be matched against horses out of his division so early in his third year. The theory is that such a horse has not yet reached his full development, and so is at a decided disadvantage with the older Thoroughbreds. As a result, Citation's esteem rose sharply in the eyes of the racing community, causing trainer Fitzsimmons to compare him glowingly with Man o' War and Ben Jones to exult: "This is the best horse I've ever had." Then there was the California turfman E. O. Stice, who made the first of a series of fruitless offers by breeders to purchase him. His $250,000 bid fell on deaf ears.

The next triumphs were in the Everglades and Flamingo stakes, the latter resulting in the colt's first big purse of the year, $43,500. Jockey Ted Atkinson remembered the Flamingo race all too well. He was aboard Pennant Day, when he suddenly heard a horse pounding up behind him on the final turn. "I knew it was Citation," he said, "and I got the hell out of the way. I didn't want to get run over." It was an indication of the increasing measure of respect Citation was beginning to command from those who were in a position to know and care. The victory skein was broken on April 12, with a loss to Saggy in the mud in the Chesapeake Trial at Havre de Grace. The defeat, however, could be attributed to some extenuating circumstances and could not be construed as a reflection on the horse's performance.

First, a tragic event struck Calumet, when their regular rider, Al Snider, was lost on a fishing trip in the wilds of the Florida Everglades. An emergency call went out to Eddie Arcaro to ride Citation in the six-furlong race. One writer likened it to "inviting a guy to rob a bank." Then the track turned up muddy, and Jimmy Jones cautioned Arcaro not to take any chances with the horse in this his first race aboard him. The jockey, being the pro that he was, candidly took the blame for the loss, admitting to an error in pacing judgment. He even claimed that he could have recovered from the mistake and won, but felt it would have meant punishing the horse too much and risking possible injury. It was just not worth it, what with the Triple Crown races coming along soon. "I knew Jimmy . . . didn't want me to beat up his horse," he said after the race. "You can't tell how much you're taking out of a horse in the mud." The decision was apparently a wise one, for the colt went on to capture the Chesapeake Stakes, on April 17, by four and a half lengths over Bovard, after running his rivals into the ground, and the Derby Trial, ten days later, before moving up to the Kentucky Derby.

Citation, with Al Snider up, wins over Big Day and Saggy in the Flamingo Stakes at Hialeah on March 1, 1948. Jockey Ted Atkinson, on Pennant Day, heard "Big Cy" pounding up on the final turn and "got the hell out of the way."

Derby day was clear, but the track was sloppy from an early rain. Calumet had two of its stars entered—Citation and Coaltown. The tandem was a powerful threat, since Coaltown had come back in 1948 from a throat ailment, which had curtailed his racing the year before, and had reeled off four straight sizzling wins. Therefore, the entry went off as the odds-on favorite at 2-5, but not before an earlier surprise. Presumably reasoning that since the entry would pay such prohibitively short odds it was senseless to back it, the early bettors had poured money on My Request. There was some merit to this, for the Whittaker colt was also on a four-win streak as a three-year-old, which included a clean sweep at Jamaica of the Experimental Handicap and Wood Memorial. Furthermore, the general public had had little opportunity to see what was happening before post time. It seems that betting on the Derby, the seventh race on the program, that day was being handled in the morning at special windows in a remote area of Churchill Downs. With the exception of quotations written on a nearby blackboard, no information was readily available until the tote board had been cleared of all data on the other races after they had been completed. Therefore, when the board blinked on for the Derby, it showed My Request as the favorite. The early odds may have also reflected the reservations of those who reasoned that Citation was riding two jinxes. Never before had a winner of the Belmont Futurity or the Derby gone on to take the big race as well. However, by post time the fans had apparently thought better of it and sent My Request off at almost 4-1.

Turf lore is filled with colorful tales, not the least of which is the one of Eddie Arcaro's doubts about Citation in the race, as reported by Robert Kelley. He was more favorably disposed to Coaltown, but was slated to ride Citation. He had made a wrong decision in the 1942 Derby, under similar circumstances, having elected to ride Devil Diver instead of Shut Out, who won the race. Both horses had been Greentree Stable entries. Therefore, his anxiety over the Calumet horses in 1948 was understandable. Ben Jones tried to reassure Arcaro, telling him not to worry about Coaltown. "Citation can catch any horse he can see," he said. Then, in the paddock just before the parade to the post, Arcaro is alleged to have muttered: "Gee, Ben. Are you sure I'm on the right one?" "You're on the right one," snapped Jones as he helped the jockey up.

Citation had the rail position, but his stablemate moved out fast to a commanding six-length lead in the backstretch, which gave Arcaro a few anxious moments and seeming truth to his earlier premonitions. However, he was not about to give up that easily, as he gunned for another Derby victory, one more than any other jockey had ever ridden. "I knew I had the rest of the field beat at the half-mile pole," he recalled. "I looked back and I knew the other horses were too drunk to cause us any trouble. We moved when I clucked to him, and I could see we'd move on out at Coaltown."

In a relatively short period the jockey had come to know his horse well, and what he could expect from him at the appropriate moment. He was aware that Citation was "lazy" and inclined to loaf, but at the same time was ready always to respond at the first "cluck." Therefore, he was able to push him, and bring him even with Coaltown going into the stretch. The two ran head to head in a momentary struggle, after which Citation spurted with a closing kick to finish handily four lengths in front, his "ears pricked—looking for more horses to run down," according to George Russell. Coaltown was second and My Request third.

The only real problem Arcaro had with Citation was the crowd. The colt appeared to be scared by the howling din sent up by the throng as they moved into the homestretch, and Arcaro whacked him for the first time with the whip, to keep his mind strictly on the race. "Maybe I didn't have to hit him, but I wasn't in any mood to take any chances," he said somewhat apologetically. The time was 2:05^2/$_5$ on the off footing, and the price, $2.80 for $2.00, with no place or show bets permitted. The payoff equaled that of Count Fleet, the smallest price since pari-mutuel betting was introduced at the Derby. The victory produced an extra measure of satisfaction for the principals. Calumet Farm enjoyed its third Derby win—Citation, Pensive, Whirlaway. It was the fourth for trainer Ben Jones—Citation, Pensive, Whirlaway, Lawrin. To Eddie Arcaro, it meant the fourth crossing of the finish line in front in a Derby—Citation, Hoop, Jr., Pensive, Whirlaway. As for "Big Cy," he collected $83,400, and thumbed his nose at the jinxes.

The Preakness, at Pimlico, was a breeze for the son of Bull Lea. He was the odds-on favorite, at 1-10, with only win bets permitted, as only three horses challenged him—Vulcan's Forge, Better Self, and Bovard. It had rained for two days before the race, and again he went off on a

Citation wins handily by four lengths with "ears pricked" in the 1948 Kentucky Derby. Stablemate Coaltown is second. Jockey Eddie Arcaro, who had wanted to ride Coaltown, wound up with his fourth Derby win.

Official chart of Kentucky Derby.

SEVENTH RACE
4 7 7 3 0
May   1-48—C.D

1 1-4 MILES. (Whirlaway, May 3, 1941—2:01⅖—3—126.) Seventy-fourth running KENTUCKY DERBY. $100,000 added. 3-year-olds. Scale weights. (Owner of winner to receive gold trophy.)

Gross value, $111,450.   Net value to winner $83,400; second, $10,000; third, $5,000; fourth, $2,500. Mutuel Pool, $670,833.

Index	Horses	Eq't A Wt	PP	St	½	¾	1	Str	Fin	Jockeys	Owners	Odds to $1
(47451)	CITATION	w 126	1	2	2h	2³	2⁵	1²	13½	E Arcaro	Calumet Farm	a-.40
(47189)	COALTOWN	wb 126	2	1	1⁶	13½	1½	2⁴	2³	N L Pierson	Calumet Farm	a-.40
(47326)	MY REQUEST	w 126	6	3	4h	4³	3¹½	3¹	3¹½	D Dodson	B F Whitaker	3.80
47189²	BILLINGS	w 126	5	6	5½	3½	4⁸	4¹⁵	4²⁰	M Peterson	Walmac Stable	14.70
47282³	GRANDPERE	w 126	4	4	3²	6	6	5½	5ⁿᵏ	J Gilbert	Mrs J P Adams	17.80
47451²	ESCADRU	wb 126	3	5	6	5⁶	5¹½	6	6	A Kirkland	W L Brann	7.10

a-Coupled, Citation and Coaltown.

Time, :12⅕, :23⅖, :34⅗, :46⅗, :59⅕, 1:11⅖, 1:24⅗, 1:38, 1:51⅖, 2:05⅖. Track sloppy.

	—$2 Mutuels Paid—	—Odds to $1—
Mutuel Prices { CITATION (a-Entry)	2.80 .40
COALTOWN (a-Entry)	2.80 .40
NO PLACE OR SHOW MUTUELS SOLD.		

Winner—B. c, by Bull Lea—Hydroplane II., by Hyperion, trained by B. A. Jones; bred by Calumet Farm

WENT TO POST—4:32.   OFF AT 4:32½ CENTRAL STANDARD TIME.

Start good from stall gate. Won handily; second and third driving. CITATION, away forwardly and losing ground while racing back of COALTOWN to the stretch, responded readily to a steady hand ride after disposing of the latter and drew clear. COALTOWN began fast, established a clear lead before going a quarter and, making the pace on the inside in the stretch, continued willingly, but was not good enough for CITATION, although easily best of the others. MY REQUEST, bothered slightly after the start, was in hand while improving his position to the stretch, then failed to rally when set down for the drive. BILLINGS suffered interference after the break when GRANDPERE bore to the outside, was in close quarters on the first turn when caught between ESCADRU and CITATION, then could not better his position when clear. GRANDPERE broke into BILLINGS at the start, displayed speed for a half mile, then gave way. ESCADRU, forced to take up when in close quarters entering the backstretch, could not reach serious contention thereafter and tired badly after going three-quarters of a mile.

Scratched—474514 Galedo, 126.

sloppy track. The result was a lazy time of 2:02²/₅, the slowest since the distance for the Preakness had been changed from a mile to a mile and three-sixteenths in 1925. Eddie Arcaro shrugged this off, remarking instead that it had been an easier run than in the Derby. He had tapped Citation once at the head of the stretch and again in the middle of it. He claimed the colt was under stout restraint throughout, and that at no time had there been any serious opposition. "Big Cy" merely galloped along in front until the stretch, at which point he was allowed to increase his advantage. "If that's all the competition we're going to have," enthused the jockey, "he and I are going to have a picnic."

The only real difficulty Citation faced that day was the ceremony in the winner's circle. He balked at having the blanket of black-eyed Susans draped over him for the traditional picture-taking. Jimmy Jones solved the problem by covering the colt's eyes as the flowers were put in place. The day also proved to be a cash windfall for Calumet Farm. In fact, it was the biggest haul for a stable in racing history. While Citation was picking up $91,870 at Pimlico, Calumet's Faultless was taking down $60,300 by winning the Gallant Fox Handicap at Jamaica in New York, and another stablemate, Fervent, was earning $15,000 by coming in second. All told, the afternoon's purses totaled $167,170.

Citation breezes to an easy victory in the Preakness. Only three horses opposed him.

SIXTH RACE

48755

May 15-48—Pim

1 3-16 MILES. (Riverland, May 1, 1943—1:56⅖—5—123.) Seventy-Second Running PREAKNESS STAKES. $100,000 added. 3-year-olds. Scale weights. (All eligibility, entrance and starting fees to the winner, with $100,000 added, of which $20,000 to second, $10,000 to third and $5,000 to fourth. The nominator of the winner to receive $2,500; the nominator of the second horse, $1,000, and the nominator of the third horse, $500 of the added money.)

Gross value, $134,870. Net value to winner $91,870; second, $20,000; third, $10,000; fourth, $5,000. Mutuel Pool, $191,004.

Index	Horses	Eq't	A	Wt	PP	St	½	¾	1	Str	Fin	Jockeys	Owners	Odds to $1
(47730)	CITATION	w		126	4	1	1^{1}½	1^2	1^{2}½	1^{2}½	1^{5}½	E Arcaro	Calumet Farm	.10
48359^3	VULCAN'S FORGE	wb		126	2	4	2^2	2^{2}½	3^3	2^1	2^{3}½	D Dodson	C V Whitney	30.00
(48259)	BOVARD	w		126	1	2	3^{1}½	3^2	2^h	3^2	3^{nk}	W Saunders	S W Labrot Jr	9.30
47326^3	BETTER SELF	w		126	3	3	4	4	4	4	4	W Mehrtens	King Ranch	12.60

Time, :13, :24⅘, :37⅖, :50⅖, 1:03, 1:16, 1:29, 1:43, 1:55⅖, 2:02⅖. Track heavy.

Mutuel Prices { CITATION .... $2 Mutuels Paid 2.20 .... Odds to $1 .10 ....

NO PLACE OR SHOW MUTUELS SOLD.

Winner—B. c, by Bull Lea—Hydroplane II., by Hyperion, trained by H. A. Jones; bred by Calumet Farm.

WENT TO POST—5:15. OFF AT 5:15½ EASTERN DAYLIGHT TIME.

Start good from stall gate. Won easily; second and third driving. CITATION sprinted to the front while under stout restraint, was without serious opposition, merely galloped along in front to the stretch, felt the sting of the whip twice and easily increased his advantage. VULCAN'S FORGE, raced kindly after breaking slowest of all, raced in the runner-up position to the stretch, gave way briefly to BOVARD and was easily better than the latter in the drive. BOVARD was not rushed early, exhibited a mild rally along the inside rounding the final turn, then flattened out under pressure. BETTER SELF failed to rally at any stage and apparently disliked the going.

Official chart of Preakness.

With two down and one to go for the "really big win," most trainers might have rested their horse to prepare for it without pressure. It was not so as far as Citation was concerned. Jones figured to keep him sharp by entering him in the Jersey Stakes on May 29, which he proceeded to polish off by a "mere" eleven lengths. There may have been some misgivings about this at the start of the Belmont Stakes on June 12. For one thing, seven opponents went to the post, apparently hopeful that a hole in his stamina might show up. For another, he stumbled at the bell, to give one and all conniptions. However, he steadied himself quickly, and was in front to stay at the far turn. "I just let him run a little, up that turn," related Arcaro. "Then I took him up again, because he went so fast it scared me." Citation waltzed over the finish line eight lengths ahead of Better Self, $77,700 richer and the eighth Triple Crown champion. The colt's road to the crown had been by far the easiest of them all. In reaching the goal, he also made Arcaro the only jockey ever to pilot two Triple Crown winners.

It was Ted Atkinson who subsequently revealed the cause of the stumble at the top of the race. He was sitting on Faraway in the starting gate stall next to the one occupied by Citation. "I looked over and this big dude had his left forefoot on a ledge alongside the gate. I yelled to Eddie to look, and he reached down with his whip and smacked Citation's leg." Just then, the gates opened and the startled colt lost his composure for the moment, but not enough to spoil his march to the "most glorious crown."

There was no stopping Citation now. He remained unbeaten for the rest of the year, with victories in the Stars and Stripes, Buckingham Purse, American Derby, Sysonby Mile, Jockey Club Gold Cup, Empire

It is no contest in the Belmont, as Citation is all by himself at the finish line eight lengths in front of Better Self. He won in spite of a stumble at the start.

Winning team, Citation, jockey Eddie Arcaro, and trainer Jimmy Jones, in the traditional parade to the winner's circle after the Belmont victory.

SIXTH RACE

5 0 9 6 9

June 12-48—Bel

Gross value, $117,300.

Mutuel Pool, $433,818.

1 1-2 MILES. (Bolingbroke, Sept. 26, 1942—2:27⅗—5—115.) Eightieth running BELMONT STAKES. $100,000 added. 3-year-olds. Scale weights. Nominators of winner, second and third horses to receive $2,000, $1,000 and $500, respectively. Colts, 126 lbs.; fillies, 121 lbs. (Geldings not eligible.)

Net value to winner $77,700; second, $20,000; third, $10,000; fourth, $5,000.

Index	Horses	Eq't A Wt PP St	½	1	1¼	Str	Fin	Jockeys	Owners	Odds to $1
(49854)	CITATION	w 126 1 1	1h	11	14	15	18	E Arcaro	Calumet Farm	.20
(50522)	BETTER SELF	wb 126 8 2	6²	5nk	55	36	2½	W Mehrt'ns	King Ranch	a-12.50
(50437)	ESCADRU	w 126 3 3	4½	41	2³	2³	3⁵	A Kirkland	W L Brann	6.85
50437	VULCAN'S FORGE	wb 126 5 6	7⁵	7⁴	7⁴	5⁴	4³	D Dodson	C V Whitney	15.10
49854	GASPARILLA	wb 126 7 7	5¹	3½	3¹	4h	5⁴	R Donoso	A J Sackett	a-12.50
50522²	SALMAGUNDI	wb 126 6 5	3²	6¹⁵	6³	6³	6²	E Guerin	W Helis	22.45
50645³	GOLDEN LIGHT	wb 126 4 8	8	8	8	8	7⁵	N Combest	Belair Stud	82.50
49854³	FARAWAY	wb 126 2 4	2³	2³	4½	7½	8	T Atkinson	Glen Riddle Farm	28.10

a-Coupled, Better Self and Gasparilla.

Time, :24, :48⅖, 1:12⅗, 1:37, 2:02⅖, 2:28⅕. Track fast.

Mutuel Prices {
	—$2 Mutuels Paid—			—Odds to $1—		
CITATION	2.40	2.30	2.10	.20	.15	.05
BETTER SELF (a-Entry)		3.70	2.10		.85	.05
ESCADRU			2.10			.05

Winner—B. c, by Bull Lea—Hydroplane II., by Hyperion, trained by H. A. Jones; bred by Calumet Farm.

WENT TO POST—4:45. OFF AT 4:46 EASTERN DAYLIGHT TIME.

Start good from stall gate. Won easily; second and third driving. CITATION stumbled at the break, but recovered quickly and was sent along under steady restraint and shook off FARAWAY when ready and, rounding the far turn, drew away and in the stretch run was shaken up slightly, then again drew away to finish with speed in reserve. BETTER SELF was taken under restraint in the early stages and was sent through on the inside rounding the stretch turn and disposed of ESCADRU in the final seventy yards. ESCADRU, on the outside and well up all the way, made a determined bid rounding to the stretch turn, but could not menace the winner and tired. VULCAN'S FORGE was outrun early, improved his position in the final half mile, but could not gain on the leaders. GASPARILLA was kept in a forward position from the beginning, but flattened out badly when roused rounding the far turn. SALMAGUNDI was steadied along in the running, but failed to respond when roused. GOLDEN LIGHT was outrun and was never a factor. FARAWAY was in near pursuit of the early pace, but tired badly and began to drift out and was not persevered with when beaten.

Scratched—49814² Coaltown, 126.

Official chart of Belmont Stakes.

City Gold Cup, Pimlico Special, Challenge Purse, and Tanforan Handicap. In the Sysonby Mile, no three-year-old other than his stablemate Coaltown wanted any part of him. However, the field did have some of the fastest sprinters in the land of all ages. Once again, Citation lay back, biding his time.

Rounding the far turn, with a half-mile to go, the front runners were Spy Song, Natchez, and Coaltown. Citation was fourth, trailing by some six lengths. Then he suddenly took off. Arcaro said it was like gunning a jet plane. At the head of the stretch, they had caught up to and passed the field, moving into a two-length lead. They extended this to three en route to the wire, with the jockey standing in the saddle for the last sixteenth of a mile. Jimmy Jones was somewhat puzzled. "Why did you move so soon?" he asked. "The sonofagun just took off on me," exclaimed Arcaro. It was a rather simple remark by a groom who worked for Alfred G. Vanderbilt and who had witnessed the race that really said it all. "Boss," he said, shaking his head, "that there horse just ain't human."

Respect for Citation continued to grow apace. Not one horse at all showed up to challenge him in the Pimlico Special on October 29, what with the race calling for level weights and a winner-take-all purse. It was a walkover, but Citation had to do it in grand style. According to H. P. Robertson, "He almost pulled Arcaro out of the irons to 'walk' over in 1:59⁴/₅," a time that was faster than some of the previous competitive runnings of the event. The gallop was worth $10,000, and Arcaro had his arms massaged afterward to ease the muscles that had been strained from trying to hold in the horse. The last race, and win, of the year for him was in the Tanforan Handicap at Bay Meadows, near San Francisco, on December 11. It gave him a record of nineteen victories in twenty starts, fifteen of them in succession, as he nailed down the best of everything in 1948—"Best Three-Year-Old," "Handicap Horse," and "Horse of the Year." His earnings of $709,470 topped Assault's mark of $424,195, and only Stymie and Armed had won as much as his total in their entire careers. Finally, his overall figure of $865,150 was only $53,335 short of Stymie's all-time record.

Unfortunately, the sweet was laced with bitters. After the Tanforan, he developed a "hot spot" on an ankle, which proved to be an osselet on the left fore ankle. Later, he was bothered by tendon trouble. The ailments became so persistent that he was finally forced to sit out the entire fourth-year season. Things were never the same again.

Citation takes Pimlico Special in walkover on October 29. "Big Cy" almost pulled Eddie Arcaro out of the irons even though there were no other horses in race.

Citation returned to action on January 11, 1950, winning a six-furlong race at Santa Anita, Calif., and regenerating all of the old excitement among his followers. It was his sixteenth consecutive win, the longest streak in modern racing history. This was followed by a series of tough losses, an overnight by a neck at Santa Anita, January 26; the San Antonio Handicap by a length, February 11; the Santa Anita Handicap by a nose, February 25; the San Juan Capistrano Handicap by a nose, March 4; and the Surprise Purse at Golden Gate Fields in Albany, Calif., May 17. He returned to his winning ways on June 3, when he took the Golden Gate Mile, to boost his earnings to a record high of $924,631, thus topping Stymie's mark by about $6,000. He then lost the Forty-Niners Handicap, June 17, and the Golden Gate Handicap, June 24, after which he was shipped to Chicago. Here it was discovered that he had sore ankles, so back he went to Calumet Farm for a rest.

On the surface, his 1950 record might appear to be disappointing. It was far from that. He won two of nine starts, finishing no worse than second in the others. His losses were mostly to the talented, Irish-bred Noor, who had been imported by Charles S. Howard, the owner of Seabiscuit, and who captured honors as the 1950 "Handicap Horse." Actually, Citation ran exceptionally well. He set a world's record of $1:33^3/_5$ in the Golden Gate Mile, and came in second in four world's-record runs and one track-record run. Some of the losses were attributed to the weight he was forced to give away, in addition to coming up against a hot Noor. They were: the Santa Anita Handicap, a mile and a quarter, track record of 2:00, won by Noor carrying 110 pounds to Citation's 132; the San Juan Capistrano Handicap, a mile and three-quarters, world's record of $2:52^4/_5$, won by Noor carrying 117 pounds to Citation's 130; the Surprise Purse, six furlongs, world's record of $1:08^2/_5$, won by Roman Inn at level weights; the Forty-Niners Handicap, a mile and a furlong, world's record of $1:46^4/_5$, won by Noor carrying 123 pounds to Citation's 128; and the Golden Gate Handicap, a mile and a quarter, world's record of $1:58^1/_5$, won by Noor carrying 127 to Citation's 126, the first race in which he had ever been given weight and his only bad defeat—by three lengths.

Normally, at this stage of his life, Citation should have been retired. He was not. Warren Wright, before he died during the year, had expressed the desire that the horse should be allowed to race until he topped not only Stymie's earnings record but had also become the first millionaire of the racing world. Consequently, the colt was brought out again in 1951. The first start was at Bay Meadows, on April 18, in a six-furlong race. It was his first event in about ten months, and he finished third. He came in third once more on April 26, winning only $400. On May 11, he wound up fifth in the Hollywood Premiere Handicap, the first time in forty-one races he had ever finished out of the money. He lost again on May 30, in the Argonaut Handicap, a race that was noteworthy to the Triple Crown champion only because it marked the last time he would be a loser. Apparently reaching back

Irish-bred Noor crosses the finish line ahead of Citation in the 1950 Santa Anita Handicap.

Noor (3) beats Citation by a nose in the San Juan Capistrano, March 4, 1950.

Citation becomes the first horse to win a million dollars, as he defeats the filly Bewitch in the Hollywood Gold Cup, July 14, 1951. It was his last race, and he avenged the first defeat of his career by Bewitch.

"Millionaire" Citation prances proudly before wildly cheering fans in his last public appearance, at Arlington Park, Chicago, July 28, 1951. Freeman McMillen is riding him.

into memory, he racked up three consecutive wins, in the Century Handicap, American Handicap, and Hollywood Gold Cup. He ran the latter on July 14, completed the mile and a quarter in 2:01 and won by four lengths. The purse, a guaranteed $100,000, pushed Citation's earnings well past the million-dollar level.

There was an interesting sidelight to the race. The horse Citation beat to the wire in this, his last race, was Bewitch, the filly who had hung on him his first defeat in 1947. She picked up $20,000 for her second-place finish, which made her the leading money-winner of her sex, with a total of $462,605.

Two weeks later, on July 28, "Big Cy" was formally retired. He made his last public appearance that day at Arlington Park, Chicago, in a parade before a wildly cheering throng. Well-deserved rest had come to the superb colt, after forty-five starts and thirty-two victories. On his way back to Calumet Farm, his train car was shared by Coaltown and Bewitch, also headed for retirement, a rather valuable cargo indeed. His stud record was favorable; by 1962 he had sired four $100,000 winners, including Guadalcanal and Fabius. However, by his own standard, he never produced any offspring that compared remotely to him, which caused the experts to consider his career as a stallion somewhat less than successful.

Citation, "Big Cy," died on the night of August 8, 1970, at Calumet Farm, at the age of twenty-five. He was buried near the side of his sire, Bull Lea, and his dam, Hydroplane II.

SECRETARIAT
and jockey Ron Turcotte.

SECRETARIAT
(Chestnut Colt)

Bold Ruler
{ *Nasrullah
Miss Disco

Somethingroyal
{ *Princequillo
Imperatrice

Secretariat

9

Exactly a quarter of a century elapsed, from 1948 to 1973, before American Thoroughbred racing fans were able to salute a new Triple Crown champion. He had the improbable name of Secretariat, a blazing-red coat, and such awe-inspiring performance that some were inclined to believe he was a veritable Pegasus incarnate.

This enthusiasm was stimulated, no doubt, by the twenty-five years of frustration, which saw only six horses make it to the Belmont Stakes with victories in the Kentucky Derby and Preakness, only to fail in the tortuous mile-and-a-half classic. Of these, half wound up with an assortment of ailments, provoking the cynics to start calling it the "Cripple Crown." For example, Canonero II (1971) developed a bad hock, Carry Back (1961) came back gimpy, and Tim Tam (1958) fractured a bone in a foot. Consequently, there were more than a few who were ready to write off all possibility for a new champion. If to this are added the fluke circumstances surrounding Secretariat, and his owners and trainers, it is truly a miracle that he even came into being, let alone made it to the "most glorious crown" as America's ninth Triple Crown champion.

The colt was born on March 30, 1970, at the Meadow Farm, in Doswell, Va. His owner was Christopher T. Chenery, a utilities magnate who collected board chairmanships of companies such as Southern Natural Gas. He had gone into the breeding business as an avocation in 1936, when he purchased 2,600 acres of rolling countryside some fifteen miles north of Richmond. The farm, originally known as the Meadow, had belonged to his ancestors from 1810 until they lost it during the Civil War.

Chenery had a philosophy about horses: ". . . the purchase price does not always represent what a horse is worth. It's only what some fool thinks he's worth." Therefore, in 1939, he shopped cautiously and purchased a yearling mare, Hildene, for only $750. "She showed speed," he liked to recall later on, "but stopped eight times in eight races. Then I stopped racing her." In the parlance of the track, she turned into a "blue hen," producing a string of top stakes winners and fillies, even though she went blind with her first foal. One of her distinguished sons was First Landing, who became the sire of Riva Ridge.

Seven years after this remarkable purchase, Chenery boldly shelled out $35,000 for another mare, Imperatrice, who proceeded to justify the price tag with an equally impressive lineup of offspring, including an unraced daughter, Somethingroyal, who became the dam of Secretariat. Thus, from the blood of these two mares the fortunes of Meadow Farm, Stable and Stud flourished, to the extent that from 1939 to 1972 forty stakes winners were produced, and earnings totaled $8,500,000 in purses and more than $12,000,000 in overall breeding sales and purses.

All did not progress that smoothly straight through. Financial troubles began to crop up in the 1960s, coincident with Chenery's failing health and increasing senility. By 1967, the industrialist's three children, Dr. Hollis B. Chenery, Mrs. Margaret Carmichael, and the youngest, Mrs. Helen "Penny" Tweedy, were forced to make a tough decision. Dr. Chenery, a distinguished economist with the World Bank, was for selling all of the horses and investing the money in a rising stock market. Mrs. Tweedy demurred. "We probably have the legal right to do that," she conceded, "but we know Dad wouldn't want us to give up the horses. So I don't think we have the moral right to do it." Furthermore, she continued, "The land has supported the horses, and the horses have supported the land." Finally, she pointed out that "I at least know how to read a balance sheet," from having attended Columbia University's Graduate School of Business. Her arguments prevailed, and she was given the green light to make a stab at managing the whole operation.

Her first move was to reduce the overhead, by cutting the stable from 130 to 68 horses. The next decision, however, was momentous in its future ramifications. It was whether or not to continue with an odd agreement her father had had for years with Mrs. Henry Carnegie Phipps and her son, Ogden. They were the owners of the stallion Bold Ruler, who had dominated racing for a decade in the breeding shed of Claiborne Farm as the leading American sire. So priceless did they regard his services that money could not buy "romance" with him. Rather, payment had to be made with a unique form of "currency."

"It was all part of a very complicated arrangement," recalled Mrs. Tweedy. "They agreed that each season Mr. Phipps's great sire, Bold Ruler, would be bred to two of my father's broodmares. Every two years they flipped a coin. The winner had first choice of the two foals that year and the loser had first choice the year after." As far as she was concerned, it was a bad arrangement. "It was a great deal for the Phippses, because they would end up with the offspring of the best mares in the country. It hadn't been good for Dad, though. He hadn't been lucky with his Bold Ruler foals. But, I decided since he had made the deal, I'd give it two more years."

Penny Tweedy had learned fast that crossing bloodlines can help overcome flaws in horses. So, with the advice of A. B. "Bull" Hancock, owner of Claiborne Farm, she sent two Meadow mares to Bold Ruler, Somethingroyal and Hasty Matelda. It was the former that suggested the greatest promise. The consensus was that Bold Ruler's offspring were precocious and brilliant racing at the age of two and at short distances. At three, they were disappointments, particularly when asked to run farther, as in the classic races of a mile and a quarter and more. On the other hand, Somethingroyal's sire was Princequillo, whose foals were tough, durable, long-running, but "seldom blessed with speed." As one breeder told her: "The Princequillos will run all day—and if the races get long enough and the other horses get tired, sooner or later they'll win for you."

The mating was accomplished and, in the spring of 1969, the mistress of Meadow Stable and the master of Wheatley Stable met in the office of Alfred G. Vanderbilt at Belmont Park for the coin flip. "We were joking," said Penny Tweedy, "because we both wanted to lose." It seems that both parties knew then that Somethingroyal had already foaled a filly, and was impregnated a second time. On the other hand, Hasty Matelda had had a colt, but was to be barren the next year. Therefore, whoever won the toss would have the first choice of the new foals, but would lose out the second year, since there would be only one foal. Thus, only one of the owners would wind up with two horses.

Mr. and Mrs. Ogden Phipps. Phipps flipped a coin with Mrs. Tweedy to determine the ultimate owner of Secretariat.

Ogden Phipps won the toss and, since he always preferred Meadow fillies, took the Somethingroyal foal. They named her The Bride, eventually raced her four times, and she never finished better than sixth. As one wag put it, she "couldn't outrun a fat lady with gout." By the same token, Mrs. Tweedy's new colt, Rising River, also had problems and was finally sold for $50,000. The following year, at the Meadow Farm on March 30, Somethingroyal dropped a bright-red colt foal, with three white stockings and a star. He was christened Secretariat, a name suggested by Elizabeth Ham, for thirty-five years executive secretary for the elder Chenery and formerly an employee of the old League of Nations in Geneva. Three years later, while reflecting on the subsequent turn of events stemming from this odd deal, the astute turf scribe William Rudy wrote: "On such vagaries are racing fortunes founded."

So much for the horses; now what do you do with them? It became obvious soon that her father's long-time trainer, Casey Hayes, was finding it difficult adjusting to her measures, so Mrs. Tweedy replaced him. The new man was Roger Laurin, thirty-four, son of the well-known French-Canadian trainer Lucien Laurin, who was employed by Claiborne Farm and who had taught his son everything he knew about the business. Young Laurin was operating his own public stable, and came well endorsed by "Bull" Hancock for the job. "We lost about $85,000 the first year," Mrs. Tweedy frankly admits, "but I would go into my father's trophy room and look around, and I would think that with all that breeding as a foundation Meadow Stud would have better times." There was a small profit of $65,000 the second year, but until Riva Ridge showed up it was strictly a "holding operation."

Some bright spots did enter the picture, nevertheless, not the least of which was the new youngster on the farm, Secretariat. The first time she saw him gamboling in the fields, she made a succinct entry in the book she kept on her horses: "Wow!" He was big, bright-eyed, barrel-chested, with legs that "promised to be straight and flawless." Farm manager Howard Gentry enjoyed watching him, too, because "he always liked to lead the field, even when he was running with other yearlings across the pasture."

By June 1971, when everything seemed to be settling down to a smooth routine, another far-reaching decision was made. Young Roger Laurin suddenly quit as trainer, lured away by the Phippses to replace their own trainer, who had died of a heart attack. The Wheatley Stable was a great opportunity for him and he grabbed it but, in doing so, added a bit of chutzpah and nepotism to the situation by suggesting his father, Lucien, as his replacement. Penny Tweedy was hardly enthused. Lucien Laurin, who by now was no longer with Claiborne Farm and was operating a public stable, was pushing sixty and on the verge of retiring. He had, in fact, booked a European vacation for his wife and himself.

"Mrs. Tweedy was reluctant at first to take on a trainer who might stay only a couple of months," admits Laurin, "but Mr. Hancock told her: 'He'll stick around. He's a good trainer and he'll stay.' " He must have been a good judge of character, because the trainer did choose to stay, bringing a wealth of experience to the Meadow horses. Laurin, a native of St. Paul Joliette, Quebec, was a jockey from 1920 until 1942, and thereafter a trainer with a reputation for converting slow or lame mounts into winners. By 1971, he had amassed the impressive record of winners in 1,137 races with earnings of $6,434,303.

In taking over the training assignment, he brought ten Meadow Stable horses to his barn, including Riva Ridge, Upper Case, and Quill Gordon, all promising Thoroughbreds, who joined stakes winner Spanish Riddle, whom he was training for another owner. An assessment of the checkerboard moves by the trainers caused *The Blood-Horse* to comment wryly: "A man can repay to his father all that he owes him, but Roger Laurin that day came as close to evening the score as a man can expect to come." Eight days later, Lucien sent out his first Meadow horse, Riva Ridge, for his first race as a two-year-old. "The colt was bumped, raced greenly and was not impressive," finishing seventh, hardly an auspicious start for both trainer and horse. It was a wholly different story by year's end, when the colt was named "Best Two-Year-Old" and Penny Tweedy and Lucien Laurin could indulge themselves in the luxury of dreaming: "Triple Crown."

They did not know it at the time, but they had the wrong horse in mind. Riva Ridge did, in fact, go on to win the 1972 Kentucky Derby and Belmont Stakes, but faltered in the Preakness because of a distaste for mud. However, down on the Virginia farm a young colt was getting set to make his move into the racing wars and to historic fame and fortune.

"It was when he was a yearling, playing in the fields, that I first suspected. And by the time he left the farm as a two-year-old, I was sure he was one of the best we'd ever raised," is the way Howard Gentry recalled the fateful moment when Secretariat "left home." Lucien Laurin was somewhat more philosophical, when he studied the big frame of the colt. Along with the size came an insatiable appetite. He ate anything that resembled food, and grew quite chubby. This simply meant that the horse would have to be brought along more slowly. "You have to have more forbearance with a fat horse," he said.

The training progression more than substantiated this. In his early workouts, Secretariat would trail his stablemates. Gradually, he caught up to them. Finally, by late spring, he moved ahead, prompting the trainer to seek out the impatient Mrs. Tweedy and happily break the good news. "He's ready to run." In fact, Laurin was so impressed with the horse he began to wonder if he were not permitting his own ardor to delude him. "He was so damned good-looking that I said to myself he probably wouldn't be worth ten cents as a racer." The response he got from the owner was a typical sample of human foible. After all the impatience and anxiety at preparing for the moment, she said she would not be able to stay for the race, that she had to be away on business. "I'll wait," Laurin said quietly. "I think you ought to be here when he runs." The comment made Helen Tweedy sit up and reflect. Laurin normally was a rather taciturn individual who wasted few words. Therefore, she reasoned, he must have something special for her to see, so she arranged to be in New York on July 4 for the colt's debut at Aqueduct.

It was a five-and-a-half-furlong sprint for two-year-old maidens, colts, and geldings, and like Riva Ridge's first race a year before, it was a nightmare, only more so. Coming out of the gate another horse bumped into Secretariat and knocked him sideways, at the same time pinching him back with no place to run. "He came this close to being knocked down," related jockey Paul Feliciano. "If he wasn't such a strong horse, he would have fallen." Despite the rough handling, he managed to finish a credible fourth, making up seven of eight lengths in the last quarter-mile. He also learned a lesson about competing at the track, which he never forgot. "It's no kidding," commented Laurin sometime later. "He sure remembered because, in his second start, he took himself back out of the gate . . . took himself back out of trouble." Indeed he did, but then he ran for daylight and won handily by six lengths. On July 31, two and a half weeks later, at Saratoga, he showed he meant business by winning a six-furlong allowance by a length and a half. This race also marked his first ride by Ron Turcotte, who from then on became his regular jockey. Turcotte was the second French Canadian on the Tweedy-Laurin team. A native of Grand Falls, New Brunswick, he became an apprentice in 1961, began riding in the United States in 1964, and proceeded to rack up more than $1,000,000 in purses. He did right well for the team in 1971 and 1972 aboard Riva Ridge, giving the Chenery family their first Kentucky Derby victory.

With two quick wins under his belt, the time arrived for Secretariat to prove that now he was to be taken seriously. The test would be his first stakes event, in the six-furlong Sanford on August 26 against his first real competition. The favorite was Linda's Chief, at 3 to 5, who had reeled off five consecutive victories. Only five horses were entered, and Secretariat proved he was fearless as well as swift. Seemingly trapped going into the final turn, reported Joe Nichols in the New York *Times,* the "Meadow colt gave a spectacular exhibition as he knifed his way between horses in the stretch to flash into the lead and score by 3 lengths." An ecstatic Ron Turcotte refused to hide his elation on later reflection. "That was the day he convinced me. When a horse is going a quarter in 26 seconds, you're forcing him, pushing him. At 24 or 25, you're working together with him. But when it's faster than that, you're picking his head up and he's pulling harder, putting everything into it, and it's a really good feeling. That's the way it is with Secretariat." The win provided the Meadow Stable with an added heady taste of success, because Secretariat followed Upper Case and classic winner Riva Ridge as the third stakes-winner racing for them in 1972.

The impressive wins by Secretariat sent a faint quiver through the racing community. There was no question but that the horse was a major factor to be reckoned with, particularly in the six-and-a-half-furlong Hopeful Stakes coming up on August 26. The race is one of the more important of the year. As the name implies, it can hopefully give a clue on potential champions: twelve former Hopeful winners captured the Belmont Stakes, while since 1936 fourteen were voted "Best Two-Year-Old."

Just about everyone pegged Secretariat the heavy favorite. The only one seemingly in the dark about him was the copy editor of the New York *Daily News,* who, on the day of the race, published an improbable headline:

> FILLY SECRETARIAT 1-2 PICK
> IN $86,550 HOPEFUL

The colt won in typical fashion, for him, shooting from last place to a five-length victory. His time of 1:16$^1/_5$ was $^3/_5$ second slower than the stakes and track record.

The faint quiver now became a distinct quake. For the first time, some began to talk of him as a "super horse." Kent Hollingsworth, editor of *The Blood-Horse,* in marveling at the end-of-the-race surge, said: "Secretariat . . . has demonstrated a lick not seen since Damascus approached the last turn trailing by about thirteen lengths and came out of it six lengths on top to win the 1967 Travers by twenty-two lengths in track-record time." Even Lucien Laurin began to believe. "Secretariat, the two-year-old, is better geared for immortality than Riva, the three-year-old." And so it was, coming up to the prestigious Belmont Futurity on September 16.

Only six horses dared to face him, the odds-on favorite, which provoked Michael Strauss of the New York *Times* to report: "Even members of the Baker Street Irregulars, a group devoted to the perpetuation of the memory of Sherlock Holmes, who made their annual appearance at the Big B . . . could find nothing mystifying about the installation of Secretariat as an overnight 2 to 5 choice." If anything, it was "an easy-does-it performance," even though he was next to last on the far turn. "My horse broke all right," remarked Turcotte, "but took himself back like he has been doing, but not so much this time. Maybe he's beginning to forget that bumping he got in his first race." Stop the Music made a brief move at him, but to no avail, at the end of the six and a half furlongs. The victory was worth $83,320, bringing his total to a respectable $162,580 for the year, and marked the first back-to-back wins by the same stable in thirty years. Riva Ridge, with Turcotte riding, too, had won the race the previous year.

There are five stakes races which are regarded as barometers for determining the best of the two-year-olds. They are the Hopeful, Futurity, Champagne, Laurel Futurity, and Garden State. Any horse that can take these, or most of them, will win the title hands down and in all probability wind up "the wealthiest horse in the country." Secretariat had a good leg on the title, by dint of wins in the first two of the five. Consequently, he came up to the $125,000-added Champagne Stakes at Belmont Park, October 14, New York's richest race for juveniles, as the 7 to 10 favorite. However, there were some doubters or wishful dreamers. "Secretariat is just about everyone's choice for leading two-year-old colt," pondered William Rudy in the New York *Post*, "but he has not scared anyone out of today's race at one mile. In fact, the fields opposing him keep getting bigger." Only four challenged him in the Sanford, six in the Futurity, and now eleven made up the field in the Champagne. There were some, too, who felt the big colt was tiring at the end of the Futurity, when Stop the Music charged him in the stretch, an opinion no doubt fired by the widely held theory that Bold Ruler's offspring could not handle longer distances.

"For the first time in three years, a disqualification turned champagne into vinegar for a great two-year-old in the . . . Champagne Stakes," is the way one writer summed it up. "Belmont ended Saturday not with a bang but with a whimper, as the best horse was disqualified," another disheartened scribe began his report. To put it more bluntly, 31,494 fans were in a state of shock. Secretariat did, in fact, race home two lengths in front and drawing out, but the "steward inquiry sign" flashed immediately, and then indicated that the colt had been dropped to second and Stop the Music had won.

The race had started in typical fashion. Secretariat ran last down the backstretch, biding his time until the far turn. Then, as William Rudy, in *The Blood-Horse*, described it: "Three-sixteenths of a mile from the finish . . . Secretariat was moving strongest between horses in a move that had brought him from last place. Stop the Music, racing inside of him, had made his move, too, and for fifty yards or so the two colts had raced stride for stride with Secretariat having just a bit of an advantage over his stubborn rival. At that point, Ron Turcotte . . . went to the whip and hit the Meadow Stable colt right-handed. The colt ducked in sharply" and seemed to bump Stop the Music. When Turcotte switched his whip to his left hand, the horse straightened out and went on to finish in front. The jockey was dumbfounded, since he could not recall Secretariat ever ducking in before in a race. Laurin, somewhat bitter, commented that the colt "never had to be hit before" so why now, especially since he appeared to be on his way to a win anyhow. For Mrs. Tweedy, the outcome was a terrible disappointment. "This was to be Secretariat's coronation race, he had the two-year-old championship in the bag," she lamented. Laurin's bitterness was further evidenced by his recalling how the colt had been "knocked against the gate and met with all kinds of traffic" in his first start. The decision of the stewards stood, nevertheless.

The sour taste of the race was washed away, however, when Secretariat emerged on the track two weeks later. "Saturday, October 28, at Laurel was designed for young lovers—and the bettors loved it," waxed *The Blood-Horse*. "The nation's two outstanding two-year-olds, La Prevoyante and Secretariat, ran on the same program, and each was backed down to 1-10." La Prevoyante was a Canadian-bred filly, owned by electronics magnate Jean-Louis Levesque. She had won all of her eleven races to date, nine of them stakes, was the only two-year-old filly ever to win more than eight straight, was certain of being named "Champion Two-Year-Old Filly" and was in the running for "Horse of the Year" honors. She was competing that October Saturday in the $121,990 Selima Stakes.

Secretariat also had quite a bit on the line. He was a shoo-in for "Best Two-Year Old" honors. But, he was also competing for "Horse of the Year," not only against the fetching filly but against the three-year-olds Riva Ridge and Key to the Mint, which two were to duel it out in the Jockey Club Gold Cup at Aqueduct that same day. In essence, the day was a track fan's dream, for the best of America's Thoroughbreds would be in action in New York and Maryland. It augured a weekend of decision by the pollsters, whose minds no doubt would be influenced by the results of the day.

Lucien Laurin had a moment of decision of his own. He was torn between two loves—should he stay in New York with Riva Ridge, or should he go to Laurel to be with Secretariat? Not only did he choose the chestnut colt, but he also assigned Ron Turcotte as his jockey. He was not disappointed. Secretariat again made an unhurried start, in his first experience with a sloppy track, kept to the outside and handled the track as though he were out for a morning breeze. He loped home by eight lengths to the good, in 1:42⁴/₅ for the mile and one-sixteenth, just ¹/₅ second slower than the track record. Turcotte looked back over his shoulder in mid-stretch and saw nothing. As they say, he was "lookin' and cookin' "; it was no contest. It was also sweet revenge over Stop the Music, who finished second and to whom he had given up first place in the Champagne Stakes on the foul claim. After the race, Lucien Laurin once more tried to explain his colt's hangup, stemming from the knocking-about he had experienced in his first race. "It happened near the three-eighths pole; apparently it made him gun-shy, because when he gets to the three-eighths pole now he turns on the gas regardless of what distance he is running."

La Prevoyante apparently had no such problems. She merely took off, spread-eagled the field by fourteen lengths, and coasted home for her twelfth win, at the same distance, in 1:46²/₅. It brought her earnings to $417,109, and made her the only two-year-old to win so many times in an undefeated season since Colin did it in 1907. Her owner, after the race, either wittingly or not, voiced a prediction on Secretariat's future that was to make headlines throughout the following year. "I know Mrs. [Helen] Tweedy very well. The deal has already been made. La Prevoyante will be bred to Secretariat the first year they are at stud."

Meadow Stable was considerably less fortunate in New York, where Riva Ridge was soundly thrashed in the Jockey Club Gold Cup. He came in three lengths behind Key to the Mint, who, in turn, lagged behind Autobiography by fifteen lengths. The loss suggested unhappy tidings in the year-end balloting.

The last race of the year for Secretariat, the Garden State Stakes in New Jersey, went as expected. Going off at 1-10, he "left the players laughing," after first "giving them a mass attack of jitters as he dawdled along in last place during the early stages of the race," was Gene Ward's colorful account of the race in the New York *Daily News*. It was only when the track announcer voiced what by now was a familiar refrain during his races—"Here comes Secretariat with a big rush on the outside"—that they headed for the win windows. Rudy Turcotte, Ron's brother who raced Angle Light to a second-place finish three and a half lengths behind, for one fleeting moment had an illusion of an upset in the making. "Then I looked over my shoulder," he recalled, "and saw those blue and white checkers on the outside. I knew if Secretariat was close to me with a quarter of a mile to go it was all over for me."

Voting for champion horses is conducted by a poll of the handicappers of the Thoroughbred Racing Associations, the staff of the *Daily Racing Form*, and members of the National Turf Writers Association. Until 1971, each group held its own voting, and prior to that the distinguished chronicler of the turf, Walter S. Vosburgh, made the selections. The 1972 nominees produced a rare ballot-box battle. It was no contest as far as champion two-year-old colt and filly were concerned. It was for top honors that the voting became somewhat sticky. "Much has been made of the contest between the two-year-old colt Secretariat and the two-year-old filly La Prevoyante for Horse of the Year Honors," reported *Sports Illustrated*, ". . . but less excitable members of the racing fraternity felt that either choice was unrealistic. No two-year-old, they argued, could properly be named horse of any year. It was as illogical as naming a particularly brilliant college junior as Man of the Year. Promise and precocity are not the same as mature achievement, and a two-year-old colt or filly is essentially promise."

The final tally, as a result, was something of a mishmash, in which Secretariat received 77 votes to La Prevoyante's 56, with the TRA and DRF favoring the colt. On the other hand, NTWA members submitted 58 ballots for "Horse of the Year," with 26 going to the filly, 21 to the colt, and 11 to the Chilean-bred Cougar II. There seemed to be a consensus that while the filly indeed had won all twelve of her races, Secretariat, in chalking up seven victories in nine starts and winning $456,404, had had tougher opposition. Thus, in taking turfdom's top award, the Eclipse Trophy, Secretariat became only the third two-year-old to achieve this feat. The others were Native Dancer (1952) and Moccasin (1965). In addition, he was the fifth home-bred champion for C. T. Chenery's Meadow Stable, following in the footsteps of Hill Prince, First Landing, Cicada, and Riva Ridge.

The one disappointment for Meadow Stable was Riva Ridge, who failed in his bid for the three-year-old title, losing out to Rockeby Stable's Key to the Mint. After having won the Belmont Stakes, Riva Ridge was victorious only once more during the rest of the year, in the Hollywood Derby, which obviously must have affected the balloting. *Sports Illustrated* seemed to object. "Now a new controversy rages over why Key to the Mint was picked instead of Riva Ridge, who won the Kentucky Derby and the Belmont Stakes, the two most prestigious races for three-year-olds. What it all comes down to, obviously, is that races and reputations are won on the track, not in the polling places."

With the start of 1973, a year that was to see Secretariat produce some of the most spectacular turf histrionics and headlines ever recorded by a three-year-old Thoroughbred in America, Lucien Laurin was no longer hesitant about the future. "I want another shot at the Triple Crown," he stated boldly, "and I think this colt . . . is going to give me a real look at our classics again. He doesn't have to carry his track around with him, either. He has handled all kinds . . . " he concluded, in an obvious allusion to Riva Ridge's problems with racing in mud.

Three days into the new year, Christopher T. Chenery, the founder of Meadow Stable, was dead at the age of eighty-six. His demise created a mountainous tax problem for the heirs. Although he had arranged for the orderly transfer of most of his assets, the taxes on the horses owned by him would have been so prohibitive that they would have necessitated a dispersal sale. As things stood, it was apparent that the "Secretariat bloodline was the most salable asset" of the Meadow operation. A little over a month later, therefore, it was announced that Secretariat had been syndicated for the unheard-of sum of $6,080,000. It was a world-record price, and it made the colt the most valuable breeding prospect in the history of Thoroughbred racing anywhere. The previous high was $5,440,000, the price attached to the European champion Nijinsky II in 1970.

Hollis Chenery had prevailed this time. "My brother's an economist," said Penny Tweedy, "and it made him nervous to think of owning an asset worth $6,000,000 that depended on a single heart beat." The syndication was put together by Seth Hancock, twenty-four-year-old son of A. B. "Bull" Hancock, who had also died. It called for thirty-two shares in the horse, each worth $190,000. Two would be retained by Mrs. Tweedy, two by the Chenery Corporation, a family-owned enterprise, and the other twenty-eight would be offered to breeders.

Several of the biggest breeding farms balked at the price, but the shares were quickly subscribed to by Thoroughbred owners in the United States and throughout the world. Each share-owner received the privilege of sending a mare to Secretariat once a year for the rest of his life, commencing with the start of the breeding season in February 1974. It was further stipulated that the colt would be allowed to continue racing until November 15, 1973, with the Meadow Stable retaining all purses won.

Mrs. Tweedy was somewhat philosophical about the price. "I guess the price was based on the Macy's basement theory; $190,000 sounded more reasonable than two hundred." Seth Hancock was more practical. "I'd say it wasn't really a gamble. Even if he doesn't win the Triple Crown, he's worth the money. He's got all three things you want in a sire: pedigree, looks, and performance." The records would tend to belie this, however, since many past two-year-old champions failed to duplicate their form at three.

Despite the controversy surrounding the price, Penny Tweedy nevertheless maintained an admirable candor about the syndication deal. "Secretariat was really a sort of deus ex machina for us. He came along at exactly the right time. And what I thought was particularly nice was that Mr. Phipps was the first subscriber to the syndicate." Phipps was somewhat less sanguine. "It's unlikely that any of his offspring will be as good as Secretariat, but then again a horse doesn't have to be that good to be successful." He may have been thinking of the foal he wound up with following the coin toss with Mrs. Tweedy in 1969. He may also have been thinking of what an expert breeder once said: "What you really need to get a good foal is a male horse, a female—and a lot of luck."

Commercial breeders in the syndicate, perhaps more than the others, could expect a quick return on their investment. It was possible for them to receive six-figure sums for Secretariat foals at Saratoga or Keeneland yearling sales. If the colt raced well in 1973, they could easily recoup with just three or four foals.

It was also revealed at the time that there would be heavy insurance coverage against anything happening to the horse. The fact is, he was covered for his entire syndication value, which called for a premium of $500,000 for 1973 alone. When Penny Tweedy indicated that Secretariat was insured against everything, from illness to infertility, one sportswriter wanted to know: "Where do you go to apply for that infertility policy?" Another found it hard to cope with the price. "In the bullish world of horse breeding," wrote Steve Cady in the New York *Times,* "buying Secretariat at $190,000 a share makes as much sense as buying I.B.M. at $431."

The big red horse made other headline news early in 1973, even though he was still residing at his winter training quarters at Hialeah. On January 11, Kenneth Noe, Jr., handicapper for the New York Racing Association and the Jockey Club, released his figures for the Free Experimental Handicap. Some 137 Thoroughbreds, including 67 fillies, were evaluated, and Secretariat was assigned 129 pounds. Only five other horses had topped him since the handicapping was begun in 1933 by Walter Vosburgh. They were: Bimelech, 130 (1939); Alsab, 130 (1941); Count Fleet, 132 (1942); Native Dancer, 130 (1952); and Bold Lad, 130 (1964).

The time was finally at hand for Secretariat to start moving to the track. He arrived in New York early in February, and was immediately prepared for his three-year-old debut in the Bay Shore at Aqueduct. He was fit; he had grown amazingly over the winter, having added an inch and a quarter to his height in six months. Laurin was worried. "I knew he had filled out well over the winter, he was training well and he was sound. But, still, until they race again, you wonder." He could have saved himself the concern. The colt drove through a sloppy track and a traffic jam of horses to win by four and a half lengths, on St. Patrick's Day, March 17. "It told us all we wanted to know," sighed Penny Tweedy with relief. "It told us that he still has the heart, the will, the courage to win, that he still knows how to win. This is the greatest test, when they come out as three-year-olds." After the race, Ron Turcotte for the first time admitted the growing pressure when he told Pete Axthelm of *Newsweek*: "I never thought that six million would feel so heavy."

His second outing was on April 7, in the Gotham Mile. Here, he proved he was warming up to the task by equaling the track mark of 1:33²/₅, while carrying 126 pounds, which prompted one reporter to look upon the results as " . . . just another preliminary exercise of the kind made by circus acrobats as they limber up for their more spectacular maneuvers." In winning both the Gotham and the Bay Shore, he became only the third horse ever to be victorious in both races. This brought him to the important Wood Memorial, on April 20. At a mile and an eighth, it would be the longest race for him thus far, and it would match him against the other best-rated three-year-old in the country, Sham. This flashy bay had a peculiar record. He was a flop early in his juvenile year, and was auctioned off for $200,000 to Sigmund Sommer, a real-estate and construction businessman. He finally broke his maiden on December 9 at Aqueduct, and then polished off three more wins in five tries, to earn $115,250. His last victory was on March 31, when he beat Linda's Chief in the Santa Anita Handicap, in 1:47, a fifth of a second faster than the mark at Aqueduct for the same distance and the distance of the Wood Memorial.

The race, traditionally, is regarded as the most important in the East before the Kentucky Derby, and is supposed to indicate the probable favorite of the "Run for the Roses." Three of the eight previous Triple Crown winners, Gallant Fox, Count Fleet, and Assault, used the Wood as the springboard to their final climb to glory. Therefore, in 1973, it had an extra measure of excitement when Sham and Secretariat were entered. "Seldom do two three-year-olds rated as the best in the land meet before the Derby," wrote William Rudy in the New York *Post*.

As the day of the race approached, a first-class rhubarb erupted. Secretariat was to be paired with his stablemate Angle Light, who was also trained by Laurin but owned by Edwin Whittaker. There was talk that Sham would have two running stablemates, Knightly Dawn, who had acted as his pacemaker in the Santa Anita, and Beautiful Music, the three owned by Sommer. In all, it appeared that eleven horses would be running, which caused the venerable Charles Hatton to voice some disgust in his column in the *Daily Racing Form* on April 19: "We hope it will narrow down to a horse race, not another donnybrook." Since the race is started on the first turn of the track, and since it is only for nine furlongs, he feared a "bloody awful scrimmage for position."

It was his hope, rather, that the race would be "virtually horse-against-horse, in the old tradition exciting to contemplate" between Sham and Secretariat. He went on to say that there "is nothing in the Rules of Racing to prevent a horse from bringing his gang with him, so long as they are paid-up eligibles. But the Wood is supposed to decide who had the best horse, not the most horses." He concluded by writing that "neither Sham nor Secretariat strikes us as the sort who need blockers," and that he did not think Frank "Pancho" Martin, Sham's trainer, really wanted to run two horses, let alone three.

The following day, Martin was quoted as saying that he would likewise prefer it if only the two colts ran. "I am running Knightly Dawn only because Lucien is running Angle Light. I will not run an entry if he will take out the other horse." He also boasted that he felt Sham was the best in the race. "I am going to give Secretariat a good try," he cried. "We have to try him and this is the time to do it." He even offered to bet Laurin $5,000 that Sham would win, so confident was he.

Hatton, in the meantime, kept up his drumbeat of complaint. " . . . there still were indications the stage would be cluttered by a lot of spear carriers when the protagonists, Sham and Secretariat, make their entrance," he warned. Then, he went on to lambast the caliber of the horses, proclaiming that some "could not get a job pulling the track harrow." Finally, he predicted that "we shall not be surprised if the tote board lights up with foul claims like Times Square on Saturday night." It was on the morning of the big race, however, that he threw out his most telling barbs. He quoted Lucien Laurin as saying earlier in the week about his horse's chances: "The only way they can beat him is to steal it," while, at the same time, reporting that the track stewards were determined that nobody was going to "purloin the race."

The volatile Martin roared with anger, and that morning scratched both Knightly Dawn and Beautiful Music. He later explained his reason. "But after the remark in the paper, I don't want to be a friend of his. I never made a remark about him. He called me a thief. I didn't call him a thief." He also claimed Laurin was in effect saying that Sham could not beat Secretariat without help. Lucien Laurin, on the other hand, explained that he could not withdraw Angle Light, because he had a different owner and, therefore, each of his two horses had "to run his own race." As for his "steal" remark, this was merely track parlance, which meant that by opening a long early lead with a false pace, or by setting a very slow pace to preserve his strength for the stretch run, a horse could just manage to throw a favorite off his race plan and sneak home in front. Throughout the protracted argument, all Helen Tweedy could say was: "From here on out it's Tums and Rolaids." It was a most prophetic comment.

Only eight horses went to the post, with the entry of Secretariat and Angle Light the 3-10 favorite. When the race was over, 43,416 people, the largest crowd of the season, could not believe what they had just seen. They were dumbstruck. Angle Light scored a smashing upset, finishing a head in front of Sham, and four lengths over Secretariat. He had come out fast and had stayed in front all the way. Jockey Jacinto Vasquez did in fact slow the pace and "steal the race from Sham and Secretariat." Bob Ussery, on sixth-place Flush, gave the clue in noting the time for six furlongs. "When they went 1:12 and change, it was good night. Any good horse can finish after that, and Angle Light is a good horse." A disappointed, puzzled Ron Turcotte could only say that his mount "just didn't have his punch today. I had him clear on the backside and I tried to move him up, but he didn't respond when I hit him at about the half-mile pole." He tried again after a wide turn into the stretch, but the colt only lugged in a bit and lacked his usual kick. Sham also seemed to be wanting in a finishing drive, although his jockey, Jorge Velasquez, felt he would have won in a longer race. Obviously caught in the middle, the rider had to worry about letting Angle Light get away, while making sure he had enough left to cope with Secretariat's expected late charge. As for Lucien Laurin, he looked like the world had come to an end, not like the trainer of a horse who had just won $68,940. He was so dazed by Secretariat's futile stretch run, that he did not realize which horse had won. It was Mrs. Tweedy who told him: "You won it, your horse was first." "Pancho" Martin, too, felt that his jockey had been conned by the slow pace, and Mrs. Tweedy said it "looked to me as though we were racing one horse, Sham, and forgetting the rest of the field." Furthermore, she had the uncomfortable experience of having had in her box ten bankers from the Chase Manhattan Bank, which had become co-executor of the Chenery will. The outcome of the race could have made her wonder if she still had a "friend at the Chase."

Angle Light (front right) scores a stunning upset over Sham (center) and Secretariat (left) in the Wood Memorial.

Needless to say, the press had a field day with the speculations on Secretariat's future, even though he had come in first in his previous ten races. "So Secretariat is only human after all, though the squeamish might insist he's only equine. Racing people and the racing public had begun to regard this newest folk hero as invincible," is the way Red Smith viewed it in the New York *Times*. Gene Ward, in the New York *Daily News*, was more cutting. "This was the horse that was going to win the Triple Crown for the first time since Citation turned the trick in 1948. This was the syndicated marvel whose backers had invested $6,000,000, and Ron Turcotte, his rider, just didn't want to admit that it was the horse's own fault—he got beat." Whitney Tower, in *Sports Illustrated*, looked ahead to the Kentucky Derby. "It may not be necessary to start the race in rows, Indianapolis 500 style, but following Secretariat's defeat a lot of guys are going to be cranking up three-year-old maidens from New England to Nevada and shipping them to Louisville." Pete Axthelm in *Newsweek* was of the opinion that " . . . the brilliant colt seemed a very shaky proposition as an even-money Derby favorite," while *Time* intoned that the Derby shaped up "as more of a horse race than the smart money had previously predicted. . . . In fact, a modicum of suspense was needed to save the Derby from tedium," and that element apparently was now present.

The doubts, concerns, bewilderment, and second-guessing engendered by the Wood Memorial followed all of the principals to Churchill Downs. Opinions and predictions were available by the yard. Most prominent among these, of course, was the old shibboleth of Bold Ruler sons, that none had ever won a Derby. Laurin and Turcotte tried simply to write off the Wood as just "a bad race thrown in by a good horse," who would fire up in the Derby. The diminutive trainer, however, was highly incensed over reports that Secretariat had some heat in his legs and was below form. "Last week," he lamented, "Jimmy the Greek claimed my horse was standing in ice with knee trouble and there was talk of laying odds that the colt wouldn't get to the Derby. . . . Secretariat has not been put in ice," he pouted, "and there's nothing in the world wrong with him." Still, with twenty-eight syndicate members looking over his shoulder at his every move with their six-million-dollar investment, the pressure was intense. He took to taking sleeping pills for the first time, but still had sleepless nights.

Some other distinguished trainers offered little solace. Jimmy Jones, for example, who helped saddle eight Derby winners including Citation, was unimpressed with all of the horses in the Derby. "It doesn't measure up as a good field. There are some good horses, no great ones. No superstars." Referring to the Wood, he added: ". . . a great horse will win under any conditions—slow track, fast track, mud, slow pace, fast pace. Citation was that kind of horse. He was an arrogant rascal. He could lick them all any time, and he knew it." What was needed now was another Citation or Whirlaway to win the Triple Crown. Then there was Horatio Luro, who had trained Northern Dancer when he won the 1964 classic and set the still-standing 2:00 mark. He said,

". . . a horse of Secretariat's 'blocky' build would not be his first choice in selecting a 1¼-mile horse." There was also the theory that Laurin had not raced the big colt enough before the Derby. "Pancho" Martin also got in his jabs, by renewing his $5,000 bet offer to the little white-haired ex-jockey-trainer. He also said he would run just Sham.

The bay colt was, in fact, shaping up as a growing favorite. The day before the race, fans at Churchill Downs gave him a slight edge against the Secretariat–Angle Light entry. They had bet $44,915 on Sham as against $41,711 on the entry. The other horses came in for short shrift. Gene Ward had a rather dim appraisal of them, after he selected Sham, My Gallant, and Secretariat in that order. He said Angle Light had had a nosebleed, Royal and Regal had a blister, and Shecky Greene was said by his critics to be able to "travel a mile and a quarter only in a van."

In New York, interest in the horse heated up. The Off-Track Betting Corporation reported $1,131,724 in bets on Friday and, by eleven a.m. on the day of the race, $1,648,940. A secretary refused to support the big red colt because "you can't make money with him." However, a United Nations Soviet executive ignored the warning. It was also reported that the OTB office on "flaky" 42nd Street was outdrawing its neighbors, the Roxy Burlesk and a double-feature sex bill of "Hetro Sexuals" and "Street of a Thousand Pleasures."

Derby Day, May 5, 1973, for the ninety-ninth running of the renowned classic, opened with a record and never quit. At the outset, 134,476 people poured through the turnstiles of Churchill Downs, the biggest crowd ever. They then charged the betting windows to plunk down a total of $7,627,965 on all of the day's races, which topped all previous American marks, and $3,200,000 on the Derby alone, also a record. In New York, a record $3,050,194 in bets were received by the OTB. The gross value of the race was $198,880, with $155,050 going to the winner, making it the richest of all Kentucky Derbys. Thirteen Thoroughbreds marched to the post, the first time in thirteen years that exact number of horses was entered. Angle Light was in the number two position, Sham in number four and Secretariat in number ten. He and Angle Light went off at 3-2, with Sham the second favorite at 5-2.

Secretariat came out of the gate slowly as usual, cut sharply to the rail and settled back to last place as the field came past the stands. Near the first turn, Bill Hartack, on Warbucks, shouted at Turcotte: "Stay out, stay out, stay away," apparently remembering the big colt's veering during the Wood Memorial. Secretariat began to pick up horses on the backstretch and went to the middle of the pack. Sham, in the meantime, had moved into second and remained there. On the far turn, Sham went into the lead, while Secretariat continued to loop the field on the outside, finally moving up to the leader, "his handsome head held low, heavy muscles grouping and stretching beneath the glistening coat." At that moment, to Gene Ward, the "real Secretariat stood up and ran over Sham . . . careening past horses as though they were standing still." In the final furlong, it was a two-horse race. They met eye-to-eye at about the three-sixteenths pole and, although Sham "held on with courage," the big colt inexorably drew away. "Secretariat had his blood up, the Wood Memorial was behind him," reported *The Blood-Horse,* and he swept down the stretch to a record-breaking victory by two and a half lengths. The time was 1:59^2/$_5$, which stripped ^{3}/$_5$ second from the old mark. An incredible performance, awe-inspiring, monumental as any ever in the history of the race, was the consensus of the press, particularly since Secretariat and Sham "ran a classic in a non-American way—the last part faster than the first part." Secretariat was clocked in 0:23^1/$_5$ for the final quarter, to break the mark of 0:24 for that distance set by Whirlaway in the 1941 Derby. He ran the first quarter in 0:23^2/$_5$.

Sham, for his part, also ran a remarkable race. He was timed at 2:00, thereby tying the old record, and finished eight lengths in front of Our Native. He completed the first mile in 1:36^1/$_5$, which meant he, too, ran the last quarter in less than 0:24. In fact, he became the fastest losing horse in the history of the Derby. To put it another way, he had run the Derby faster than ninety-seven winners. His achievement was even more startling considering his mishap at the start. Another colt, Twice a Prince, had acted up in the starting gate, disturbing Sham and causing him to bang his head against the side of his stall. On his return to the barn, his mouth was bloodied, with two teeth dangling by a thin strip of his gum, causing trainer Frank Martin to remark that he looked "like a four-legged hockey player."

Secretariat completes a remarkable record-breaking race ahead of Sham in the 1973 Kentucky Derby. He stripped ^{3}/$_5$ second from old mark, and ran the last quarter in 0:23^1/$_5$.

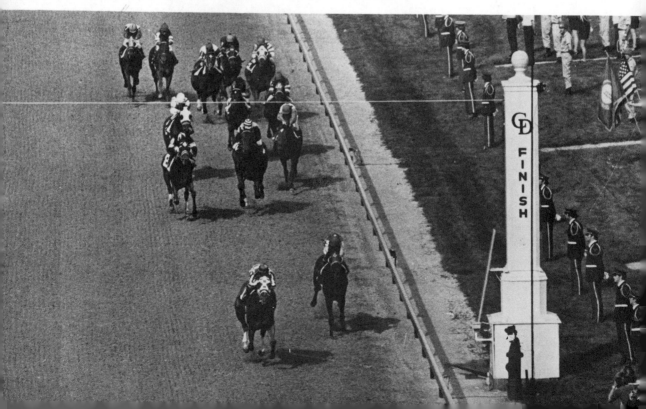

NINTH RACE
CD
May 5, 1973

1¼ MILES. (2:00). Ninety-ninth running KENTUCKY DERBY. SCALE WEIGHTS. $125,000 added. 3-year-olds. By subscription of $100 each in cash, which covers nomination for both the Kentucky Derby and Derby Trial. All nomination fees to Derby winner, $2,500 to pass the entry box, Thursday, May 3, $1,500 additional to start, $125,000 added, of which $25,000 to second, $12,500 to third, $6,250 to fourth, $100,000 guaranteed to winner (to be divided equally in event of a dead-heat). Weight, 126 lbs. The owner of the winner to receive a gold trophy. Closed with 218 nominations.
Value of race, $198,800. Value to winner $155,050; second, $25,000; third, $12,500; fourth, $6,250.
Mutuel Pool, $3,284,962.

Last Raced	Horse	EqtAWt	PP	¼	½	¾	1	Str	Fin	Jockeys	Owners	Odds to $1
4-21-73⁷ Aqu³	Secretariat	b3 126	10	11h	6½	5¹	2¹½	1¹	12½	RTurcotte	Meadow Stable	a-1.50
4-21-73⁷ Aqu²	Sham	b3 126	4	5¹	3²	2¹	1½	2⁶	2⁸	LPincayJr	S Sommer	2.50
4-26-73⁶ Kee²	Our Native	b3 126	7	6½	8¹½	8¹	5h	3h	3½	DBrumfield	Pr'ch'd-Thom's-R'q't	10.60
4-26-73⁶ Kee⁵	Forego	3 126	9	9¹½9½	6½	6²	4½	42½		PAnderson	Lazy F Ranch	28.60
4-28-73⁷ CD²	Restless Jet	3 126	1	7¹½7h	10¹½	7¹½	6¹½	52½		MHole	Elkwood Farm	28.50
4-28-73⁷ CD¹	Shecky Greene	b3 126	11	1¹½1¹³	1¹½	3³	5¹	6¹½		LAdams	J Kellman	b-5.70
4-26-73⁶ Kee⁶	Navajo	b3 126	5	10¹½10¹14	8¹½	8²	7no			WSoirez	J Stevenson-R Stump	52.30
4-26-73⁶ Kee⁷	Royal and Regal	3 126	8	3¹	43	43	4¹	7¹½	83½	WBlum	Aisco Stable	28.30
4-26-73⁶ Kee¹	My Gallant	b3 126	12	8h11¹½12³	11²	10½	9h			BBaeza	A I Appleton	b-5.70
4-21-73⁷ Aqu¹	Angle Light	3 126	2	4h	5¹½	7¹	10¹½	9¹½10¹½		JLeBlanc	E Whittaker	a-1.50
5- 1-73⁸ CD⁵	Gold Bag	b3 126	13	2h	2h	3½	9¹	11¹	11no	EFires	R Sechrest-Gottdank	68.30
4-28-73⁷ CD⁶	Twice a Prince	b3 126	6	13	13	13	13	12²	12¹½	ASantiago	Elmendorf	62.50
4-26-73⁶ Kee³	Warbucks	3 126	3	12¹½12³	9h	12¹½13	13			WHartack	E E Elzemeyer	7.20

a-Coupled, Secretariat and Angle Light; b-Shecky Greene and My Gallant.

Time, :23⅖, :47⅖, 1:11⅘, 1:36⅕, 1:59⅖ (new track record). Track fast.

$2 Mutuel Prices:

1A-SECRETARIAT (a-Entry)	5.00	3.20	3.00
5-SHAM		3.20	3.00
8-OUR NATIVE			4.20

Ch. c, by Bold Ruler—Somethingroyal, by Princequillo. Trainer, L. Laurin. Bred by Meadow Stud, Inc. (Va.).
IN GATE—5:37. OFF AT 5:37 EASTERN DAYLIGHT TIME. Start good. Won handily.

SECRETARIAT relaxed nicely and dropped back last leaving the gate as the field broke in good order, moved between horses to begin improving position entering the first turn, but passed rivals from the outside thereafter. Turcotte roused him smartly with the whip in his right hand leaving the far turn and SECRETARIAT strongly raced to the leaders, lost a little momentum racing into the stretch where Turcotte used the whip again, but then switched it to his left hand and merely flashed it as the winner willingly drew away in record breaking time. SHAM, snugly reserved within striking distance after brushing with NAVAJO at the start, raced around rivals to the front without any need of rousing and drew clear between calls entering the stretch, was under a strong hand ride after being displaced in the last furlong and continued resolutely to dominate the remainder of the field. OUR NATIVE, reserved in the first run through the stretch, dropped back slightly on the turn, came wide in the drive and finished well for his placing. FOREGO, taken to the inside early, veered slightly from a rival and hit the rail entering the far turn, swung wide entering the stretch and vied with OUR NATIVE in the drive. RESTLESS JET saved ground in an even effort. SHECKY GREENE easily set the pace under light rating for nearly seven furlongs and faltered. NAVAJO was outrun. ROYAL AND REGAL raced well for a mile and had nothing left in the drive. MY GALLANT, outrun at all stages, was crowded on the stretch turn. ANGLE LIGHT gave way steadily in a dull effort and was forced to check when crowded by GOLD BAG on the stretch turn. GOLD BAG had good speed and stopped. TWICE A PRINCE reared and was hung in the gate briefly before the start and then showed nothing in the running. WARBUCKS was dull.

Official chart of Kentucky Derby.

Ron Turcotte, in the jockey room after the hectic festivities, let go with some pent-up sarcasms, apparently reflecting some of the feelings of the Meadow Stable team. "He ran pretty good for a crippled horse. You know something, he might have run that in 1:56 if he was all right."

The result of the race produced a number of new and significant statistics and equaled others. It was the first time that the same owner-breeder-trainer-jockey combination had saddled two consecutive Derby winners. It also meant consecutive winning mounts for groom Eddie Sweat and exercise rider Charlie Davis. Mrs. Tweedy became the fourth breeder and third owner with consecutive winners. Lucien Laurin was the fourth trainer with consecutive winners. Ron Turcotte became the first jockey in seventy-one years to have back-to-back victories. Secretariat was only the second two-year-old champion since Needles (1956), and the second Free Experimental topweight since Middleground (1950), to fulfill his juvenile promise by taking the Derby. He was the second Virginia-bred horse since Reigh Count

(1928) to win the Derby. Of particular interest to breeders, he destroyed the myth about Bold Ruler's sons.

There was a wholly different attitude toward Secretariat, as the Preakness approached two weeks later. By then, the opposition dwindled down to just five, with the owners and trainers of some exhibiting considerably more respect. Bill Resseguet, owner of Our Native, stated: "I'm going to tell my jockey to hold onto Secretariat's tail and see if we can get second money." Fred Menke, owner of Deadly Dream, candidly admitted: "Our best chance is if the others collapse." Buddy Delp, trainer of Ecole Etage, had a unique race plan. "We'll try to go to the head. That's where he likes to be. And we're going to put high-speed roller skates on him so he'll be able to stay in front." Sham's Frank Martin simply said: "Anybody that beats him will have to do some running." There would be no excuses.

The day of the Preakness was clear and bright, and a record crowd of 61,657, 15,000 in the infield alone, invaded the track and invested it with a carnival atmosphere, replete with rock bands, dance contests, and a special promotion by the Baltimore Colts football club to honor their ace quarterback Johnny Unitas. The Harry M. Stevens Company even came out with a special black-eyed Susan drink of vodka, rum, and fruit juice, to match the mint julep of Kentucky. Even Bob Marisch, of the Baltimore *Sun*, was motivated to uphold civic pride and espouse the importance of the Maryland classic. He wrote of a Louisville newsman quoting Irvin S. Cobb's famous description of the Kentucky Derby: "But, what's the use? Until you go to Kentucky and with your own eyes behold the Derby, you ain't never been nowhere and you ain't never seen nothin'." Marisch countered with an Ogden Nash rhyme:

> The Derby is a race of autocrat sleekness
>   For horses of birth to prove their worth to run in the Preakness
> The Preakness is my weakness.

The tight turns of the Pimlico track are always items of concern for trainers. On the day before the race, Lucien Laurin discounted this hazard for his horse, and vowed not to fall into the same trap he had with Riva Ridge in 1972. "I may not win tomorrow, but I'll guarantee you I won't lose ten lengths in the first turn. And I'll make every one of them run every step of the way." He did.

Secretariat went off as the 5-10 favorite, and "looked like a mine of pure gold . . . instead of a mere $6,000,000," to Joe Nichols. He broke well, and sat back in fourth place, five and a half lengths behind the leader, Ecole Etage. After the first quarter, going into the first turn, the pace seemed slow to Turcotte. He chirped, and his mount accelerated, going three-wide around horses to the dismay of the fans and near heart failure for Lucien Laurin. Later, Turcotte revealed that Secretariat seemed to feel the pace, too, and drew out on his own.

Laffit Pincay, Jr., had Sham running well, and was waiting for Turcotte to apply the whip. "He went by us flying in the backstretch," he recalled, hardly expecting the move so early in the race. With three-quarters of a mile to go, the chestnut colt took the lead and headed for home, never touched by the whip. Pincay figured he might have a chance at the top of the stretch, because of Secretariat's early move. He never did. For Turcotte, the biggest threat he faced was the crowd in the infield, some of whom began to climb the rail. To prevent his horse from being spooked, he cocked his head to the right, so that the move and the blinkers would block out the turmoil on the left.

It was a delightfully easy victory by two and a half lengths over Sham and ten and a half over Our Native, marking the first time in the history of the Preakness that the 1-2-3 horses duplicated exactly the windup of the Derby. The official time was announced as 1:55, which set off an unusual controversy. In the stands, two staffers of the *Daily Racing Form* timed the race with their own stop watches and came up with 1:53$^2/_5$, better than the record of 1:54 set by Canonero II in 1971. The track's time was recorded electronically. The embarrassed track officials stood by their guns until two days later, when they changed the time to 1:54$^2/_5$. It was explained that the official track clocker had also timed the race manually, and that was his result. The decision seemed to be a compromise, although many felt that Secretariat was being finessed out of a record-breaking credit.

Jockey Ron Turcotte hand-rides Secretariat to a two-and-a-half-length victory over Sham in the Preakness. Our Native was third, thus duplicating the 1-2-3 finish of the Kentucky Derby.

Trainer Lucien Laurin and owner Helen Tweedy lead Secretariat and Ron Turcotte to the winner's circle following the Preakness victory. The race produced hot controversy over whether or not the colt had broken the record.

Official chart of Preakness.

EIGHTH RACE
Pim
May   19, 1973

1 3/16 MILES. (1:54). Ninety-eighth running PREAKNESS STAKES. SCALE WEIGHTS. $150,000 added. 3-year-olds. By subscription of $100 each, this fee to accompany the nomination. $1,000 to pass the entry box, starters to pay $1,000 additional. All eligibility, entrance and starting fees to the winner, with $150,000 added, of which $30,000 to second, $15,000 to third and $7,500 to fourth. Weight, 126 lbs. A replica of the Woodlawn Vase will be presented to the winning owner to remain his or her personal property. Closed Thursday, Feb. 15, 1973 with 194 nominations.

Value of race $182,400. Value to winner $129,900; second, $30,000; third, $15,000; fourth, $7,500.
Mutuel Pool, $922,989.

Last Raced	Horse	EqtAWt	PP	St	1/4	1/2	3/4	Str	Fin	Jockeys	Owners	Odds to $1
5- 5-73⁹ CD¹	Secretariat	b3 126	3	6	4½	1½	12½	12½	12½	RTurcotte	Meadow Stable	.30
5- 5-73⁹ CD²	Sham	b3 126	1	4	3³½	4³	2¹½	2⁵	2⁸	LPincayJr	S Sommer	3.10
5- 5-73⁹ CD³	Our Native	b3 126	4	5	5ʰ	5⁸	4³	3³	3¹	DBrumfield	Mrs M J Pritchard	11.90
5-12-73⁶ Pim¹	Ecole Etage	b3 126	6	1	1¹½	2²	3½	4¹⁰	4¹⁰	GCusimano	Bon Etage Farm	11.30
5- 5-73⁷ Pen¹	Deadly Dream	b3 126	2	3	6	6	6	6	5³	ASBlack	Wide Track Farms	35.50
5-12-73⁶ Pim⁵	Torsion	3 126	5	2	2½	3ʰ	5¹⁴	5³	6	BMFeliciano	Buckland Farm	39.00

Time, :24⅖, :48⅕, 1:11⅖, 1:35⅗, 1:54⅖. Track fast.
(Daily Racing Form Time 1:53⅖ New Track Record).

$2 Mutuel Prices:

3-SECRETARIAT	2.60	2.20	2.10
1-SHAM		2.20	2.20
4-OUR NATIVE			2.20

Ch. c, by Bold Ruler—Somethingroyal, by Princequillo. Trainer, L. Laurin. Bred by Meadow Stud Inc. (Va.).

IN GATE—5:40. OFF AT 5:40 EASTERN DAYLIGHT TIME. Start good. Won handily.

SECRETARIAT broke well and was eased back and relaxed nicely as the field passed the stands the first time. He was guided outside two rivals entering the clubhouse turn and responding when Turcotte moved his hands on the reins, made a spectacular run to take command entering the backstretch. SECRETARIAT was not threatened thereafter and was confidently hand ridden to the finish. SHAM broke to the right and brushed with DEADLY DREAM leaving the gate, then drifted in and hit the rail entering the clubhouse turn. Pincay swung SHAM out entering the backstretch and roused him in pursuit of the winner but he could not threaten that rival in a game effort. OUR NATIVE, reserved between rivals early, rallied to gain the show. ECOLE ETAGE, hustled to the lead, gradually weakened after losing the advantage. DEADLY DREAM stumbled then was brushed by SHAM just after the break and was outrun thereafter. TORSION, stoutly rated early, could not menace when called upon.

(The :25, :48⅘, 1:12, 1:36⅕ and 1:55 as posted by the electric timer during the running was invalidated after a 48-hour interval by a stewards' ruling, and the above time reported by official timer E. T. McLean Jr. was accepted as official. **Scratched—The Lark Twist.**

After the race, Laurin and Turcotte explained their strategy. Both felt that they had lost the Wood Memorial when Turcotte restrained Secretariat at the start of the race, which seemed to confuse the colt. Now, they "let the horse run his own race." For "Pancho" Martin, it was another cruel blow. Although he refused to offer any excuses, it was a fact that Sham ran into some more bad luck at the start of the race. He brushed with Deadly Dream coming out of the gate, and then hit the rail on the clubhouse turn. "I just have to see him go in the big one at Belmont, where there's plenty of room on the track," he moaned. Clem Florio, in the New York *Post,* found it easier to explain Martin's dilemma in baseball terms. He "understandably finds it difficult to accept his .300 hitter had been overshadowed by one that can bat .400 with only one eye open."

Winning the race broke a jinx for Laurin. It was his first Preakness. In the happy glow of victory, he commented: "I thought Mrs. Tweedy did not charge enough for membership in the syndicate. I suggested $250,000 and I guess I'm right now, eh?" Apropos of this, one such member told Seth Hancock that he had, indeed, been offered a quarter of a million for his share. As for the Tweedys, the day was a succession of rather odd experiences. Their car was smacked into in the parking lot; there were no Meadow Stable credentials at the track, so they had to pay their way in; Mrs. Tweedy's arm was burned by a cigarette; and Mr. Tweedy's pocket was picked. Later, Jack Tweedy remarked: "Boy, we needed to win this one today, just to get even."

Early in June, as the date for the running of the 105th Belmont Stakes neared, it appeared as though newsmen were searching lexicons and thesauri for appropriate adjectives with which to describe the wondrous attributes of Secretariat. His tremendous wins in the Kentucky Derby and Preakness, once and for all, dispelled any notions of his ability to go on and take the Triple Crown. One could be accused of blasphemy if he were even to suggest that remotest of possibilities. His popularity was at such a seething boil that three national magazines, *Time, Newsweek,* and *Sports Illustrated,* featured him in cover stories within the same week. The remarkable coincidence impelled *Newsweek*'s editor, Osborn Elliott, to remark: "We're going from Watergate to Starting Gate."

"He has a neck like a buffalo, a back as broad as a sofa. . . . At full speed, this huge and powerful combination of bone and muscle and glistening red chestnut coat covers just an inch short of twenty-five feet in a single stride," marveled *Time.* The editors sagely concluded that his success was a "compound of good genes, good training and good luck." Pete Axthelm, in *Newsweek,* waxed somewhat more poetic. "Secretariat generates a crackling tension and excitement wherever he goes. Even in the kind of gray weather that shrouds lesser animals in anonymity, Secretariat's muscular build identifies him immediately; his glowing reddish coat is a banner of health and rippling power. Magnificent enough at rest . . . when he accelerates . . . he produces a breathtaking explosion that leaves novices and hardened horsemen alike convinced that, for one of those moments that seldom occur in any sport, they have witnessed genuine greatness." To New York *Post* columnist Larry Merchant, "Secretariat is the kind of Big Horse that makes grown men weep, even when they are flint-hearted bettors, even when he goes off at 1-10. He is the apparently unflawed hunk of beauty and beast that they search for doggedly in the racing charts every day, and never seem to find. His supporters rhapsodize over him as though he is a four-legged Nureyev, extolling virtues of his musculature, his grace, his urine specimens." If he were to lose the Belmont, Merchant warned, the "country may turn sullen and mutinous."

All of these platitudes notwithstanding, it was a simple occurrence on the Belmont track early one morning that really mattered. In a one-mile workout, Secretariat was clocked in 1:34$^4/_5$, just 1$^1/_5$ slower than the track record. When he returned to the barn Willie Wright, his "walker," announced that the colt was jumping, happy, playful, and not at all tired. It was a signal of things to come on June 9.

Secretariat roared out of his rail post position like a demon possessed. He faced only four challengers, of which Sham was the one to give him any concern. This time there was no settling back; this time he was the leader and moving. They had gone past the grandstand for two furlongs, when an hysterical fan screamed at him: "You can't win a Belmont with a quarter in :23$^3/_5$." Into the clubhouse turn they slammed with all indications that it was shaping up as a match race, as Sham ran head and head with him, even moving into the lead momentarily. They had straightened out into the backstretch at the half-mile pole, and a shiver of fear gripped Lucien Laurin. The second quarter's time was a searing :22$^3/_5$ seconds. The worrisome trainer knew that "Belmonts, by modern customs, are not for front-runners," and that since 1950 no horse who had led after a half-mile in this classic had managed to finish first. In fact, his greatest fear was that his horse might stop in the last quarter, as so many potential wonders of the past had. It was at this moment in the race that Secretariat seemed to ignite a second-stage rocket within him, and off he streaked. Turcotte took a quick look behind, and saw Sham and the others drop back swiftly and fade in size. One mile into the race, the two were quite alone, some seven lengths in front.

When they moved into the homestretch, Turcotte spotted the fraction times on the tote board, and suddenly realized there was a record to be had. He ducked his head down, tightened his grip on the reins, and for the only time in the race really rode Secretariat through the last one-eighth of a mile to the wire. The 69,138 fans, watching with incredulity a Thoroughbred racing within himself, ignored the 90-degree heat and humidity and went wild with excitement as he barreled home a fantastic thirty-one lengths ahead of his next pursuer, Twice a Prince, in the startling time of 2:24. It was an unbelievable record, shattering Gallant Man's 1957 mark by 2$^3/_5$ seconds. His time for the mile was 1:34$^1/_5$, which topped his Derby time of 1:36$^1/_5$, while his mile and a quarter was $^2/_5$ second faster than his Louisville run.

Secretariat slams into the clubhouse turn, leading Sham and the rest of the field at the start of the Belmont Stakes.

He flies into the final turn and home stretch, all four feet off the ground, far out in front of the field.

Jockey Ron Turcotte turns to see what happened to the rest of the opposition as he guides Secretariat to an incredible thirty-one-length victory and the Triple Crown.

EIGHTH RACE

Bel

June   9, 1973

1½ MILES. (2:26⅖). One Hundred-fifth running BELMONT. SCALE WEIGHTS. $125,000 added. 3-year-olds. By subscription of $100 each to accompany the nomination; $250 to pass the entry box; $1,000 to start. A supplementary nomination may be made of $2,500 at the closing time of entries plus an additional $10,000 to start, with $125,000 added, of which 60% to the winner, 22% to second, 12% to third and 6% to fourth. Colts and geldings. Weight, 126 lbs.; fillies, 121 lbs. The winning owner will be presented with the August Belmont Memorial Cup to be retained for one year, as well as a trophy for permanent possession and trophies will be presented to the winning trainer and jockey. Closed Thursday, Feb. 15, 1973, with 187 nominations.

Value of race $150,200. Value to winner $90,120; second, $33,044; third, $18,024; fourth, $9,012.
Mutuel Pool, $519,689. Off-track betting, $688,460.

Last Raced	Horse	EqtAWt	PP	¼	½	1	1¼	Str	Fin	Jockeys	Owners	Odds to $1
5-19-73⁸ Pim¹	Secretariat	b3 126	1	1h	1h	17	120	128	131	RTurcotte	Meadow Stable	.10
6- 2-73⁶ Bel⁴	Twice a Prince	3 126	4	45	410	3h	2h	312	2½	BBaeza	Elmendorf	17.30
5-31-73⁶ Bel¹	My Gallant	b3 126	3	33	3h	47	32	2h	313	ACorderoJr	A I Appleton	12.40
5-28-73⁸ GS²	Pvt. Smiles	b3 126	2	5	5	5	5	5	4¾	DGargan	C V Whitney	14.30
5-19-73⁸ Pim²	Sham	b3 126	5	25	210	27	48	41½	5	LPincayJr	S Sommer	5.10

Time, :23⅗, :46⅕, 1:09⅘, 1:34⅕, 1:59, 2:24 (new track record) (against wind in backstretch). Track fast.

$2 Mutuel Prices:

2-SECRETARIAT	2.20	2.40
5-TWICE A PRINCE		4.60	...

(NO SHOW MUTUELS SOLD)

Ch. c, by Bold Ruler—Somethingroyal, by Princequillo. Trainer, L. Laurin. Bred by Meadow Stud, Inc. (Va.).

IN GATE—5:38. OFF AT 5:38 EASTERN DAYLIGHT TIME.   Start good. Won ridden out.

SECRETARIAT sent up along the inside to vie for the early lead with SHAM to the backstretch, disposed of that one after going three-quarters, drew off at will rounding the far turn and was under a hand ride from Turcotte to establish a record in a tremendous performace. TWICE A PRINCE, unable to stay with the leaders early, moved through along the stretch approaching the rail and outfinished MY GALLANT for the place. The latter, void of early foot, moved with TWICE A PRINCE rounding the far turn and fought it out gamely with that one through the drive. PVT. SMILES showed nothing. SHAM alternated for the lead with SECRETARIAT to the backstretch, wasn't able to match stride with that rival after going three-quarters and stopped badly.   Scratched—Knightly Dawn.

Exacta (2-5) Paid $35.20; Exacta Pool, $274,110; Off-Track Betting, $334,273.

Official chart of Belmont Stakes.

The superlatives for America's new Triple Crown champion were endless. One called it the greatest performance by a racehorse in this century. Another ranked it with such great sporting events as Joe Louis's one-round knockout of Max Schmeling and the Olympics feats of Jesse Owens, and likened the smashing of the old record equivalent to Joe Namath tossing ten touchdowns in one game or Jack Nicklaus coming in with a 55 in the U.S. Open. Kent Hollingsworth, editor of *The Blood-Horse,* wrote: "He ran so far beyond known reference points, he left us with no measurable comparison." As for the other participants in the race, Ed Bowen saw them as "merely moving yardsticks whose only function was to provide a measure of Secretariat's mastery."

There were sidelights galore, before and after the Belmont Stakes. Mrs. Helen Tweedy drew spontaneous applause from the crowd when she entered her box, as if they were paying tribute to a queen. In the last sixteen runnings of the Belmont, eight favorites had been defeated, which gave some pause to wonder at Secretariat's odds of 1-10, the only horse since Citation to be so heavily favored to win the Triple Crown. Twice a Prince, who had created such a rumpus in the stall at Churchill Downs and upset Sham, was led into the starting gate blindfolded. After the race, Ron Turcotte said he had noticed during the warmup that Sham was not striding impressively, so he "decided to deliver Secretariat's knockout punch early." The Belmont Stakes had a theme song of its own for the first time, when the band played "Sidewalks of New York" as the horses came onto the track.

Following the presentation ceremonies, Secretariat was taken to the New York State Racing Commission Test Area, where saliva was swabbed from his mouth into a basin, causing an onlooking woman to exclaim: "To think they're treating him like any other horse." Ron Turcotte, ever the loyal Canadian and hockey enthusiast, crowed: "This horse is like Boom-Boom Geoffrion, big and bold." Mrs. Tweedy offered a typically feminine comment. "It seems a little greedy to win by thirty-one lengths." Sigmund Sommer, owner of Sham, candidly admitted to being so terribly saddened by the defeat that he went home after the race, had a few drinks, and then cried. Laffit Pincay, Jr., his jockey, said he refused to punish his horse in a vain attempt to try to take second and fell back. The crowd was so thick at the paddock that Lucien Laurin could not get through to help Turcotte into the saddle, so his assistant trainer, Benny Hoefner, handled this chore.

In the course of the Triple Crown races, the New York *Times'* Tom Rogers ran across and traced a continuing story that graphically illustrated the sagacious ingenuity of horse players. At seven-thirty a.m. on the day of the Kentucky Derby, a man carrying an attaché case stepped from a taxi in front of the Times Square OTB parlor. He bet $5,000 in cash on Secretariat, then took his cab to the airport and flew to Churchill Downs to witness the race. He did the same thing on the day of the Preakness, only this time he bet $10,000 on Secretariat. He was playing a hunch that OTB would pay off more than the tracks. It did. Churchill Downs paid $5 to OTB's $5.80, so he wound up with a profit of $2,000. Pimlico paid $2.60 against $2.80 which gave him $1,000 profit. On Belmont Stakes day, the same bettor, who by now had been dubbed "The Masked Marvel," again arrived, at seven-twenty a.m. He now he pulled out $26,000 in $100 bills. "He said he wanted to bet $35,000 on Secretariat to win and $5,000 on an Exacta ticket with Secretariat to win and Sham to place." He also produced $10,000 in win tickets on Secretariat in the Preakness, with a payoff value of $14,000, to make up for the additional money he needed. It took the clerk ten minutes to punch out 400 tickets for the bets, at which time he revealed he was hoping for a win price of $2.40. As so often happens with ingenious schemes, he could not anticipate the unexpected. He could not foretell that OTB would funnel all bets into the Belmont tote system a half-hour before post time, making its payoffs the same as the track's. The result was a loss of $1,500 for the man, when his win bet on Secretariat paid off at 1–10 odds, or $3,500, but his Exacta was a $5,000 loser. Had OTB kept its betting pool separate, Secretariat would have paid $2.40 to win, which would have doubled his take to $7,000, thereby assuring him a final profit for the day of $2,000.

In becoming America's ninth Triple Crown winner, the big colt suddenly became the object of intense scrutiny. His every move, the decisions of Mrs. Tweedy and Lucien Laurin, were discussed, analyzed, and second-guessed, resulting in stories, headlines, and controversy. Leading off was the decision to race him at Arlington Park in Chicago in what was called the $125,000 Arlington Invitational. The race was dreamed up by John F. Loome, president of the track, with the approval of Mrs. Tweedy and Laurin, who thought it would be nice to let the people in the Midwest see Secretariat run. Also, Mrs. Tweedy insisted on televising the race, and it was scheduled for June 30, with the owner and trainer set to provide the commentary for ABC-TV's "Wide World of Sports." His opposition would be Our Native, My Gallant, and Blue Chip Dan, two of whom he had already beaten soundly, and the third had won only two minor races in his career. The prizes would be $75,000, $30,000, and $20,000, respectively, for the first three across the line. Laurin justified the race, too, by claiming it was getting difficult to keep Secretariat inactive. "If I don't run this horse he's going to hurt himself in his stall."

News of the race brought no cheers. It was considered little more than an exhibition, a "manufactured race." The complaint was that the colt had not beaten older horses yet and had not carried high weight. Therefore, it hardly could be classified as his "finest hour." "To be Horse of the Century," wrote Kent Hollingsworth, "Secretariat must meet every genuine challenge. The only such challenge left for Secretariat, in all the world, is the one and a half miles, uphill and down around irregular turns, clockwise, at weight for age against Europe's best classic and older horses, the Prix de l'Arc de Triomphe, the greatest prize of all, run the first Sunday in October, in Paris."

Chicago's Mayor Daley disagreed, and issued a two-hundred-word proclamation declaring it "Secretariat Day." The colt's first visit to Middle America produced a sell-out crowd of 41,223. One reporter wrote: "Chicago hasn't had an animal as celebrated as Secretariat since Mrs. O'Leary's cow." Another, describing the security precautions, claimed he was "surrounded by the most formidable band of bodyguards since Al Capone's day in Chicago."

To nobody's surprise, Secretariat "casually circled the small field and galloped away by nine lengths, without urging from Ron Turcotte," in the mile-and-an-eighth event. With only win bets allowed, and with Secretariat paying off at the legal minimum of $2.10 for $2, the track had a minus pool of $17,941.35. Not enough had been lost on the other horses, who had been running as one entry. He was timed in 1:47 flat, $1/5$ second off the track record by Damascus in 1967, while carrying 126 pounds to 120 for the others. The victory brought his total earnings to $970,242.

Ten months later, Kenny Noe, Racing Secretary for the New York Racing Association, in a discussion with the New York *Daily News'* Gene Ward about his handicapping of the 1974 Metropolitan Mile at Belmont, revealed what was perhaps the real reason why Secretariat's next race after the Triple Crown was won was in Chicago. Noe was talking about assigning Forego 134 pounds. "That's the worst weight I've ever put on a horse," he said, "except for the 136 I assigned Secretariat for the mile-and-a-quarter Dwyer last July. But Meadow Stable didn't accept the weight and it went for the match race in Chicago instead." This recalled Samuel Riddle's decision to retire Man o' War after his third year of racing, rather than risk the expected heavy weights the colt would surely have been laden with if he participated in the 1921 handicap races.

Just prior to leaving for Chicago, the colt made news of another sort. It was announced that the William Morris Agency, the world's largest talent agency, would now represent him in deals for posters, statues, and other merchandising items, and that brought some rather caustic comments. According to Dave Anderson, "up there where the William Morris Agency executives wheel and deal for Elvis Presley, Sophia Loren, Bill Cosby, Don Rickles, Pearl Bailey, and the Jackson Five, a new client has been added to, if the old clients will pardon the expression, the stable. . . . But the William Morris Agency, accustomed as it is to merchandising sex symbols, won't accompany Secretariat to stud. . . . 'The creative efforts of our clients are solely and completely their property,' " he quoted from the agency's framed pledge. Frank Beerman, in the show-business bible *Variety,* put it another way. "Secretariat, the Triple Crown racehorse, may be in show biz up to its seventeen-hands-high withers now that its owner, Penny Tweedy, has signed with the William Morris Agency to represent it. But there are no 'National Velvet' acting roles in its future, she says. 'The horse is an athlete,' she said, 'and anything he does will probably have to be at a race track in a setting natural to him.' " Beerman figured that in the spring Secretariat "will lightly be turned to thoughts of love and will hardly have time for extracurricular activities at those prices."

The news kept tumbling forth unabatedly from Meadow Stable. Early in July it was announced that Riva Ridge, their four-year-old star who had become the twelfth Thoroughbred to earn a million dollars, had been syndicated for $5,120,000, the thirty-two shares worth $160,000 each. His was the third highest deal of this sort, behind Secretariat and Nijinsky II. It seemed to be the season for these things, as Sham was also split up at $90,000 a share, or a total of approximately $3,000,000. Finally, Jack Krumpe, president of the New York Racing Association, announced that a match race between Secretariat and Riva Ridge had been set for September 15. It would be called the Marlboro Cup, since Philip Morris, Inc., manufacturer of the cigarette of that name, had put up $200,000 as a purse. CBS would televise, and the distance would be at a mile and an eighth, with weights to be announced in the future. The story was that racing secretaries Kenny Noe of New York, Frank Kilroe of Hollywood Park, and Kenneth Lennox of Monmouth Park had been polled, and they had voted unanimously for Riva Ridge as the best opponent for Secretariat. Penny Tweedy added to this that she had always wanted to see the two run, and had agreed with her father's heirs to donate both purses to charity. The winner was to receive $200,000, and the loser $50,000, the latter to be put up by the NYRA. Jack Krumpe further stated, "There will be a race, rain or shine," bearing in mind, no doubt, Riva Ridge's disdain for mud. Thus, this would be the first match race in New York since

Armed beat Triple Crown winner Assault by eight lengths on September 27, 1947.

The whole idea started to blow up almost as soon as it was born. The NYRA stewards put a damper on it by stating that it would have to be only an exhibition, since match races involve separate interests or owners. Racing fans were unimpressed, because there could not be any betting. They called it just a publicity stunt. "It's a funny situation," mused one trainer. "The winner will be whichever horse the trainer wants to win." Others asked which of the two horses Ron Turcotte would choose to ride.

Adding to the woes of the "matchmakers" was the totally unexpected defeat of Riva Ridge by a 56-1 outsider, Wichita Oil, in a mile-and-a-sixteenth overnight grass race at Saratoga on August 1, even though he had been the 1-2 choice and had broken the record in the Brooklyn Handicap in his last start. This shocking news had Gene Ward wondering: "What Will TV People Think If Secretariat Loses?" He was referring to the upcoming prestigious Whitney Stakes on August 4. Since CBS had bought four races for televising—the Whitney, Marlboro Cup, Woodward, Jockey Club Gold Cup—the "network biggies are very unhappy about the Riva Ridge defeat," he wrote, "but should Secretariat get his lumps Saturday there is going to be one helluva explosion. Madison Avenue and the television folk just don't like anything or anybody to mess with their carefully plotted scripts."

It happened. The Whitney Stakes was virtually a replay of the Wood Memorial. Onion, a four-year-old gelding who had never won a stakes race and was a lightly regarded 6-1 choice, pulled off a masterful upset over the 1-10 favored Triple Crown champion. The feat left everyone gasping. He won by a length over Secretariat, who just barely made second by a half-length, and it was the first race since the Derby that Turcotte went to the whip. The second-guessing was furious. During the days preceding the race, it was reported that Laurin was worried about the distance, a mile and an eighth, the same at which he lost in the Wood. This was also his first competition against older horses, and Secretariat had not had any real competition since his battles with Sham in the Derby and Preakness. Onion, with Jacinto Vasquez in the saddle, moved out front at the start, kept the pace slow, and had enough left to withstand a challenge by Secretariat in the stretch. Coincidentally, it was Vasquez who had also ridden Angle Light to a victory over the red colt and Sham in the Wood, eliciting from him the comment: "I'll make the Hall of Fame yet, beating these famous horses."

The historic defeat was compared to the losses by Man o' War to Upset, his only career loss, in the 1919 Sanford, and Gallant Fox to the 100-1 shot Jim Dandy, in the 1930 Travers, both at Saratoga too. It also brought out the verbal knives. "Super Horse? No. They All Get Beat," headlined William Rudy in his New York Post column. He claimed the horse was carrying "the incalculable burden of being a golden equine god, a running machine who could turn it on at any

The four-year-old gelding Onion, ridden by Jacinto Vasquez, pulls off a masterful defeat of Triple Crown champion Secretariat (right) in the Whitney Stakes at Saratoga.

time, run that one fast furlong that kills the opposition." Gene Ward felt "some of the living legend label peeled away." Ed Bowen claimed there was "no horse so great as to be assured of constant success." As for the forthcoming Marlboro match race, some facetiously thought it should be between Onion and Wichita Oil instead, that since Marlboro and the New York Racing Association were left with two tarnished champions, the fans might find it more intriguing to watch the Marlboro Man race a Camel. for Secretariat, the defeat also prevented him from becoming a millionaire, his total earnings with the $11,847 second-place money reaching $982,089.

Jack Landry, group vice president of marketing for Philip Morris, is credited with having come up with the idea for the match race between Secretariat and Riva Ridge. He told of how he first admired Secretariat in 1972, when he won the Sanford Stakes, and of how the idea for the match race came to him after the Belmont. Then, before the Whitney and after Riva Ridge had lost just four days earlier, he told reporters: "If Secretariat loses, you'll see one dead man lying in the middle of the track—me."

He did not die. Rather, he went into a huddle with all of the principals involved, and came up with a new idea that met with public approval. The Marlboro Cup would be an invitational affair, with the best horses in the country asked to participate. First prize would be

$150,000, second $55,000, third $30,000, and fourth $15,000. It turned out, indeed, to be the greatest gathering of top horses ever. They were Secretariat, Riva Ridge, Onion, Cougar II, Key to the Mint, Kennedy Road, Tentam, and Annihilate 'em. Together, they had won $4,544,335 in purses and sixty-three stakes. Riva Ridge and Cougar II had topped the million mark in earnings. The only poor relation was Onion, who had won "only" $124,657, but was the one horse who had beaten Secretariat. The red colt was the only three-year-old in the lot. The race was also the first rich venture into outside commercial sponsorship for a major New York turf event. Since the Belmont track was presenting the $100,000 Beldame Handicap on the same card, the purses for the nine races of the day came to over $451,800, making it the richest afternoon in Thoroughbred history.

Secretariat was pronounced fit, following a bout with the flu. He was found to have a virus after the Whitney, which may have contributed to his upset defeat and which caused him to miss six days and a couple of workouts before the match race. Despite this, he was assigned 124 pounds. Riva Ridge had the highest impost, 127 pounds. According to weight-for-age scales, therefore, the three-year-old in theory was carrying the top weight in the race and was giving his stablemate 2 pounds to the good. Ron Turcotte was on Secretariat and Eddie Maple on Riva Ridge, and Lucien Laurin told them in the paddock: "I want to finish one, two, and I don't care who finishes first." Mrs. Tweedy, however, differed. "Secretariat needs to win more than Riva Ridge. He needs to prove he can give weight and win a handicap."

Secretariat started with the others, then settled into fifth place on the outside. Onion took the lead and Riva Ridge stayed with him. Going into the far turn, Riva Ridge made his move, as did Secretariat. The stablemates ran head and head at that point, and it became a match race between the two after all. At the three-sixteenths pole, Eddie Maple recalled, "I saw a big red head and body coming right at me and there was nothing I could do about it. It was a helpless feeling." Secretariat crossed the finish line in front by three and a half lengths and in a new world record time of 1:45^2/$_5$ for a dirt track, to better the mark of 1:46^1/$_5$ set by Canonero II against Riva Ridge in the 1972 Stymie Handicap.

The crowd of 48,023 wildly embraced their hero once more. William Rudy called him a "great horse" and assumed "the doubters are satisfied now," no doubt forgetting his own doubts about the colt following the Whitney. Gene Ward summed it up best when he wrote: "Not even on Madison Avenue, where they live on dreams, could they have hoped for a dream race with the dream horse winning in record time." The win made Secretariat the thirteenth millionaire Thoroughbred in turf history, at $1,132,089, and the eighth on the all-time winners list.

Two weeks later, "Super Red," as some were calling him, threw his fans into another paroxysm by losing the mile-and-a-half Woodward Stakes to a four-year-old, who was winning only his seventh race in

Secretariat barrels home in record-breaking time to take the Marlboro Cup at Belmont. The race featured the top horses of the country, with the Triple Crown champion the only three-year-old. The time of 1:45²/₅ was a new world's record on a dirt track for a mile and an eighth. The purse made Secretariat the thirteenth "millionaire" Thoroughbred.

thirty-two starts. Prove Out went off at 16-1, and gave the three-year-old star 7 pounds by carrying 126. His trainer was Allen Jerkins, the same man who had sent out another outsider, Onion, in the Whitney to clobber the red colt. Secretariat looked good down the backstretch, on a sloppy track, maintaining a couple of lengths' lead. Then Prove Out moved up on him on the far turn and never quit, winning by four and a half lengths.

Lucien Laurin was furious over the slow time. Jorge Velasquez, the winner's jockey, confirmed this. He said he slowed the pace, hoping to save his horse and take second money. "When I saw Ron whipping the choochoo train," he recalled, "I thought for the first time I had a shot. I went to the whip, too. But instead of the choochoo taking off and running away from me, it was my horse who took off. He just kept on running."

To prove his point, Laurin referred to the :50 time for the half-mile, compared to the :45³/₅ of the Marlboro Cup race. It was the equivalent of twenty-five lengths, he fumed. Call it coincidence or oddity, but it was a fact that Secretariat apparently did not take to stakes races whose names begin with the letter "W." His only losses in 1973 were in the Wood, Whitney, and Woodward.

New York's last glimpse of Secretariat in action was in the $100,000 Man o'War Stakes on October 8 at Belmont Park, and he left his fans

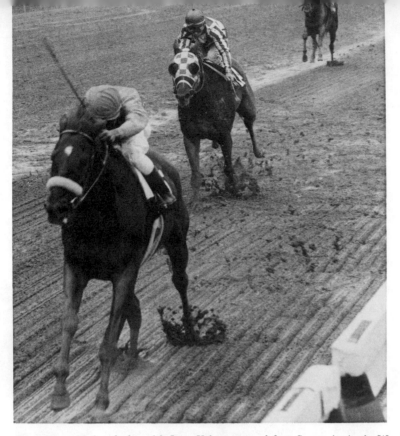

Prove Out, a 16-1 underdog with Jorge Velasquez up, defeats Secretariat in the Woodward Stakes. Cougar II is third. It was the third stakes race with a name beginning with the letter "W"—Wood, Whitney, Woodward—lost by Secretariat.

on a high note. The race marked his first on turf. Tentam was the horse to beat, since he had set a world record for a mile and an eighth on turf. Once more, the Laurin-Turcotte strategy after a loss that resulted from a slow pace was to keep everyone honest. Secretariat dashed to the front within a quarter of a mile and never let go. "Every time Tentam moved up, Turcotte chirped and Secretariat responded," said William Rudy. He ran smoothly and roared home ahead by five lengths in a new course record of 2:24⅘, faster by ⅗ second. There was an element of revenge in the win. Trainer Allen Jerkens, whose colts had beaten Secretariat in the Whitney and Woodward, saw his Triangular come in fourth, some thirteen lengths in the rear.

The time was fast approaching for Secretariat to hang up his racing shoes. He had been given until November 15, and his twenty-eight syndicate owners were waiting patiently, not without some trepidation. As long as he raced, there was always the possibility of injury. Fittingly enough, Lucien Laurin picked the Canadian International Championship, on October 28, for his last outing. The race is held at the Woodbine Track near Toronto, about 200 miles from Kenilworth Park, where Man o' War had run his last race, the match race with Triple Crown champion Sir Barton in 1920. There was a certain amount of nationalism in the choice, as well, since both Laurin and Turcotte were Canadian, and this would be the big colt's first race in the Dominion. It is run on the Marshall Course, which is a combination of turf, dirt, and turf strips, at a mile and five-eighths, a furlong longer than the Man o' War States.

Unfortunately, the plans did not gel as desired. Ron Turcotte was grounded for interference in a race on Wednesday of that week. He was slated to ride Riva Ridge, in his last race, in the two-mile Jockey Club Gold Cup on Saturday, at Aqueduct, and then fly to Canada to wind up Secretariat's career. Consequently, Eddie Maple, the Ohio farm boy who had ridden 8,000 races and won more than $7,000,000, was selected for the two chores. Riva Ridge's finale was a fiasco. He finished last to Prove Out, who now could boast of having beaten Meadow Stable's two millionaires. Riva Ridge's record thus was seventeen wins in thirty races, two classic victories, a world record for a mile and three-sixteenths, and earnings of $1,111,347.

Sunday at Woodbine was cold, windy, enshrouded in drizzle and mist. Despite the inclement weather, 35,117 people turned out. They were well rewarded. With stiff competition expected from Kennedy Road, who had set a track record in the Hollywood Gold Cup the previous week, Secretariat stormed home with ease after having opened a twelve-length lead, in 2:41$^4/_5$, only $^4/_5$ second off the track record. Frank Deford waxed eloquent in describing the race for *Sports Illustrated:* "Hard by the hedge, snorting steam in the raw twilight like some mythical beast running across a faded storybook, he drove home alone through the mist and almost, it seemed, out of the low lake clouds, and won at his leisure, from here to there." The last race was good for $92,775, bringing his total earnings to $1,316,808 and making him the fourth leading money-winner in turf history. It was the sixteenth victory in twenty-one starts, in only sixteen months since he first started to race and barely three and a half years since he was foaled. His third year was the richest single season ever for a horse, with nine of twelve wins and $860,404 in purses, topping the mark of $817,941 set by Damascus in 1967. He established another record of sorts along the way. It was estimated that some $100,000 in uncashed pari-mutuel win tickets, including 5,617 from the Belmont Stakes worth $14,597, were being held by racing fans as mementos. A Canadian collector, in fact, ran an advertisement in the *Daily Racing Form,* offering $20 for a winning ticket from the Preakness with a face value of merely $2.60.

Secretariat paraded in regal panoply at the Aqueduct track in New York on November 6. Dressed in silks, in the time-honored, traditional ritual of American turfdom reserved for Thoroughbred heroes who were retiring from the racing campaigns, with his jockey, Ron Turcotte, on his back, the chestnut colt made his last public appearance before 32,990 loudly and fervently cheering fans. His next stop would be the Claiborne Stud Farm in Kentucky, where he would live out the rest of his days as a stallion in luxurious, lazy splendor, with the appetizing thought that each year thirty of the best Thoroughbred mares would be brought to him for his favors. The mere thought of it whetted the typewriters of newsmen, and they came up with some affectionate chidings. Their copy referred to him as "the most celebrated sex sym-

bol since Errol Flynn, or anyway, Joe Namath." Since this was the day
New Yorkers were voting for a new mayor, they joked that he would
"probably win in a walkover" if he were a candidate. They even reported that his fan mail had included a postcard signed "Fiji," which
read: "I can't wait." She was one of the elite broodmares who would be
"dating" him in 1974. "For the big horse, it's all fun now," concluded
another story. Penny Tweedy was asked for her schedule the next day,
and she sadly replied: "I don't know, a hangover, I guess."

*Secretariat, with Ron Turcotte in the saddle, parades in silks at Aqueduct in his last public appearance be-
fore retiring to stud.*

On November 11, the Meadow Stable's two equine millionaires, Secretariat and Riva Ridge, were flown to Lexington and let out on the
fields of Claiborne Farm, not, however, before they were given tran-
quilizers. "We had to do it," said the Claiborne manager. "You just
don't turn out colts who are fresh off the track like that. They're liable
to run through a fence or something."

Early in December, Secretariat had his first sex experience, with a test Appaloosa mare. Thereafter, he underwent a series of fertility tests, called for by the syndicate terms. By the end of the year, too, his value was enhanced with his being named "Champion Three-Year-Old Colt," "Champion Grass Horse" and "Horse of the Year." He was only the tenth Thoroughbred of this century to win successive "Horse of the Year" awards. Since 1936, only Challedon (1939-1940), Whirlaway (1941-1942), and Kelso (1960-1961) had been so honored.

But all was not well down on the farm. Rumblings were heard which jarred the syndicate. The tests were not coming up with the desired results. It was hardly appropriate as a Yuletide greetings telegram that Seth Hancock, manager of the syndicate, sent to the breeders on Christmas Eve. It read: "Veterinarians have requested additional 60 days to complete Secretariat [or Riva Ridge, whichever applicable] fertility tests and are unanimously optimistic about final results. Request your approval to extend time to March 1, 1974, subject to insurance underwriters' approval of similar extension. Please wire or cable your consent. Regards. Seth."

The fact was that although Secretariat exhibited a fondness for the females, according to young Hancock, like "any well-adjusted three-year-old colt," microscopic studies revealed the presence of spermatogonia, immature cells, in his semen. It was the same with Riva Ridge. By February 1974, Hancock advised the subscribers of the syndicate that the colt had failed to pass the fertility test in an unqualified manner, and that the original agreement was "forthwith terminated." Then it was announced that two of the three test mares he had been mated with were in foal. Finally, a new agreement was offered to the breeders who chose to remain in the syndicate. It was stipulated that if 60 percent of the mares were in foal by September 1, not counting mares who had been barren the last two years or were more than sixteen years old, the syndicate would stand as originally formed and unpaid fees would be due.

This steady stream of news bulletins from Paris, Ky., was too much for television sportscaster Dick Schaap. On his NBC-TV News program, he said, somewhat indiscreetly, that Secretariat and Riva Ridge were "the most famous pair of stablemates since Joseph and Mary." The studio's switchboard quickly lit up with calls from irate listeners. Cardinal Cooke deplored the attack on Catholicism and Christian symbols, and Schaap was put on the air twice the following day to express his abject apologies. On top of this, Claiborne Farms faced another problem. Joe Taylor, its manager, reported that he had received so many letters from people wanting to purchase the Appaloosa mare in foal to Secretariat that he had decided to sell the mother and fetus. "I want to get her off my neck," he said. "The mare doesn't even have a name. She is called No. 24 and was chosen because she happened to be in heat at the time." Sealed bids by special-delivery letter were suggested.

As he approached the end of his racing career, Secretariat was being called "the horse of the century" and, quite naturally, was being compared to Man o' War, who has worn that title since 1919. While "Super Red's" racing record compares favorably with that of "Big Red," the experts reason that his true test of greatness will only come in years ahead, when the talents of his offspring will be seen. Man o' War's heritage has never been surpassed by any other Thoroughbred stallion. Secretariat's first foals will not reach the racing tracks until 1977, at which time they may give the first indication of how strong his bloodline will be. Only time will tell, and Secretariat, down on the farm at the age of four, just embarking on a career as a stallion, had an abundance of that.

Epilogue

They Were Only Human

*The most glorious crown is
set with false diamonds.*
—Corneille: *Héraclius,* I (1647)

Adulation of heroes has been the
fancy of sports fans from time immemorial. Physical attributes, prowess and noble achievements have provided fodder for endless debate,
argument, and comparison. With it all, however, none of these heroic
figures ever could be deemed to be the ultimate paragon. Each in his
own way and time exhibited some flaw that marred an otherwise perfect image. So it could be said of the nine super horses who make up
the elite Triple Crown club. While these equine giants represented the
finest of their breed and fully deserved the accolades they accumulated,
the truth is that some failings manifested themselves in each which, to
stretch the application of the phrase, may be excused by the simple fact
that after all "they were only human."

There is an old axiom which says in effect that anyone who reaches
the top of the heap is fair game to those who would like to climb to the
pinnacle. If reaching the summit is impossible, then the next best thing
is to embarrass the champ, or best him in one fashion or another. Of
the handsome nine, for example, four were directly challenged to
match races, and all four lost in head-to-head duels—Sir Barton to
Man o' War, War Admiral to Seabiscuit, Whirlaway to Alsab, Assault
to Armed.

When Hollywood was grinding out horse-racing sagas in years gone
by, the film moguls' image of the Thoroughbred was one of rugged
mien, unexcelled beauty, and tremendous will and stamina. Very often, he was raised under the most difficult of conditions, by poor owners and amateur trainers. Despite these shortcomings, he was strong as
iron, met all competitors head on and unflinchingly, never missed a
race, and prevailed over all adversities.

With the exception of two, the Triple Crown winners would have
flunked any screen test for one of these roles. They had their problems.
Sir Barton's feet constantly hurt, causing him to be irascible. Omaha
went lame within a few months after he captured the crown, and never
again raced in the United States. War Admiral sheared off a piece of
his forefoot in the Belmont Stakes, and was out of action from June to
October. Whirlaway hurt his leg at the end of his third year of racing,

which rushed his retirement the following spring. The great Count Fleet struck himself in the left fore ankle, which created a splint and abruptly ended his racing career. Assault injured a foot as a yearling, and walked as though he were about to fall down. He also suffered a kidney ailment in his third year and a leg splint in his fourth year. Citation had tendon trouble, which kept him from racing during his entire fourth year. The only ones who came off relatively easy were Gallant Fox and Secretariat, who were retired after their third years, which no doubt saved them from some of the miseries of the trade they might have encountered if they had continued to race in their fourth year.

In the business of breeding Thoroughbred horses, a fine stallion obviously is a vital commodity. Should he be a top stallion, then he is an extremely valuable asset to the breeding farm. The measure of a stallion's potential at the outset is twofold: his lineage and his racing record. Most Thoroughbreds have excellent family trees, some better than others, but all respectable. It is when a Thoroughbred reaches stardom as a champion that he becomes sorely in demand for services as a stallion. In this capacity, he can bring in untold wealth to his owner. For example, with today's inflationary pressures on prices, a top stud can command as much as $10,000 to $15,000 for one breeding. These matings can involve between thirty and forty mares per year per stallion. Therefore, when consideration is given to the fact that the ability of a stud may continue for as long as twenty years, a little simple arithmetic will produce a rather staggering figure on his earning potential, long after his racing days are over. It is because of such statistics that Secretariat was able to command over $6,000,000 when syndicated, or why Canonero II, who was just another horse before his victories in the Kentucky Derby and Preakness, could be sold for $1,500,000 to the King Ranch.

Needless to say, the racing accomplishments of America's Triple Crown winners made them extremely attractive for stud duty when they were retired. Alas, history records that they posted rather dismal batting averages as sires, for the most part. Sir Barton was a flop, eventually winding up at a U.S. Remount Station in Nebraska, with stud fees of $5 to $10. Gallant Fox was only moderately successful, not enough to get excited over the results. Omaha became a tourist attraction in Nebraska. Whirlaway did well at first at Calumet Farm, but came to an untimely end in France, when he suddenly dropped dead after a breeding session. Assault shocked his owner, as tests proved him to be sterile. That is, he was incapable with Thoroughbreds, but somewhat more productive with Quarter horses on the open Texas ranges. Citation was only so-so at stud. On the other hand, War Admiral and Count Fleet enjoyed tremendously effective years, more than balancing the deficiencies of their colleagues. The verdict is still out, insofar as Secretariat is concerned. His sterility tests late in 1973 and early 1974 did not produce hosannas from the breeders, and it would not be until

1977 that his first get would reach the tracks. Some clue might be had then about his prowess as a sire.

They Had Charisma

"The Sultan of Swat," "Broadway Joe," "The Brown Bomber," "The Golden Jet," "Wilt the Stilt." Ask any sports fan to identify these individuals, and the chances are he will answer unhesitatingly, left to right: baseball's Babe Ruth, football's Joe Namath, boxing's Joe Louis, hockey's Bobby Hull, and basketball's Wilt Chamberlain. It is commonplace for imaginative sportswriters, with a flair for turning a phrase, to create special "monikers" for heroic athletes by which, in time, they are almost more identifiable than by their legal names. Usually, the appellations reflect the hero's special prowess, physical mien, or personality.

With the exception of one, the Triple Crown champions were so honored. While their names may not be as easily identifiable as the ones above, as far as the general public is concerned, they have special significance for racing buffs.

Gallant Fox	"The Fox of Belair"
Omaha	"The Belair Bullet"
War Admiral	"The Mighty Atom"
Whirlaway	"Mr. Longtail"
Count Fleet	"The Fleet"
Assault	"The Clubfooted Comet"
Citation	"Big Cy"
Secretariat	"Super Red"

Sir Barton never made the list with a special name. He was not a particularly endearing colt, being rather irascible and aloof, refusing to allow people or pets to cotton up to him. This may very well have been due to his constantly aching feet. However, it would appear to be an unkind cut of fate that the Thoroughbred who began this whole business of America's Triple Crown should not be dignified with some sort of special identification. He is assuredly deserving of it. So, to America's first Triple Crown champion, we herewith dub him:

Sir Barton	"The Tender-Toed Typhoon"

Dearth of Triple Crown Champions

One dominant question pervades any discussion of the American Triple Crown. Why has there been such a dearth of winners? While it is true that the supply has not been in overabundance, it is equally true that America has not fared too poorly through the years. Actually, for a while, the champion Thoroughbreds were coming along at a rather regular clip. It was only after 1948 that the stream suddenly dried up. If it is any solace to American turf buffs, they might take note of the fact that the British have not done much better. Yes, they have had many more of their own Triple Crown winners, but they have been at the sport a lot longer. The fact is, they suffered a thirty-five-year famine before Nijinsky II won the British Triple Crown in 1970, ten years longer than the American drought from 1948 until the appearance of Secretariat in 1973. For the British, this represented only the fifteenth champion since their first was crowned in 1853.

The following are the respective winners of the British and American Triple Crowns:

ENGLAND	AMERICA
1853—West Australian	1919—Sir Barton
1865—Gladiateur	1930—Gallant Fox
1866—Lord Lyon	1935—Omaha
1886—Ormonde	1937—War Admiral
1891—Common	1941—Whirlaway
1893—Isinglass	1943—Count Fleet
1897—Galtee More	1946—Assault
1899—Flying Fox	1948—Citation
1900—Diamond Jubilee	1973—Secretariat
1903—Rock Sand	
1915—Pommern	
1917—Gay Crusader	
1918—Gainsborough	
1935—Bahram	
1970—Nijinsky II	

The answer to the question of why so few is simple. There is just too much competition these days. A Triple Crown champion today has to be that much better than were his predecessors, if he is to prevail over the field in the three "jewel" races. This state of affairs is due largely to the fantastic growth of Thoroughbred racing in America since early in the century.

For example, in 1920 there were a total of 4,032 horses of all ages who were starters in races throughout the country. By 1970, this figure had risen to 49,087. In 1920, too, there were 1,022 racing days in the year, while in 1970 these had reached the 6,242 mark. Concomitant with this tremendous expansion was the constantly growing demand for more and more Thoroughbreds to fill out the racing programs. Needless to say, the breeding farms answered the call. In 1916, the year Sir Barton was born, 2,128 foals were dropped. In 1970, approximately 25,000 foals entered the world. And every foal has an equal crack at the Triple Crown, provided the owner feels that his horse is good enough to justify the cost and bother involved in preparing for the three races.

To put it in another perspective, there were 1,035 colts in Sir Barton's crop who were racing in 1919, the year he won the Triple Crown. That was the number of Thoroughbred horses, of the same age and sex, who were competing with him at the same time. The statistic is pertinent, since to date only colts have won the title. These colts were among the total of 2,128 foals who were born in 1916. By 1970, the number of colts in crop had jumped to 10,683, out of the approximately 25,000 foals.

The following chart indicates the number of colts in crop, and the total number of foals produced in the years of America's Triple Crown champions:

TRIPLE CROWN YEAR		COLTS IN CROP	TOTAL CROP	
1919	Sir Barton	1,036	2,128	(1916)
1930	Gallant Fox	2,046	4,182	(1927)
1935	Omaha	2,567	5,256	(1932)
1937	War Admiral	2,424	4,924	(1934)
1941	Whirlaway	2,761	5,696	(1938)
1943	Count Fleet	2,991	6,003	(1940)
1946	Assault	2,940	5,923	(1943)
1948	Citation	2,860	5,819	(1945)
1973	Secretariat	10,683	25,056	(1970)

It is evident from the above statistics that the boom in producing Thoroughbred horses went into high gear after 1948, resulting in a greater increase in competition among the equine population than ever before.

Records and Earnings of Triple Crown Champions

Nobody can gainsay that the Triple Crown champions of America earned their keep. For the most part, they had reasonable total earnings by the time they reached the end of their racing days, although some were at more heady plateaus than others. The reasons for this disparity are twofold, and make it well-nigh impossible to attempt to rate one horse against the other on the basis of how much money they garnered. First, not all of the horses campaigned the same number of years. Second, the value of stakes purses leaped enormously through the years from 1918 to 1973.

None of the owners fared poorly. In some respects, the earlier earnings could be compared favorably with the larger, later takes, simply because the dollar was worth a great deal more then. Of all the owners involved, three split honors for the greatest success. Samuel Doyle Riddle had the unique pleasure of experiencing victory and defeat on two sides of the fence. In 1920, his Man o' War toppled the Triple Crown champion Sir Barton in their match race. Then, in 1937, he enjoyed the thrill of owning a Triple Crown winner, War Admiral. The following year, he found himself on the short end, when his horse was defeated by Seabiscuit in their match race. William Woodward became the first double winner, with Gallant Fox and Omaha. Warren Wright, Sr., matched this record with Whirlaway and Citation.

The following are the campaign records of each of the Triple Crown champions:

	Year	Age	Starts	1st	2nd	3rd	Unplaced	Earnings
SIR BARTON	1918	2	6	0	1	0	5	$ 4,113
	1919	3	13	8	3	2	0	88,250
	1920	4	12	5	2	3	2	24,494
			31	13	6	5	7	$116,857
GALLANT FOX	1929	2	7	2	2	2	1	$ 19,890
	1930	3	10	9	1	0	0	308,275
			17	11	3	2	1	$328,165
OMAHA	1934	2	9	1	4	0	4	$ 3,850
	1935	3	9	6	1	2	0	142,255
	1936	4	4	2	2	0	0	8,650
			22	9	7	2	4	$154,755
WAR ADMIRAL	1936	2	6	3	2	1	0	$ 14,800
	1937	3	8	8	0	0	0	166,500
	1938	4	11	9	1	0	1	90,840
	1939	5	1	1	0	0	0	1,100
			26	21	3	1	1	$273,240
WHIRLAWAY	1940	2	16	7	2	4	3	$ 77,275
	1941	3	20	13	5	2	0	272,386
	1942	4	22	12	8	2	0	211,250
	1943	5	2	0	0	1	1	250
			60	32	15	9	4	$561,161
COUNT FLEET	1942	2	15	10	4	1	0	$ 76,245
	1943	3	6	6	0	0	0	174,055
			21	16	4	1	0	$250,300

ASSAULT	1945	2	9	2	2	1	4	$ 17,250
	1946	3	15	8	2	3	2	424,195
	1947	4	7	5	1	1	0	181,925
	1948	5	2	1	0	0	1	3,250
	1949	6	6	1	1	1	3	45,900
	1950	7	3	1	0	1	1	2,950
			42	18	6	7	11	$675,470
CITATION	1947	2	9	8	1	0	0	$155,680
	1948	3	20	19	1	0	0	709,470
	1949	4	0	0	0	0	0	000,000
	1950	5	9	2	7	0	0	73,480
	1951	6	7	3	1	2	1	147,130
			45	32	10	2	1	$1,085,760
SECRETARIAT	1972	2	9	7	1*	$0	1	$456,404
	1973	3	12	9	2	1	0	860,404
			21	16	3	1	1	$1,316,808

*Champagne Stakes—penalized from first to second for interference.

Purses of Triple Crown Races

It costs an owner today over $11,000 to start a Thoroughbred in the Kentucky Derby, Preakness, and Belmont Stakes. The fees for the Derby are $100 to nominate, $4,000 to pass the entry box, and $3,500 to start. The Preakness fees are $100, $1,000, and $1,000, and the Belmont fees are $100, $250, and $1,000, respectively. These costs, of course, do not include the other related expenses—transportation, stall space at the tracks, training, etc. Is it worth it? The following tells the story of what the Triple Crown was worth in dollars to each of the champions and their owners:

	KENTUCKY DERBY	PREAKNESS	BELMONT STAKES	TOTAL
Sir Barton	$ 20,825	$ 24,500	$11,950	$ 57,275
Gallant Fox	50,725	51,925	66,040	168,690
Omaha	39,525	25,325	35,480	100,330
War Admiral	52,050	45,600	˙38,020	135,670
Whirlaway	61,275	49,365	39,770	150,410

Count Fleet	60,725	43,190	35,340	139,255
Assault	96,400	96,620	75,400	268,420
Citation	83,400	91,870	77,700	252,970
Secretariat	155,050	129,900	90,120	375,070

Times of Triple Crown Victories

	KENTUCKY DERBY	PREAKNESS	BELMONT STAKES
Sir Barton	2:09$^4/_5$	1:53*	2:17$^2/_5$**
Gallant Fox	2:07$^3/_5$	2:00$^3/_5$	2:31$^3/_5$
Omaha	2:05	1:58$^2/_5$	2:30$^3/_5$
War Admiral	2:03$^1/_5$	1:58$^2/_5$	2:28$^3/_5$
Whirlaway	2:01$^2/_5$	1:58$^4/_5$	2:31
Count Fleet	2:04	1:57$^2/_5$	2:28$^1/_5$
Assault	2:06$^3/_5$	2:01$^2/_5$	2:30$^4/_5$
Citation	2:05$^2/_5$	2:02$^2/_5$	2:28$^1/_5$
Secretariat	1:59$^2/_5$	1:54$^2/_5$	2:24

*The Preakness was raced at a mile and an eighth from 1911 to 1925.

**The Belmont Stakes was raced at a mile and three-eighths from 1906 to 1925.

Near Misses

On seven different occasions, the owners of seven Thoroughbreds might have been impelled to mutter softly to themselves, "There, but for the grace of God, go I," as they witnessed in abject disappointment the unfolding of the ceremonies in the winner's circle, following the running of the Belmont Stakes. These were the seven years in which high-flying hopes and expectations for capturing the Triple Crown were dashed to smithereens, as each of the promising candidates came a cropper in the mile-and-a-half torture test. Each of the seven horses had won the Kentucky Derby and the Preakness, only to flunk out at Belmont Park. They were the near misses, so close, yet so far.

BELMONT STAKES FINISH

1944—Pensive	second to Bounding Home
1958—Tim Tam	second to Cavan
1961—Carry Back	seventh to Sherluck
1964—Northern Dancer	third to Quadrangle
1966—Kauai King	fourth to Amberoid
1969—Majestic Prince	second to Arts and Letters
1971—Canonero II	fourth to Pass Catcher

There were fourteen other horses who won two out of the three "jewels," but they lost either the Kentucky Derby or the Preakness, and so were never really in the running for the crown. They were:

1923—Zev	twelfth to Vigil, Preakness
1931—Twenty Grand	second to Mate, Preakness
1939—Johnstown	fifth to Challedon, Preakness
1940—Bimelech	second to Gallahadion, Kentucky Derby
1942—Shut Out	fifth to Alsab, Preakness
1949—Capot	second to Ponder, Kentucky Derby
1950—Middleground	second to Hill Prince, Preakness
1953—Native Dancer	second to Dark Star, Kentucky Derby
1955—Nashua	second to Swaps, Kentucky Derby
1956—Needles	second to Fabius, Preakness
1963—Chateauguay	second to Candy Spots, Preakness
1967—Damascus	third to Proud Clarion, Kentucky Derby
1972—Riva Ridge	fourth to Bee Bee Bee, Preakness
1974—Little Current	fifth to Cannonade, Kentucky Derby

Finally, nine horses were victors in two of the "jewels," but failed to start in all three of them. They were:

1877—Cloverbrook	did not start Kentucky Derby
1878—Duke of Magenta	did not start Kentucky Derby
1880—Grenada	did not start Kentucky Derby
1881—Saunterer	did not start Kentucky Derby
1895—Belmar	did not start Kentucky Derby
1920—Man o' War	did not start Kentucky Derby
1922—Pillory	did not start Kentucky Derby
1932—Burgoo King	did not start Belmont Stakes
1936—Bold Venture	did not start Belmont Stakes

GLOSSARY

Throughout this narration, various terms and phrases, commonly used in Thoroughbred racing circles, have been employed to describe situations, conditions, or events. Some of the terms may be rather remote in meaning for the unindoctrinated. It is for their benefit, through the courtesy of the Thoroughbred Racing Associations, that the following definitions and explanations are offered:

The Thoroughbred

HORSE: Among Thoroughbreds, a male animal five years old or more.

COLT: A male Thoroughbred through his fourth year.

FILLY: A female Thoroughbred until the age of five.

MARE: A female Thoroughbred five years old or more.

BROODMARE: A mare who becomes a mother.

FOAL: A Thoroughbred prior to his first birthday. For the sake of uniformity and to avoid confusion, the birthdays of all foals are established as of January 1 of each year.

WEANLING: The foal, when he is separated from his mother in the fall of his first year.

YEARLING: The Thoroughbred after he celebrates his first New Year's Day.

TWO-YEAR-OLD: The Thoroughbred on January 1 of his second year, when he becomes eligible to race.

JUVENILE: A two-year-old horse.

SOPHOMORE: A three-year-old horse.

STALLION: A male horse not castrated.

GELDING: A castrated male horse.

STUD: A stallion used for breeding. Also a breeding farm.

SIRE: A Thoroughbred's father.

DAM: A Thoroughbred's mother.

PRODUCE: A dam's collective offspring.

GET: The collective offspring of a sire, or stallion.

PRODUCER: The term applied to a mare, when one of her sons or daughters has won a race. On the other hand, a stallion is not officially a sire until one of his get has won.

FAMILY: The female side of a Thoroughbred pedigree.

LINE: Horses traceable to a common paternal ancestor are said to form a particular line.

Color

BAY: This color varies from a light yellowish tan (light bay) to a dark rich shade, almost brown, and between these a bright mahogany. While occasionally a horse is listed as "dark bay or brown," the bay can usually be distinguished by black points—a black mane and tail and shadings of black low on the legs.

BROWN: Sometimes difficult to separate from black or dark bay, this color usually can be distinguished by noting fine tan or brown hairs on the muzzles or flanks.

CHESTNUT: This varies from light washy yellow to a dark live color, between which will come brilliant red, gold, and copper shades. A chestnut never has black points, mane, or tail.

BLACK: Doubt between a dark brown or black can usually be resolved by noting fine black hair on the muzzle.

GRAY: A mixture of white hairs and black. A gray foal will sometimes appear to be black at birth, but will lighten with age. To produce a gray, one or both of the parents must be gray. However, a gray parent does not necessarily mean the offspring will be gray.

ROAN: This is a mixture of white hairs and chestnut or white bay. It is considered a variation of gray. Depending on their color, such a horse is sometimes referred to as "strawberry roan" or "blue roan"; but for registration purposes they are listed as roan.

DUN: A rare color among Thoroughbreds, varying from mouse color to a golden dun, and generally accompanied by black points and a black stripe down the spine.

WHITE: Perhaps the rarest color among Thoroughbreds. The first white to be registered by the Jockey Club was in 1963, a filly by Ky. Colonel—Filly O'Mine, appropriately named White Beauty.

(Although black shows up with the hero's horse in fables, the color is rare among Thoroughbreds. There is also no indication that color has any bearing on a Thoroughbred's racing ability. Bay is predominant among Thoroughbreds, followed by chestnut and brown, the last frequently appearing to be black. About 90 percent of registered Thoroughbreds are bay, brown, or chestnut, with the remainder as gray, roan, or black.)

Races

STAKES RACE: Originally a "Sweepstakes," in which the owners put up "stakes," such as a nominating fee, entry fee, and starting fee, all of which went to the winner. Today, the race track adds money to these stakes. This is called added money, and can range from a few thousand to more than $100,000. In most stakes races today, the original fees paid by the various owners still go to the winner along with the major share of the added money. The second, third, and fourth horses (and in some cases horses finishing farther back) earn a portion of the added money.

HANDICAP RACE: A race in which the racing secretary assigns the weight to be carried by each horse, according to his evaluation of the horse's potential. In theory, these weight assignments put all the contestants on an equal basis. Some of the major stakes races are run under handicap conditions.

ALLOWANCE RACE: While some stakes races are run under allowance conditions, the allowance race usually refers to an event in which the weight carried is determined by the amount of money and/or the number of races won by a horse during a specified time.

CLAIMING RACE: Any horse entered in a claiming race is subject to purchase, for the amount for which the horse is entered, by any owner who has started a horse at that particular race meeting. In some such races, the claiming price will have a range of $1,000 or $2,000, with weight allowances made for horses entered at the lower price. The claiming race is a method of classifying horses in order to produce races involving competition of equal ability. When a horse wins easily while running among $3,000 claimers, he is usually moved up in value to avoid his being claimed. Many good stakes horses have evolved from the claiming ranks, the most notable perhaps being Stymie, a $1,500 claim, who went on to win $918,425.

MAIDEN RACE: A race for horses that have never won.

FUTURITY: A stakes event for two-year-olds for which they are entered as foals.

PRODUCE RACE: One to be contested by the produce of horses named at the time nominations for the race are closed.
> (With the exception of the early closing of stakes events, and a few special races in which specific horses are invited to compete, entries for races are usually made the morning of the day prior to the race.)

OVERNIGHT RACE: A race in which entries close 72 hours (exclusive of Sundays) or less before the post time for the first race on the day the race is to be run.

OAKS: A stakes event for three-year-old fillies, named for the ancestral estate of England's Lord Derby.

At the track

ALSO-RAN: A horse that does not finish among the first three.
BACKSTRETCH: The straightaway on the far side of the race track.
BANDAGES: Bandages or cloth wrappings on a horse's legs, not neces-

sarily denoting lameness or infirmity. Many trainers keep their horses in standing bandages at all times as protection. They are also used in racing for protection and support.

BARRIER: The starting gate is sometimes referred to as the barrier. Before the invention of the starting gate, the horses stood behind several ropes stretched across the track, which when raised with the ringing of a bell and the dropping of a flag started the race.

BLINKERS: Once called the "rogue's badge," blinkers are a common piece of racing equipment today. The eye cups on the blinkers, depending on modifications, block side and rear vision in either or both eyes. The use or disuse of blinkers must be approved by the stewards and the change reported on the official program.

CLUBHOUSE TURN: The turn to the right of the grandstand, so called because the clubhouse is usually to the right of the general stands.

COLORS: The jockey's silk or nylon jacket and cap provided by the owner. Distinctive colors are registered by the owner with the Jockey Club and with the state racing authority. The practice of using individually registered colors was introduced at Newmarket, England, in 1762.

DEAD HEAT: Where the photo-finish camera shows two horses inseparable at the finish, the race is declared a "dead heat" or tie.

EIGHTH POLE: The pole one-eighth of a mile before the finish line.

ENTRY: Two or more horses in a race, owned by the same stable, or trained by the same trainer, are termed an "entry" and coupled as a single betting unit, a bet on one being a bet on both.

FAR TURN: The turn off the backstretch.

FAST: A race track at its best condition is said to be fast.

FIELD: This word has two meanings in racing. The entire group of starters in a race are known collectively as the "field." However, a "field horse" is one of a group designated by the racing secretary in a case where there are more starters than there are betting units provided by the pari-mutuel equipment. Rightly called the "pari-mutuel field," this group runs as a single betting unit. For example, in the Kentucky Derby of 1971, while there were only twelve betting units, actually there were twenty-two horses running. Therefore, the horses twelve through twenty-two were paired and were the "field horses."

FURLONG: One-eighth of a mile. Originally a "furrow long" or the length of a plowed field.

HAND: A unit of four inches by which a horse's height is measured, placing one hand above the other from the ground to the withers, or the point where the saddle sits. A horse that measures sixteen hands is five feet, four inches tall at the withers.

HANDICAPPER: One who assigns the weights to be carried in a handicap race.

HANDILY: A horse working or racing with ease and without urging is said to be going handily.

HOMESTRETCH: The straightaway leading to the finish.

IN THE MONEY: A horse finishing first, second, or third is "in the money."

INFIELD: The area within the inner rail of a race track.

IRONS: The stirrups are referred to as irons.

ODDS ON: Odds of less than even money ($1 to $1). A winner at a payoff of under $4 is "odds-on."

PADDOCK: The area at the race track where the horses are saddled and viewed prior to a race. A fenced-off field on a farm.

POST: The starting point of a race.

POST POSITION: A horse's position in the starting gate from the inner rail outward, which is decided by a drawing at the close of entries the day prior to the race.

POST TIME: The time at which all horses are required to be at the post and ready to start.

PURSE: Technically, a race to which the owners do not contribute to the prize. There was a time when the prize money was contained in a purse and hung on a wire which crossed the finish line. The terms "taking down a purse" and "going under the wire" once had literal meanings.

QUARTER POLE: On a one-mile track, the pole at the turn into the stretch a quarter of a mile before the finish.

RACING SECRETARY: The official who makes up the conditions for the races and assigns the weights for handicap races.

SCALE OF WEIGHTS: An arbitrary set of weights to be carried by horses of a certain age at a certain time of year at a certain distance.

SCRATCH: To withdraw a horse from a race. There is a deadline for scratches, after which permission must be obtained from the stewards.

SEX ALLOWANCE: In all races other than handicaps, or where conditions state otherwise, fillies and mares are allowed weight below the scale, usually 3 pounds for two-year-old fillies and 5 pounds for fillies and mares three years and up, prior to September 1, and 3 pounds thereafter.

STAYER: A horse that can run well at longer distances.

WALKOVER: A rare occurrence in which only one starter goes to the post and is required only to gallop the distance of the race to be declared the winner and collect the purse, or a prescribed portion thereof, depending on the rules in effect.

WEIGHT-FOR-AGE: A type of race in which horses carry scale weight, or weight assigned arbitrarily according to age, distance, and month of year.

WIN BY A NOSE: The expression "win by a nose" became official in 1937, when the New York Racing Commission made the nose the official part of a horse in a photo-finish, to end any dispute which might occur over outstretched feet or foot.

Horse Ailments

BLEEDER: A horse suffering a nasal hemorrhage resulting from a ruptured throat vein.

BOWED TENDON: A rupture of tendon fibers due to strain of one or both flexor tendons, which extend down the back of the cannon and pastern bones. Bowed tendons become inflamed, sore, and swollen.

BREAKING DOWN: A general term for going lame in a workout or in a race, due to any ailment or injury causing a horse to go lame while running, most often a bowed tendon.

FILLED: A swelling accompanied by heat usually in the limb area.

FIRING: An operation in which a hot metal tip is inserted many times under the skin in the area of the trouble, such as bowed tendons, splints, osselets, or arthritic conditions. It is done under local anesthesia.

OSSELETS: Arthritic growths in and around the fetlock joint (ankle). When acute, the fetlock joint becomes visibly inflamed and swollen. The condition usually affects both front ankles.

SPLINT: An inflamed, oval enlargement on the splint bone, located along the sides of the cannon bone, just below the knee of the foreleg, and the hock of the hindleg.

CONFORMATION OF HORSE

Bibliography

Books

Alexander, David. *The History and Romance of the Horse.* New York: Cooper Square Publishers, 1963.

Anderson, C. W. *Thoroughbreds.* New York: The Macmillan Co., 1942.

Beckwith, B. K. *Seabiscuit, the Saga of a Great Champion.* San Francisco: Wilfred Crowell, Inc., 1940.

Corum, Bill. *Off and Running,* edited by Arthur Mann. New York: Henry Holt & Co., 1959.

Craig, Davis. *Horse-Racing—The Breeding of Thoroughbreds and a Short History of the English Turf.* London: J. A. Allen & Co., Ltd., 1963.

Hervey, John. *Racing in America—1922-1936.* Written for the Jockey Club, printed privately. New York: the Jockey Club, 1937.

Hervey, John. *American Race Horses—1936.* New York: Sagamore Press, 1936.

Hervey, John. *American Race Horses—1937.* New York: Sagamore Press, 1937.

Hervey, John. *American Race Horses—1938.* New York: Sagamore Press, 1938.

Kelley, Robert F. *Racing in America—1937-1959.* Written for the Jockey Club. New York: North Press, 1960.

Newman, Neil. *Famous Horses of the American Turf, Vol. 1—1930.* New York: The Derry-dale Press, 1931.

Palmer, Joe H. *American Race Horses—1946.* New York: Sagamore Press, 1947.

Palmer, Joe H. *American Race Horses—1947.* New York: Sagamore Press, 1948.

Palmer, Joe H. *American Race Horses—1948.* New York: Sagamore Press, 1949.

Palmer, Joe H. *American Race Horses—1950.* New York: Sagamore Press, 1951.

Palmer, Joe H. *American Race Horses—1951.* New York: Sagamore Press, 1952.

Parmer, Charles B. *For Gold and Glory—The Story of Thoroughbred Racing in America.* New York: Carrick and Evans, Inc., 1939.

Rice, Grantland. *The Tumult and the Shouting—My Life in Sport.* New York: A. S. Barnes & Co., 1954.

Robertson, H. P. *The History of Thoroughbred Racing in America.* Englewood Cliffs, N. J.: Prentice-Hall, Inc., 1964.

Rogrigo, R. *The Racing Game—A History of Flat Racing.* London: Phoenix Sports Books, 1958.

Ross, J. K. M. *Boots and Saddles—The Story of the Fabulous Ross Stable in the Golden Days of Racing.* New York: E. P. Dutton & Co., Inc., 1956.

Russell, George B. *Hoofprints in Time.* South Brunswick, N. J.: A. S. Barnes and Co., 1966.

Summerhays, R. S. *Summerhays' Encyclopedia for Horsemen.* London, New York: Frederick Warne & Co., Ltd., 1962, 1966.

Underwood, Tom R., and Day, John I. *Call Me Horse—Interesting Humorous and Informative Notes and Anecdotes About Horse Racing and Breeding.* New York: Coward-McCann, Inc., 1946.

Vesey-Fitzgerald, Brian Seymour. *The Book of the Horse.* London: Nicholson & Watson, 1946, 1947.

Vosburgh, W. S. *Racing in America—1866–1921.* Written for the Jockey Club, printed privately. New York: the Jockey Club, 1937.

The American Racing Manual. Compiled and published by *Daily Racing Form,* Triangle Publications, Inc.

Encyclopaedia Britannica (1959).

New York Times Encyclopedic Almanac (1970).

Newspapers and Periodicals

New York *Times*—1920—Oct. 10, 13, 15

        1930—Mar. 20; Apr. 4, 27, 29; May 10, 12, 17, 18, 19; June 7, 8, 28, 29; July 12, 13; Aug. 10, 16, 17, 18; Oct. 2, 28

        1938—Apr. 6, 7, 8, 9, 10, 13, 14, 15, 17, 18, 19, 26, 29; May 12, 23, 25, 26, 29; Sept. 20, 21; Oct. 6, 16, 28; Nov. 1, 2

        1941—Aug. 10

        1942—Oct. 4, 10, 11

        1943—Apr. 14, 16, 18, 19, 20; May 1, 2, 3, 5, 9, 11, 23; June 6; Dec. 19

        1950—July 14

        1953—Apr. 8

        1972—July 5; Aug. 17, 27; Oct. 15, 29; Nov. 19; Dec. 27

        1973—Jan. 5, 12; Feb. 16, 27, 28; Mar. 18; Apr. 1, 8, 21, 22, 23, 24; May 2, 3, 4, 5, 6, 7, 8, 15, 19, 20, 21, 22; June 2, 3, 8, 9, 10, 11, 21, 26, 29, 30; July 1, 8, 10, 23, 27, 28; Aug. 2, 5; Sept. 11, 12, 15, 16, 29, 30; Oct. 2, 9, 26, 27, 29, 30, 31; Nov. 4, 7, 12; Dec. 4

        1974—Feb. 19, 25; Mar. 4, 8, 11

New York *Daily News*—1972—Jul. 31; Aug. 1, 17, 26; Sept. 15, 16, 17; Oct. 14, 15, 26, 29; Nov. 19, 22

        1973—Mar. 17, 18, 19; Apr. 8, 16, 22, 23; May 5, 6, 7, 20; June 7, 8, 9, 10, 11, 28; July 1; Aug. 4, 5, 6; Sept. 16, 30; Oct. 9, 27, 28

        1974—Feb. 15; May 24

New York *Post*—1972—Sept. 18; Oct. 14, 25, 30; Nov. 20

        1973—Mar. 16, 19; Apr. 4, 9, 21; May 1, 3, 5, 7, 21; June 6, 9, 11, 28; July 27; Aug. 6; Sept. 17; Oct. 1

        1974—Feb. 14, 19, 20

New York *Herald Tribune*—1938—Apr. 6, 9, 12, 13, 15, 16, 17, 26; May 8, 24, 25, 26, 28; Oct. 6, 23, 28, 30, 31; Nov. 1, 2

New York *Journal-American*—1938—Mar. 16, 30; Apr. 7, 9, 10, 12, 15, 18, 26; May 21, 25, 29; Oct. 7, 30; Nov. 1, 23

        1945—Aug. 6

        1953—Apr. 7, 9; May 3, 9, 11; June 8

New York *World-Telegram*—1938—Apr. 7; May 10, 21, 25, 31; Oct. 6, 31; Nov. 1, 2, 3

New York *Journal*—1930—May 10, 17

New York *Daily Mirror*—1941—May 8, 11, 12
New York *American*—1930—May 18; June 8
Baltimore *Sun*—1938—Nov. 2
                1973—May 17, 20
Louisville *Courier-Journal*—1973—May 2, 6
Morning Telegraph—1938—Mar. 16, 30; Apr. 7, 9, 10, 12, 15, 18, 26; May 21, 25, 29;
                Oct. 7, 30; Nov. 1, 2, 3
            1950—July 13
Daily Racing Form—1973—Apr. 19, 20, 21, 23; June 11
Newsweek—1938—May 30; June 6, 11; Nov. 14
            1973—Apr. 2; May 7, 14; June 11, 18
            1974—Jan. 7
Time—1973—May 7; June 11, 18
Sports Illustrated—1972—Oct. 23
                1973—Jan. 8; Apr. 30; May 7, 28; June 11, 18; Aug. 13; Sept. 24;
                Oct. 8; Nov. 5
                1974—Feb. 18
Blood-Horse—1936—July 25; Nov. 28
            1938—Jan. 1, 8, 15, 22; Feb. 5, 12, 16; Mar. 5, 12, 26; Apr. 2, 9, 16, 30;
                May 7, 14, 21, 28; June 4, 18; July 9, 23, 30; Aug. 6, 20, 27; Sept.
                3, 24; Oct. 8, 22, 29; Nov. 5
            1940—Aug. 17; Oct. 5, 12, 26; Nov. 23
            1941—Feb. 15; May 3, 9, 10, 17; June 14, 28; July 26; Aug. 2, 16, 23, 30;
                Sept. 20, 27; Dec. 13, 20
            1942—Mar. 14; Apr. 18; May 2, 16, 23; June 6, 20, 27; July 4, 11, 25;
                Aug. 8, 15; Sept. 5, 19, 26; Oct. 3, 10, 17, 31; Nov. 7, 14, 21, 28;
                Dec. 19
            1943—Jan. 9; Mar. 6; Apr. 24; May 8, 15; June 12; July 3, 10, 17; Aug.
                7
            1944—Jan. 22; July 29
            1947—May 31; July 29
            1950—July 15, 29; Aug. 5
            1951—Jan. 6; July 14; Oct. 20; Nov. 3; Dec. 22
            1953—Apr. 11
            1954—Nov. 20
            1969—Mar. 29; July 2, 12
            1970—Apr. 15, 25; Oct. 24
            1971—June 7; Sept. 27
            1972—Mar. 20; May 8, 15; Aug. 28; Sept. 4, 16, 17, 25; Oct. 14, 23; Nov.
                6, 27
            1973—Jan 1, 15; Mar. 5, 12, 26; Apr. 16, 30; May 14, 28; June 4, 18, 25;
                July 2, 9; Aug. 6, 13, 20; Sept. 24; Oct. 8, 15; Nov. 5; Dec. 10, 24
            1974—Jan. 7, 16; Feb. 11, 18, 25
American Horseman—1974—Mar.
Western Horseman—1971—Jan.
Spur of Virginia—1971—Summer   *Horsemen's Journal*—1971—June
Turf and Sport Digest—1938—Feb., May   *New Yorker*—1940—Sept. 28
                1952—Sept.   *Variety*—1973—July 4

INDEX